HATED

WITHOUT A REASON

THE REMARKABLE STORY OF
CHRISTIAN PERSECUTION
OVER THE CENTURIES

PATRICK SOOKHDEO

Isaac Publishing
McLean, VA

Hated Without a Reason: The remarkable story of Christian persecution over the centuries

First edition, April 2019

Published in the United States of America by Isaac Publishing
6729 Curran Street, McLean, Virginia 22101
isaac-publishing.com

Library of Congress Control Number: 2019901436

ISBN: 978-1-7321952-4-0

Interior design and layout by Words Plus Design

Printed in the United Kingdom

There were others who were tortured, refusing to be released so that they might gain an even better resurrection. Some faced jeers and flogging, and even chains and imprisonment. They were put to death by stoning; they were sawn in two; they were killed by the sword. They went about in sheepskins and goatskins, destitute, persecuted and mistreated – the world was not worthy of them.

Hebrews 11:35-38

FROM THE AUTHOR

Many friends and colleagues around the world have helped to shape this book. I am most grateful for their information, interpretation and analysis, for the obscure documents they have managed to unearth, and for their editorial skills. Wise and insightful comments made to me in numerous conversations that were not directly connected with this book have also helped to guide my thinking. There are far too many people to name them all, but I would like to express particular thanks to Rev. Canon Albrecht Hauser, Caroline Kerslake, Mark McNaughton, Rev. Canon Dr Vinay Samuel and Rev. Canon Dr Chris Sugden.

The writing of this book has been a moving, humbling, inspiring and challenging experience for me. My hope and prayer is that readers will find it not only informative but also an uplifting, devotional work.

CONTENTS

Chapter 1

INTRODUCTION

Two thousand years after Christ lived on earth, an enormous volume of material is available for anyone who wants to study the persecution of His people. Whole libraries could be devoted to this one subject. Some denominations have a particularly deep appreciation of the privilege of suffering for Christ. Like the apostles, they would rejoice to be counted worthy of suffering for Christ.[1] They also find encouragement and build up their faith by remembering the faith of those who suffered for Him in the past as recorded, for example, in chapter 11 of Hebrews. These denominations, such as the Coptic Orthodox of Egypt and Roman Catholics, have many devotional materials that focus on the suffering of those who have gone before. Protestants have little but *Foxe's Book of Martyrs*, and even this is seldom read today.

A single book, like *Hated Without a Reason*, cannot try to cover the entire scope of this glorious and uplifting history. This book must therefore be selective. The aim has been to choose aspects of the story which will give a flavour of the whole, and which will show something of the faith, something of the courage and something of the scale of suffering of our Lord's faithful followers. It will also show something of the consuming hatred of their persecutors, the tenacity of their efforts to damage and destroy the Church, and the ruthless and inventive cruelty of some of their methods.

The Coptic Orthodox Church has been called the "Church of Martyrs" because so many believers have died for their faith in Egypt. The stories of some will be told in this book,[2] but these are just a tiny fraction of the total. During the reign of Roman Emperor Diocletian, almost a million men, women and children died for Christ in Egypt.[3] To commemorate their faithful sacrifice, the Coptic Church decided to begin its calendar at the year 284 AD, the first year of Diocletian's blood-soaked reign. In their calendar this is the year 1 AM (*anno martyrii*, in the year of the martyrs).

Only God knows the full extent of suffering for the Name of Christ. But even if we consider merely what is known and recorded, it is striking that certain individuals, in certain times and places receive (well-deserved) honour and acclaim, while others, who were just as brave and faithful, are neglected and all but forgotten. Therefore, the selection in this book deliberately includes examples from the times and places of Christian persecution that are less often written about.

Some chapters focus on time periods and some on geographical areas, which vary in length according to their content. Some subjects are divided between two chapters. For example, the greater part of the story of the persecution of Christians in China appears in chapter 9 "China" but the final part, with the advent of Maoism, is found in chapter 13 "The Long Twentieth Century".

It has not been possible to give every part of the world the attention it may deserve. Examples from Africa are scattered across a number of chapters but, sadly, space has not permitted a full study of the persecution of Christians in that vast continent. The primary persecution in Africa was for many years the martyrdom of foreign missionaries. At the same time there were notable instances of African Christians also suffering and dying for Christ, such as the "Buganda martyrs".[4] In recent decades the Christians of northern Nigeria have experienced increasing violence from angry Muslim mobs, from ethnic Fulani herdsmen and from Boko Haram militants. The latter now spreading out further across West Africa, and various other Islamist terror groups operate in other parts of Africa. There is also anti-Christian persecution at the hands of the followers of traditional African religions. Africa's smaller neighbour Madagascar has a heroic but little known past of faithful Christian endurance of terrible persecution.

Madagascar's Queen Ranavalona I

Christians in Madagascar suffered greatly under Queen Ranavalona I who, on 26 February 1835, banned the practice of Christianity by Malagasy people. Her husband King Radama had welcomed British missionaries, and a Church was planted. But after he died in 1828, the queen gradually introduced more and more repressive measures. Her 1835 decree specified the death penalty for owning a Bible, meeting with other Christians to worship, or refusing to deny Christ. Those caught were either imprisoned, condemned to hard labour, fined, subjected to the "Tangena Ordeal" or executed in various cruel ways. In one public execution, 15 Christian leaders were dangled from ropes over a ravine about 50 metres deep. When they refused to deny Christ, the ropes were cut. It is impossible to know the exact number of Christians formally executed during Queen Ranavalona's reign (perhaps between 80 and 200) but in addition many Malagasy Christians died from the Tangena Ordeal. In this Ordeal, the accused was forced to swallow poison extracted from tangena nuts; their guilt or innocence was determined by the way their body reacted.

Western missionaries left Madagascar soon after the 1835 decree and did not return until after the queen's death in 1861. The Church grew faster under Queen Ranavalona (a time of persecution but no missionaries) than it had in the relaxed days of King Radama (missionaries but no persecution).

PERSECUTION BY CHRISTIANS

Unfortunately, the subject of persecution *by* Christians cannot be entirely glossed over. Chapter 6 "When Christians became the Persecutors" looks at the classic example of this: when Christianity gained dominance within the Roman Empire in the fourth century and within a few decades became the official state religion. It is shocking to see how quickly the persecuted became the persecutors, not only of non-Christians but even of fellow Christians with other doctrinal beliefs.

There are, sadly and shamefully, all too many historical and present-day examples of Christian-on-Christian persecution and violence. Many readers will think immediately of the Huguenots, the Reformation, the Counter-Reformation, the Thirty Years' War and other European events. Yet there are many examples from other parts of the world.

A few of the other internecine conflicts that have bedevilled the Christian community throughout most of its history – when those who call themselves Christians have turned upon others who call themselves Christians because of differences of belief or ideology or church practice or authority – are mentioned in chapter 13. It is good to note that in the twenty-first century the Catholics have apologised for their treatment of Pentecostals under twentieth-century fascism[5] and the Lutheran Church has apologised for how their forebears persecuted the Anabaptists.

However, much healing still needs to be done with regard to how Christians have seen each other. Thankfully the Church has gone beyond the use of the sword to settle internal disputes, but, in many cases, proper reconciliation and forgiveness have yet to be achieved.

Lutherans apologise to Mennonites

In July 2010,[6] the Lutheran Church formally apologised to the Mennonite Church and asked their forgiveness for what the early Lutherans had done in the sixteenth century to the Anabaptists, whom the Mennonites see as their predecessors.

The Anabaptists were pacifists who also held that baptism should only be given to those who had repented and believed in Christ's atoning work on the cross (therefore not to babies). This seemed heresy to Lutherans, Calvinists, Anglicans and Catholics alike. The Protestants demanded that Anabaptists should be imprisoned or expelled and, occasionally, that they should be executed. Catholics routinely saw execution as the appropriate penalty, and thousands of Anabaptists were indeed killed, while many others fled.

Another issue that Christians cannot ignore is how the Church has responded to those who are outside her, i.e. to those of other religions and beliefs. Sadly, the persecuted became the persecutor and so a tragic history has evolved. Examples from the Roman era are given in chapter 6, but unfortunately it did not stop there. In India, the Portuguese, having demolished the Hindu civilisations in Goa and Buddhist civilisations in Sri Lanka, turned their attention to cruelly persecuting innocent Hindus (and others) under the Goa Inquisition, which continued almost uninterrupted from 1560 to 1820. There are parallels also with Catholic treatment of Amerindians of South America and with Protestant treatment of Africans in South Africa, Muslims in Indonesia, and Native Americans. It is right and proper that the Church faces her mistakes and does not consider the persecution she suffers in isolation from her own actions.

Bearing all these issues in mind, this book will nevertheless keep its main focus on the persecution of Christians by those who do not term themselves Christians. The Lord Jesus told His disciples that the world would hate them because they belonged to Him, and that the world hated Him and His Father without cause.[7]

CHURCH AND STATE

The early Church existed alongside those, both from Judaism and from the Roman Empire, who sought her destruction.[8] Yet she not only survived but thrived. Utilising the Jewish communities scattered around the Mediterranean and even further afield, navigating the roads and the trade routes of the Roman Empire, she was able to take the Gospel to multitudes. Though enduring much pain, suffering and martyrdom, the Church was established without the use of the sword, without financial assistance form the powerful, and without the protection of the state. Whilst Paul could appeal to Caesar, ultimately Caesar was to put him to death.

As the Church evolved throughout history, she became dependent on the state. In fact, in many contexts she became inextricably linked to the state. This meant that when the state persecuted those who were deemed its enemies, the Church was more often than not complicit. Alternatively, the Church could use the state to pursue her own ends. Church leaders became the instruments of punishment instead of the instruments of salvation. Over centuries, from Christendom to city-states, to nation-states, and then to colonial empires, this pattern continued. The Church was able to use colonial structures and resources, as well as the ever expanding networks of trade and communication, to take the Gospel – and often with considerable success. However, this fundamentally changed the Church's mission. For the Gospel no longer came from a weak and vulnerable Christian community as in the early Church. Now the Gospel came with the protection of a state, often an invading state. If anti-Christian persecution came, then the power of that state could be applied to punish the persecutor.

The model of an alliance between Church and state had important exceptions. Moravians, Anabaptists, Mennonites and Free Church missionaries, including such remarkable men as Hudson Taylor, identified with the people of their chosen calling and did not seek the support or help of those governments in their evangelistic or other missionary work. They – and certain other Christians – strongly condemned some of their government's overseas policies, for example, the British imposition of opium on the people of China. This was highlighted by Richard Chenevix Trench, Dean of Westminster, in his sermon at Westminster Abbey on 7 October 1857, Britain's "day of national humiliation".[9] Dean Trench condemned this as one of Britain's national sins.[10]

Yet it is equally true that many Christians saw colonial power as God's gift to facilitate the proclamation of the Gospel and establishing the Church of Jesus Christ. Perhaps they compared it with the practical advantages of the Roman Empire in the first century for making known the Gospel in those days. Sometimes the results were catastrophic. The Berlin Conference (1884-85) handed over Congo to King Leopold of Belgium on the understanding that the Church would care for the people, but the Belgians inflicted appalling atrocities on the Congolese population. The Boxer Rebellion in China in 1900 occurred because colonial powers sought to divide and exploit China and impose Christianity. The rebellion unleashed nationalistic forces which were to engulf Christians, both nationals and missionaries, who died in considerable numbers. These facts of history are not to be forgotten, because they must serve as warnings for us today.

Sadly, the Church, in her history, has given much cause for others to hate her. But if we are to take seriously the words of the Lord Jesus to be "hated without reason", except for the reason that we bear His Name, then we must seek to be faithful to that Lord, to deny ourselves, to take up our cross and to walk in His footsteps in life and in death.

Chapter 2

THE PERSECUTION OF JESUS

"If they persecuted me, they will persecute you also." (John 15:20)

> O sacred head, once wounded,
> With grief and pain weighed down
> How scornfully surrounded
> With thorns, Thine only crown![11]

The persecution of our Lord, which Christians have sung of in their hymns ever since He lived on earth, was foretold hundreds of years earlier in the Old Testament. The pain, shame and rejection of the "man of sorrows" are described with almost unbearable clarity by Isaiah.[12] And even earlier, David wrote of the hideous details that later believers recognised in the crucifixion – the pierced hands and feet, the people staring and gloating, and the heart-rending cry of the abandoned Son, who in His extremity could perhaps no longer remember the eternal purpose for His agony of body and spirit: "My God, my God why have you forsaken me?" (Psalm 22:1)

When a baby just a few weeks old, more prophecies were given about what Jesus was to endure before His work on earth was finished. He was to be "a sign that will be spoken against", said old Simeon to Mary, adding, "And a sword will pierce your own soul too." (Luke 2:34-35)

Some 30 years later, Jesus began His ministry and was soon beset with misunderstanding, hostility, attempted assassination, plots, betrayal and desertion by his closest circle of friends. In Gethsemane we are privileged to get a glimpse of His mental and spiritual anguish as He wrestled with the literally "dread-full" burden of foreknowledge of what was to come (John 18:4). He who was pure and perfect would within hours be carrying the weight of the sins of the world, and dying slowly by the most painful method the Romans had devised. It is little wonder that His sweat was like drops of blood (Luke 22:44).

All these precious truths are well known to Christian believers. But less well known is the outrageous injustice of the legal process to which He was submitted between arrest and execution.

TWO LEGAL SYSTEMS ACCOMPLISHED HIS DESTRUCTION

The Gospels record many details about the series of court trials that our Lord Jesus faced in the hours before His crucifixion. His case was batted to and fro between two legal systems, religious and secular — the ancient law of Moses and the law of Rome, which by this time was highly developed. As H.B. Workman says, "to accomplish His destruction they were both violently wrested into injustice".[13]

The Jerusalem Sanhedrin was the supreme Jewish council and court of justice which, in New Testament times, comprised up to 70 scribes, elders, priests and other respected citizens, presided over by the high priest, making a maximum membership of 71. A quorum of 23 had to be present to conduct any business. The Jerusalem Sanhedrin had no jurisdiction in Galilee, so it was not until Jesus crossed into Judea that He came under their control.

Of course, at this time both Galilee and Judea were part of the Roman Empire and thus the Roman authorities had ultimate power. But it was Roman policy to govern through local institutions and in Judea they sought to appease local feeling as much as possible. So the Sanhedrin was allowed to exercise their judicial functions. The only thing they needed Roman permission for was to enact a death sentence; this permission was usually granted by the Roman procurator (governor) more or less automatically, in line with the policy of pleasing the local people.

LEGAL ARREST

Jesus was arrested on the Thursday night. This was apparently a legal and legitimate arrest by the Sanhedrin, on the charge of causing a riot in the Temple when He threw out the money-changers. The Sanhedrin obtained from the Roman procurator, Pilate, a detachment of Roman soldiers to back up the Temple police when making the arrest. Perhaps the Sanhedrin feared that the Galileans around Jesus would not recognise the authority of the Sanhedrin. Or perhaps they feared that the Temple police might hesitate to arrest the man whose words they must have heard and whose deeds they may have seen. The Roman soldiers were not inhibited by any prior experience of Jesus and duly arrested Him, handed Him over to the officers of the Sanhedrin and left the scene.

ILLEGAL INTERROGATION

Jesus was then taken before Annas to be questioned (John 18:12-13,19-24). This was strictly against Jewish law, which banned any preliminary private interrogation. Annas was a former high priest who had been deposed by the Roman procurator about 15 years earlier for carrying out a death sentence without getting the procurator's permission. However he appeared to retain immense authority in the eyes of the Jewish community, presumably because in Jewish law a high priest is appointed for life. Indeed he was still sometimes called "the high priest". Annas would have taken a personal financial hit from Jesus' action in throwing the money-changers out of the Temple.

ILLEGAL TRIAL – GUILTY VERDICT

Next Jesus was taken before some members of the Sanhedrin, headed by the actual high priest, Caiaphas, who happened to be the son-in-law of Annas (Matthew 26:57-67). Assuming that at least 23 members had assembled, this was marginally less illegal than the hearing before Annas. However it was against Jewish law to hold a trial at night. It was also against Jewish law to hold a trial for a capital offence on the eve of a Sabbath or to hold any trial during a major festival (such as Passover). Furthermore, it was against Jewish law to accept testimony from witnesses who disagreed with each other even slightly (Mark 14:56).

Another short hearing was begun at daybreak, but no witnesses were called, which broke the Jewish laws requiring two or three witnesses and forbidding the use of the accused's confession. So this hearing was in effect just the formal announcement in daylight of the decision taken during the night (Luke 22:66-71; Mark 15:1). A further contravention of Jewish law was the fact that the Sanhedrin did not adjourn for twelve hours before giving their guilty verdict as required in cases where "guilty" would lead to a death sentence.

LEGAL TRIAL – NOT GUILTY VERDICT

As we have seen, the Sanhedrin had to get their death sentences rubber-stamped by the Roman procurator. These requests were usually just nodded through and probably would have been this time as well if the Sanhedrin had stuck to the charge of blasphemy on which they had found Jesus guilty (Mark 14:64). However, when they brought the case to Pilate they changed the charge from blasphemy to treason. This might have been because they did not want Jesus to die by stoning (the punishment laid down in Jewish law for blasphemy) but by crucifixion, which was reserved by the Romans for executing slaves and the worst criminals. Crucifixion was considered the most shameful method to die, not only by the Romans but also by the Jews.[14]

Once the charge of treason was mentioned, Pilate could not consider the matter an internal Jewish religious issue. He was obliged to hold a formal trial himself and look at the case again without reference to the Sanhedrin's findings. High treason against the emperor was the most serious offence in Roman law. In Latin it was *crimen laesae majestatis* (the crime of lese-majesty), often called *majestas* for short. Previously, in the days when Rome was a republic, *majestas* had covered any crime against the Roman people or their security. But when the republic came to an end and Rome transisted to rule by an emperor (who gradually came to be regarded as a god), the law of *majestas* – being both broad and vague – became a powerful instrument of repression and tyranny. Disrespecting the emperor or his statue, whether by words or actions, were obvious breaches of the *majestas* law (and a major difficulty for the early Christians) but an ingenious lawyer could even make tax issues into *majestas* issues, thus incurring the penalty of banishment or death.

When the Sanhedrin first brought Jesus before Pilate, they tried to get Him condemned on a general unspecified warrant (John 18:29-30). Pilate refused to consider such a case, so they had to formulate a specific accusation and came up with three charges: subverting the nation, forbidding the payment of taxes to Caesar, and claiming to be a king (Luke 23:2). According to Roman law, each charge of an indictment had to be tried separately, and Pilate evidently decided to focus on the third as being the most comprehensive and important – important enough to carry a death sentence.

The trial before Pilate seems to have been brief. Jesus entered a plea known in modern law as "confession and avoidance" i.e. admitting to the allegation but adding further facts to neutralise the legal effect of what has been admitted. So Jesus admitted that He was a King but explained that His Kingdom was not of this world (John 18:36-37). Pilate concluded that this was merely a Jewish religious matter after all and announced his verdict: not guilty. "I find no basis for a charge against him." (John 18:38)

OVERTURNING THE LEGAL VERDICT

Pilate had conducted the trial properly according to Roman law. But his principles began to waver in the face of the outraged Jewish leadership and the baying mob. Hearing the word "Galilee" (Luke 23:5) he seized the opportunity to try to send the prisoner to the jurisdiction where the "crime" had been committed instead of where He had been arrested. Galilee did not have a Roman procurator in charge but was ruled instead, with Rome's permission, by a local king, Herod Antipas, one of the sons of Herod the Great.[15] If Pilate had done this *before* announcing his own "not guilty" verdict, it would have been a legal move. But doing so after having already acquitted the accused made it a complete travesty of justice.

Herod Antipas happened to be visiting Jerusalem at the time, so it was a simple matter for Pilate to send Jesus over to him. Prudently, however, Herod avoided getting involved with a charge of *majestas* and simply ridiculed and mocked the prisoner before sending Him back to Pilate. Then what was perhaps a still deeper mockery occurred, this time a mockery of Roman justice. Buss has described it as "a veritable phantasmagoria of injustice and brutality to the accused, of alternate conciliation and expostulation towards the prosecutors, ending in the defeat of the Judge."[16]

Normally, when pronouncing a death sentence, Roman judges would call the sun to witness the justice of their acts. Pilate, however, when he finally yielded to the crowd, followed a Jewish practice and washed his hands, throwing the responsibility of the execution on to the watching multitude (Matthew 27:24-26). So, although Jesus had been formally acquitted a few hours earlier according to proper Roman justice, He was now informally condemned to death by crucifixion for the crime of *majestas*.

TORTURE AND DEATH

One thing Jesus had escaped so far in the judicial process was torture; Pilate had not flouted Roman law to this extent. But now Pilate "had Jesus flogged and handed him over to be crucified" (Matthew 27:26). A world of agony lies in the word "flogged" for it was carried out with leather thongs loaded with balls of lead or bone spikes.

Finally we come to the crucifixion itself, a method of execution deliberately designed for maximum pain, from which the English word "excruciating" is derived. The notice fastened to His cross made clear the charge of *majestas*: "JESUS OF NAZARETH, THE KING OF THE JEWS".

Who was responsible for His death?

> Who was the guilty? Who brought this upon thee?
> Alas, my treason, Jesus, hath undone thee!
> 'Twas I, Lord Jesus, I it was denied thee;
> I crucified thee.[17]

The shame of crucifixion

Crucifixion was apparently invented by the Persians, the first known usage being in 519 BC when King Darius crucified 3,000 political opponents in Babylon. It was then adopted by Alexander the Great and his successors including the Seleucid Empire (which covered the Levant), and later by the Romans.

Romans considered crucifixion the most shameful method of execution, and it was therefore rarely applied to anyone with the status of Roman citizen unless they were guilty of treason. Jews likewise considered it supremely shameful because "cursed is everyone who is hung on a tree" (Galatians 3:13 (New Living Translation) referring to Deuteronomy 21:23). The Hebrew in Deuteronomy 21:22 could be translated either that the person to be executed "is put to death when you hang him on the tree" or that he "is put to death and thereafter you hang him on a tree". In other words, it is unclear whether the person is to be hung alive on the tree until he dies or whether he is executed first and then his corpse hung on the tree (or pole or cross – alternative meanings of the Hebrew word "tree").

One of the longest of the "Dead Sea Scrolls" is known as the Temple Scroll. It is the work of a Jewish scholar from the second century BC who created a new edition of the laws of Deuteronomy, incorporating verses from other parts of the Torah as well as priestly teaching from his own time. Here is his expanded version of Deuteronomy 21:22-23:

> If a man informs against his people, delivers his people up to a foreign nation and betrays his people, you shall hang him on the tree so that he dies. On the word of two or three witnesses shall he be put to death, and they shall hang him on the tree.

> If a man commits a crime punishable by death, and he defects into the midst of the nations and curses his people, the children of Israel, you shall hang him also on the tree so that he dies. And their bodies shall not remain upon the tree, but you shall bury them the same day, for those who hang on the tree are accursed by God and men, you must not defile the land which I gave you as an inheritance. (Temple Scroll 64:6-13)

So the Temple Scroll states clearly that someone who betrays or curses their nation should be executed by being hung alive on the tree. Rabbinic sources show that this phrase primarily meant execution by hanging on a pole. Crucifixion was another form of hanging someone on a tree.

Chapter 3

THE APOSTLES AND THEIR CONTEMPORARIES

It was not long after Christ's resurrection that persecution began for His followers, especially for the leaders of the fledgling Church. This was exactly what the Lord Jesus Himself had warned them would happen: "If they persecuted me, they will persecute you also." (John 15:20)

Some of this persecution is described in the New Testament and more is recorded in traditions passed down amongst the believers through the ages or in historical documents. The traditions of different church denominations can vary greatly, so in some cases it is very hard to know what really happened. While dates and details may be uncertain, what we can be sure of is that these brave believers witnessed and suffered for their faith. It is remarkable to consider that many of them had at one time forsaken their Master and fled when He was arrested, even – in the case of Peter – had denied knowing Him. Yet now, empowered by the Holy Spirit, they endured torment, torture and often martyrdom.

Although we know in considerable detail about Paul's persecution, for most of the others in this chapter we have little information about the details of what they endured in their years of ministry. But we know that many of them were martyred, for the fact of their glorious sacrifice was treasured by their contemporaries and passed down by them to other Christians through the ages. As martyrdom is usually the culmination of a period of persecution, we can be sure that most of the martyrs also suffered much persecution before their death. We know too of some like the apostle John who suffered persecution without it ending in martyrdom.

It is incredible to read how far these first followers of the Lord travelled as they spread the Gospel. How demanding, difficult and dangerous travel was at that time. But Jesus had commanded them to "go and make disciples of all nations" and they faithfully obeyed this Great Commission (Matthew 28:19).

The persecution began almost immediately, as we read in Acts 4 about the opposition faced by Peter and John, and in the following chapter of the harassment of all the apostles. But the Church grew. As the years rolled by, persecution became all too familiar, partly fluctuating with the whims of the current Roman emperor,[18] partly a response by Jewish or pagan religious leaders, and sometimes a response by individuals or communities angered by the likely loss of livelihoods.

How would the early Christians have felt as their oldest, most respected and experienced leaders, including most of those who had known the Lord Jesus personally, were brutally killed, one by one? Look at the cluster of martyrdoms in the 60s AD – Andrew, Matthew, Barnabas, Peter and Paul, very likely all of them grey-haired by this time. In addition James son of Alphaeus, Judas Thaddaeus, Simon the Zealot and Mark the Evangelist were also probably martyred in the first eight years of this decade, under Emperor Nero's insane cruelties.

But the patient endurance of these brave Christians only seems to have served to draw more people to the Lord Jesus whom they served.

STEPHEN, MARTYRED C. 34 AD

Stephen, who has the honour of being recognised as the first Christian martyr, was not an apostle but a deacon, appointed by the apostles to head up an area of practical ministry within the young Church (Acts 6:1-6). We know from the book of Acts that he was "a man full of God's grace and power" who "performed great wonders and signs among the people" (Acts 6:8). At a crisis point in his persecution, his enemies saw that his face was "like the face of an angel" (Acts 6:15).

Stephen's preaching of the Gospel brought him into conflict with Jews from his own Greek-speaking background. But those who argued with him "could not stand up against the wisdom the Spirit gave him as he spoke" (Acts 6:10). Consequently, they had him falsely accused of blasphemy. Stephen gave a powerful speech, outlining the history of God's people rejecting His appointed leaders, and concluded fearlessly, "You stiff-necked people! Your hearts and ears are still uncircumcised. You are just like your ancestors: You always resist the Holy Spirit! Was there ever a prophet your ancestors did not persecute? They even killed those who predicted the coming of the Righteous One. And now you have betrayed and murdered him – you who have received the law that was given through angels but have not obeyed it." (Acts 7:51-53)

This enraged the Sanhedrin, but Stephen was encouraged by a vision of heaven opened and Jesus standing at the right hand of God. Covering their ears, his former listeners dragged him out of the city and stoned him to death. As Jesus had prayed on the cross for forgiveness for those who killed him, Stephen likewise prayed, as he was being killed, that the Lord would not hold this sin against his murderers (Acts 7:54-60).

JAMES, SON OF ZEBEDEE, MARTYRED C. 44

Only a few martyrdoms are recorded in the New Testament, but one of them is James, the older brother of John. We know that these two sons of Zebedee were Galilean fishermen, amongst the very first of those called by Jesus to be His disciples. Along with Peter they made up Jesus' inner circle of three apostles who, for example, witnessed the transfiguration.

The brothers probably had impetuous and fiery temperaments, at least in their youth, as they were known as "the Sons of Thunder". Perhaps this aspect of their character is also seen in their decision to ask Jesus for the most honoured places – on either side of Him – in His Kingdom. Jesus replied by asking whether they could drink the same cup He would drink and be baptised with the same baptism, both phrases being ways of speaking of great suffering. They said they could and Jesus affirmed that this suffering would indeed come to them (Matthew 20:20-23; Mark 10:35-40). So James had an early and very personal indication that he would be persecuted, and he was indeed the first of the apostles to die for Christ.

Nothing is known of James' particular ministry between the time when he returned to Jerusalem after witnessing the ascension (Acts 1:13) and his execution about 14 years later, in the midst of a general anti-Christian persecution by King Herod Agrippa.

> It was about this time that King Herod arrested some who belonged to the church, intending to persecute them. He had James, the brother of John, put to death with the sword. (Acts 12:1-2)

PHILIP, MARTYRED C. 54 OR LATER

Philip, one of the twelve original apostles, came from the Galilean city of Bethsaida and, despite his Greek name, he was Jewish.

According to tradition, after the resurrection, Philip made a number of missionary journeys, often with his friend and fellow apostle Nathanael Bartholomew. On one such journey, when they were accompanied by Philip's sister Mariamne, they came to Hierapolis (in modern Turkey) which was the centre of a snake-worship cult. Of course, Philip and Bartholomew urged the people to turn from the snake to Jesus. Many did so, including Nicanora, the Jewish wife of the proconsul, who was sick in bed so only heard the apostles' teaching second hand. But she called on the Name of the Lord and found herself healed of her many illnesses. She got up and made her way to see Mariamne, who told her that Christ, the Sun of Righteousness, had risen upon her to enlighten her and rescue her from the snake to whom she had been given. Nicanora loudly and publicly declared her new faith, and Philip with the rest of his group prayed for her. At this point Nicanora's husband, the proconsul, arrived, apparently furious at finding his wife suddenly healed. He ignored Nicanora's impassioned plea to him to turn from snake worship, and dragged her away by her hair, saying he would first kill her and then put the "foreign magicians" to "a most cruel death".

He had Philip, Bartholomew and Mariamne whipped and then dragged by their feet through the streets to the snake temple. The snake priests, supported by a crowd of thousands, pleaded with the proconsul to punish the three Christians, whose effective preaching had devastated worship at their temple. As proof of how dangerous the "corrupters and seducers of men" were, the snake priests said, "They say, 'Live in chastity and piety, after believing in God'.

The dragons (i.e. the large snakes) have not struck them blind, or even killed them; but even the keepers of our city (the snakes) have been cast down by these men."

The proconsul did not need much persuasion. He was already thoroughly enraged by everything his wife kept telling him about Jesus being the true Light and the way she prayed all night and spoke in a strange language. He even saw a light shining around her, and when he went to look out of the window to see Jesus the Light he was almost blinded by the brightness, like lightning. "Since then, I have been afraid of my wife on account of her luminous Jesus," he said.

He ordered the public executioner to strip Philip, Bartholomew and even Mariamne to try to find whatever they used for their "enchantments". Then he had Philip crucified on a tree near the snake temple, head downwards and held by iron hooks piercing his ankles and heels. Bartholomew was crucified on a wall opposite, with nails through his hands. The two men, who had been friends even before they met Jesus, smiled at each other.

Tradition records that Philip and Bartholomew hung on the tree and the wall for six days, during which time the apostle John arrived in Hierapolis. Many dramatic events occurred, leading most of those who had opposed them to repentance. Believers then ran up to Philip, intending to take him down from the tree, but he told them to see to Bartholomew first, because he, Philip, was about to "depart from his body" to be with the Lord. Bartholomew was brought down from the wall and his life was saved. Meanwhile Philip gave final instructions for establishing a church in Hierapolis and directed who should lead it, all of which was done. Bartholomew and Mariamne departed separately to continue their missionary travels.

Although the details of this story are not accepted by all, it is widely held that Philip was martyred in Hierapolis, either around the year 54 or in the last two decades of the first century. A tomb believed to be his was discovered in 2011 by archaeologists who were excavating ancient Hierapolis.

ANDREW, MARTYRED C. 60

Andrew was a Galilean fisherman, going about an ordinary day's work, when Jesus called him and his brother Simon to follow him and become fishers of men (Mark 1:16-17). Without hesitation Andrew and Simon abandoned the safety and familiarity of what they knew in order to follow Jesus, and ultimately to follow Him to their deaths.

Andrew is recorded as having preached the Gospel far and wide: in Scythia, Colchis, Greece, Epirus and Achaia. Tradition says that, like Jesus, Andrew was crucified but in Andrew's case he was tied to the cross, not nailed, and it was an X-shaped cross, not a vertical one. This is believed to have taken place at Patras in Achaia (Greece) in about the year 60.

Foxe's Book of Martyrs describes the apostle's courage as he faced death, and records his words:

> O cross, most welcome and oft-looked for; with a willing mind, joyfully and desirously, I come to thee, being the scholar of Him who did hang on thee; because I have been always thy lover, and have longed to embrace thee![19]

Andrew hung on the cross for three days and continued to proclaim Christ, with the result that onlookers began to believe in Jesus and asked the governor that he should be taken down. The governor consented, but, by the time Andrew was taken down, he had died.

MATTHEW, MARTYRED C. 60

Around the same time that Andrew was crucified, the apostle Matthew was also martyred but in a very different place and by a very different method.

Matthew had been a tax collector – a greatly despised profession in New Testament times – until called by Jesus to follow Him, much to the consternation of the Pharisees who were scandalised by Jesus' association with "sinners".

It is believed that after Jesus' ascension Matthew, who is referred to by the name Levi in the Gospels of Mark and Luke, preached in Judea for nine years, taking the Gospel to fellow Jews. His Gospel was evidently written with a Jewish readership in mind. Matthew is also reported to have preached in Persia, Parthia and Ethiopia.

His martyrdom probably took place in Parthia or Ethiopia around the year 60, although "Ethiopia" may not mean the country in Africa of today. In one account he was stabbed in the back as he stood at the altar with his hands raised in prayer.

BARNABAS, MARTYRED C. 61

Barnabas, a Jewish Cypriot, was one of the earliest disciples in Jerusalem. His real name was Joseph but the apostles gave him the name Barnabas, meaning "son of consolation" or "son of encouragement", reflecting the beautiful character we see described in the book of Acts. He always thought the best of others, wanted to raise them up and involve them in the Lord's work, and gave generously of his own property for distribution by the apostles to other Christians in need.

The Jerusalem church leaders sent Barnabas to Antioch to build up the new church of Gentiles there. True to his character, when he arrived in Antioch "and saw what the grace of God had done, he was glad and encouraged them all to remain true to the Lord with all their hearts. He was a good man, full of the Holy Spirit and faith, and a great number of people were brought to the Lord." (Acts 11:23-24)

One of those nurtured and encouraged by Barnabas was Paul, and they worked together to teach the Christians of Antioch. Later they travelled extensively together, first to take a church offering from Antioch to Jerusalem and then to preach the Gospel. During their missionary journey, Barnabas and Paul repeatedly encountered opposition. On one occasion, in Pisidian Antioch, "almost the whole city gathered to hear the word of the Lord". The Jews were jealous and opposed the pair, inciting the city's prominent citizens against them and finally having them expelled (Acts 13:44-50). At Iconium there was a plot to stone them, but Barnabas and Paul heard what was afoot and left before the plan could be implemented. However, their enemies in Antioch and Iconium followed them to Lystra and persuaded the crowd to actually stone Paul, who was left for dead. The next day he and Barnabas moved on to the city of Derbe (Acts 14:19-20).

After this journey, Barnabas returned with Paul to the ministry at Antioch for a while. Later Barnabas returned to his homeland, Cyprus, where he established the Church. Tradition records that he was martyred, probably at Salamis on Cyprus in the year 61, being dragged out of a synagogue, where he was preaching the Gospel, by Jews who were infuriated by the success of his ministry. They stoned him to death.

How closely Barnabas' death reflects what the Lord Jesus had said would happen to His followers: "They will put you out of the synagogue; in fact, the time is coming when anyone who kills you will think they are offering a service to God." (John 16:2)

JAMES SON OF ALPHAEUS, MARTYRED C. 62

This apostle occurs in lists of the Twelve and even the Eleven (Acts 1:13) but apart from that nothing is known about him for sure. Some scholars identify him with other individuals called James, but with little supporting evidence.

There are, however, traditions that he was martyred. Some say that he was crucified by pagans at Ostrakine (El Felusiyat in the Sinai area of modern Egypt) where he was preaching the Gospel. Others say he was sentenced to death by the Sanhedrin in Jerusalem in the year 62, then thrown from the parapet of the Temple, stoned, and finally clubbed to death.

SIMON PETER, MARTYRED C. 64

Simon, to whom Jesus gave the name Peter, was martyred about four years after his brother Andrew. Three decades earlier, Simon Peter had avoided persecution by denying that he knew Jesus when Jesus was arrested and taken for trial. Earlier still, he had rebuked Jesus for predicting His persecution and death, and had received a strong rebuke from Jesus in turn for his too-human thought processes (Matthew 16:21-23).

But of course Jesus was not wrong when he gave the name "Rock" to his disciple Simon. After the resurrection, Peter was transformed and spoke out boldly. Thus he and John were the first to suffer persecution, as we shall see on page 31. The letter he wrote that is called 1 Peter in the New Testament was addressed to scattered and persecuted Christians, probably at the time of Emperor Nero, to prepare them for worse suffering to come.

After King Herod had had James killed, probably in the year 44, and saw that this "pleased the Jews", he had Peter arrested as well (Acts 12:3). But Peter was miraculously freed from jail by an angel.

Peter spent the final part of his life in Rome, where he was martyred under Emperor Nero. It is thought that he wrote 2 Peter while in prison awaiting execution. According to tradition, he was detained with the apostle Paul, and together they converted two captains of the guard and 47 others to Christianity during their time in prison. After nine months, Peter was brought for execution, given a severe flogging and then crucified with his head downwards. It is traditionally believed that Peter himself asked to be crucified upside down because he considered himself unworthy to be crucified in the same way as Jesus.

He had been prepared for his martyrdom by the risen Lord in their final meeting, in which Jesus restored Peter and put him in charge of tending the flock, also warning him, "when you are old you will stretch out your hands, and someone else will dress you and lead you where you do not want to go." (John 21:18-19)

JUDAS THADDAEUS, MARTYRED C.65

Amongst the original twelve apostles were two called Judas, one being the infamous Judas Iscariot who betrayed Jesus. The story of the other Judas, the faithful apostle, is very obscure. This is probably in part because the name "Judas" became unpopular in the early Church, for obvious reasons, and all the Judases of the early Church seem to have adopted other names, causing later believers some difficulty in trying to be sure who was who. Judas the faithful apostle is sometimes referred to as "Judas son of James" or as "Thaddaeus". John simply says he is "Judas not Iscariot".

He is always paired with Simon the Zealot, both in the New Testament and in tradition. It is believed they travelled together to preach the Gospel in Palestine and possibly further afield in the Middle East. (Judas Thaddaeus is the "St Jude" of many churches dedicated to "St Simon and St Jude".)

In all the muddle and confusion, one fact is repeated in every tradition – that Judas Thaddaeus was martyred. This may have taken place in Beirut in

25

Phoenicia (modern Lebanon) or in Persia. He may have been clubbed to death or killed with an axe. But the one repeated message is that he died for Christ.

SIMON THE ZEALOT, MARTYRED IN THE 60S?

Simon the Zealot is an even more mysterious apostle than Judas Thaddaeus. Some traditions say that he was martyred together with Judas in Beirut in about 65 AD. But there are many other alternative stories of how Simon the Zealot died. Some say he was martyred in Persia by being sawn in half. Some say he was crucified in Abkhazia on the eastern coast of the Black Sea (now a territory disputed between Georgia and Russia). Some say that Simon's crucifixion occurred in Britain, on the second of two missionary journeys he made there. Specifically, it is said that he was arrested, tried and crucified at Caistor (in modern Lincolnshire) on about 10 May 61, when Britain was under the rule of the Roman procurator Catus Decianus.

There is also a tradition that Simon died peacefully at Edessa. This would be an ironic end for someone reputed to have preached the Gospel in Egypt, Mauritania and Spain as well as all the places listed above and known for his radical and revolutionary tendencies.

PAUL, MARTYRED C. 66-67

Following his dramatic conversion on the road to Damascus, Paul went from chief persecutor of Christians to being persecuted himself. He summed up what he had suffered so far in his second surviving letter to the Corinthians, which was probably written between 55 and 57 AD. Some of these incidents are the common dangers of travel in the first century (shipwreck, bandits etc.) but the majority are anti-Christian persecution:

> I have worked much harder, been in prison more frequently, been flogged more severely, and been exposed to death again and again. Five times I received from the Jews the forty lashes minus one. Three times I was beaten with rods, once I was pelted with stones, three times I was shipwrecked, I spent a night and a day in the open sea, I have been constantly on the move. I have been in danger from rivers, in danger from bandits, in danger from my fellow Jews, in danger

from Gentiles; in danger in the city, in danger in the country, in danger at sea; and in danger from false believers. (2 Corinthians 11:23b-26)

We have further details of some of these incidents from the book of Acts, for example the Jewish plots to kill him in Damascus and Jerusalem or being attacked and beaten by angry mobs.

It has been calculated that Paul may have spent up to 25% of his ministry time in prisons of various kinds. This is all the more remarkable given that prisons in the ancient world were rarely used for punishment as such, although people were routinely stripped naked and flogged before being imprisoned and then held in painful leg irons. The normal use of a prison was as holding cells for those on remand and awaiting trial or for those convicted and awaiting execution. Tradition says that during Paul's second imprisonment in Rome, before his execution, he was held in the appalling Mamertine Prison, which could fittingly have been called the "House of Darkness". Worse still, he was being held in its underground dungeon, which had been described earlier by the Roman historian Sallust as "foul from neglect, darkness and stench, it is an altogether terrifying sight". It was here that Paul wrote the letter we know as 2 Timothy. It seems he had already had a preliminary hearing and was now awaiting his final trial, at which he expected to be found guilty and then executed. (2 Timothy 4:6-7,16)

There is a strong tradition that Paul's execution took place on the Ostian Way in Rome by order of Emperor Nero in about 66 AD, soon after writing his letter to Timothy. Because he was a Roman citizen Paul was probably beheaded rather than subjected to any more prolonged and painful death.

MARK THE EVANGELIST, MARTYRED C. 68

John Mark, the writer of Mark's Gospel, grew up in a reasonably well to do Jewish family in Jerusalem. His family home was a place where Christians gathered regularly. It was where Peter headed after the angel freed him from prison and, sure enough, he found many believers there praying for him (Acts 12:12). It may have been the same house in whose upper room Jesus had met to eat the Passover with the twelve apostles on the night He was betrayed and arrested.

The first we hear of John Mark himself is when he fled from danger and persecution on that terrible night when Jesus was arrested. He is thought to be the young man who left his garment behind – probably his nightwear – and fled naked when those who had come to arrest Jesus seized him also (Mark 14:51-52). (It was common practice at the time for an author to mention themselves briefly but anonymously in their writing.)

However, he must have been an impressive young man when Paul and Barnabas met him some years later, for they took him back to Antioch to help them in the ministry there (Acts 12:25). In about 46 AD, John Mark set off with Barnabas and Paul on what was later called Paul's first missionary journey but soon left them to return to Jerusalem (Acts 13:4-5,13). When, perhaps three years later, Paul wanted to revisit the believers along the route of his first journey, he refused to take the unreliable John Mark, so Barnabas took John Mark to Cyprus instead.

Early records show that John Mark later spent time with Peter, helping him to evangelise the northern parts of Asia Minor (modern Turkey). After this they visited Rome together to teach the Christians there. The influence of Peter can be seen in the content of Mark's Gospel.

Mark was still in Rome when Paul arrived and spent two years under house arrest, but had gone by the time Paul was serving his second prison term in Rome, this time in the unspeakable Mamertine Prison (Philemon 23-24; 2 Timothy 4:11).

According to tradition, it was Mark who brought the Gospel to Egypt and established a church at Alexandria, which was later to become an important centre of Christianity. The Coptic Church teaches that he was martyred in Alexandria in the year 68 when Easter Day coincided with a big pagan religious celebration. A pagan mob broke into the church where he was leading a communion service, tied him with rope and dragged him through the streets. By the end of the day, he was badly wounded but still alive, so the next day they dragged him over rocks and rougher ground until he was dead.

THOMAS, MARTYRED C. 72

Although Thomas has come to be known as "doubting Thomas" because of his sceptical response to the news of Jesus' resurrection, at other times he displayed deep love and faith in the Lord. John records Thomas' understanding of what Jesus had come to do, and his willingness to die with Him (John 11:16).

Thomas did indeed die for his Lord. According to tradition, his martyrdom took place in around the year 72 in south India where he had spent two decades labouring for the Gospel, and facing much opposition.[20]

MATTHIAS, MARTYRED C. 80

Matthias was the man chosen to replace Judas Iscariot as the twelfth apostle (Acts 1:21-26). We know from this that he had been a follower of Jesus from the very beginning of His ministry and had seen the risen Christ.

Apart from this the Bible tells us nothing about him, and nor do the historical records. There is a tradition that he was crucified, another that he was stoned to death, another that he was burnt to death, another that he was beheaded and another that he died of old age. There is a tradition that he died soon after his election, i.e. about the year 30, and another tradition that he died about the year 80. So there is almost nothing we can say for certain of Matthias except that as a worthy follower of Christ and an apostle, he surely preached the Gospel at a time when that was a dangerous thing to do, and most likely met with opposition and persecution, whether or not he died a martyr.

NATHANAEL BARTHOLOMEW, MARTYRED SOME TIME BETWEEN 55 AND 90

Bartholomew was one of the twelve men chosen by Jesus to be His apostles. As "Bartholomew" is a family name (meaning the son of Tolmai or Talmai) and because he is always linked with Philip in the Gospels, it is thought that he is probably the same person as Nathanael, the guileless and transparent apostle, who was called at the same time as Philip (John 1:43-45). So his name would have been Nathanael Bar Tolmai.

The fourth-century church historian Eusebius[21] records that Bartholomew evangelised in India, and left behind a copy of Matthew's Gospel in Hebrew. He is said also to have preached in Ethiopia, Mesopotamia (modern Iraq),

Parthia (in modern Iran), Lycaonia (in modern Turkey) and Armenia (a word which referred to a larger area than modern Armenia). We have already seen how Bartholomew survived crucifixion at Hierapolis, when his friend Philip's martyrdom took place.

According to tradition, Bartholomew's own martyrdom came when he was crucified a second time. This is said to have occurred in Armenia, when he was scourged, flayed, crucified upside down and then beheaded. The exceptionally cruel execution followed a series of dramatic power encounters with demons associated with the god Astaruth, to whom people went for healing of their sicknesses. One account runs:

> Then the Apostle said to the people, "Behold, the god whom you thought to cure you, does more mischief to your souls and bodies. Hear now your Maker who dwells in the heavens, and do not believe in lifeless stones. And if you wish that I should pray for you, and that all these may receive health, take down this idol, and break it to pieces. And when you have done this, I will sanctify this temple in the name of our Lord Jesus Christ; and having baptized all of you who are in it in the baptism of the Lord, and sanctified you, I will save all."

> Then the king gave orders, and all the people brought ropes and crowbars, and were not at all able to take down the idol. Then the Apostle said to them, "Unfasten the ropes". And when they had unfastened them, he said to the demon dwelling in it: In the name of our Lord Jesus Christ, come out of this idol, and go into a desert place, where neither winged creature utters a cry, nor voice of man has ever been heard. And straightway he arose at the word of the apostle, and lifted it up from its foundations; and in that same hour all the idols that were in that place were broken in pieces. Then all cried out with one voice, saying, "He alone is God Almighty whom Bartholomew proclaims."[22]

Many people became Christians but many others were outraged at the shattering of the idols. Bartholomew's gruesome death followed soon after.

Various dates have been suggested for his martyrdom including 55, 68, 70 or 90 AD. One possible location was Derbent, on the Caspian Sea (in modern Dagestan, Russia). It is interesting to note that in the fifth and sixth centuries,

Derbent became an important centre for propagating the Christian faith in the Caucasus.

JOHN

John, the disciple especially beloved by Jesus, does not seem to have travelled as widely as most of the other apostles. His early years of ministry were apparently focused in Judea, and later on he was based in Ephesus as leader of the churches in Asia Minor. He also differs from almost all the others in that he was not martyred. Tradition records that he died in Ephesus in extreme old age, perhaps around the year 100.

He did, however, endure many types of persecution during his long life. He was arrested and detained overnight with Peter in the very first recorded incident of persecution after the resurrection (Acts 4:1-22). Before long it happened again, this time with all the apostles, and an angel released them. They were immediately arrested again, brought before the Sanhedrin, flogged and released (Acts 5:17-41). All this was of course accompanied by many threats from the authorities.

John himself tells in his own words of his exile, much later in life, on the small island of Patmos, where he wrote the book of Revelation:

> I, John, your brother and companion in the suffering and kingdom and patient endurance that are ours in Jesus, was on the island of Patmos because of the word of God and the testimony of Jesus (Revelation 1:9).

It is believed he was released from Patmos and returned to Ephesus around the year 95 where he wrote his Gospel and the three letters we have in the New Testament.

Tradition fills in some examples of persecution for John between the early and late experiences that we read of in Scripture. There is a story that he was challenged to drink a cup of poison by a priest of Diana at Ephesus. Tertullian records a tradition that John was thrown into a cauldron of boiling oil at the Latin Gate of Rome, under the persecution of the Roman Emperor Domitian.[23] In both cases, John was miraculously delivered.

"A CONSTANT VISION BEFORE OUR EYES"

Eusebius, who was not only a historian but also Bishop of Caesarea, wrote in the introduction to his book on the martyrs of Palestine about the way in which he personally was inspired by the courage and character of the martyrs, who had themselves been inspired to stand firm by the words of an earlier martyr, the apostle Paul (in Romans 8:35-39). The reason he wrote his book was so that the martyrs should not be forgotten but be a "constant vision before our eyes" to inspire the Christians that came after them.

> Let us therefore, relate the manifest signs and glorious proofs of the divine doctrine, and commit to writing a commemoration not to be forgotten, setting also their marvellous virtues as a constant vision before our eyes. For I am struck with wonder at their all-enduring courage, at their confession under many forms, and at the wholesome alacrity of their souls, the elevation of their minds, the open profession of their faith, the clearness of their reason, the patience of their condition, and the truth of their religion: how they were not cast down in their minds, but their eyes looked upwards, and they neither trembled nor feared. The love of God, also, and of His Christ, supplied them with an all-effective power, by which they overcame their enemies. For they loved God, the supreme sovereign of all, and they loved Him with all their might. He, too, requited their love to Him by the aid which He afforded them : and they also were loved by Him, and strengthened against their enemies, applying the words of that confessor who had already borne his testimony before them and exclaiming "Who shall separate us from Christ? shall tribulation, or affliction, or persecution, or hunger, or death, or the sword? as it is written, For thy sake we die daily : we are reckoned as lambs for the slaughter." And again, when this same martyr magnifies that patience which cannot be overcome by evil, he says – "that in all these things we conquer for Him who loved us." And he foretold that all evils are overcome by the love of God, and that all terrors and afflictions are trodden down, while he exclaimed, and said : "Because I am persuaded that neither death, nor life, nor things present, nor things to come, nor powers, nor height, nor depth, nor any other creature, shall be able to separate us from the love of God which is in our Lord Jesus Christ."[24]

Chapter 4

TO 312 AD: HATED BY THE ROMAN WORLD

Jesus said, "If the world hates you, keep in mind that it hated me first."

John 15:18

> The fires of popular hatred were ever smouldering, liable at any moment to break into sudden flame … [the early Christians] lived under the shadow of a great hate.
>
> H.B. Workman, *Persecution in the Early Church* (1906), p.107

> So to the wild wolf Hate were sacrificed
> The panting, huddled flock, whose crime was Christ.
>
> Sir William Watson (1858-1905)

The agony of Gethsemane, the mental anguish of a rigged trial, the physical torture preceding the crucifixion, and finally the nailing of Jesus to the cross and the appalling pain were followed for Jesus by that ultimate suffering when He cried out "My God, my God, why have you forsaken me?" So, it seemed, ended a life that had shown so much promise. For many the death of Jesus was a hope devastated and a calamitous defeat.

But three days later Jesus rose triumphantly from the grave. He met with His disciples and they encountered Him in His bodily resurrection. Then this timid band of cowards and betrayers became invigorated and, as they experienced the reality of the Holy Spirit in the Upper Room in Jerusalem, so they were transformed. From lambs they became lions. Those who had lost all hope were filled with a passion and a vision of what Jesus wanted of them and what the world could become. And so, following His ascension, His disciples went out into the world to make disciples of all nations.

There were many positives in their mission, which focused firstly on the Jews, for Jesus was a Jew and they themselves were Jews so it was the natural starting place. Commencing with Jerusalem, they took the Gospel to the Jewish diaspora that had been scattered around the then known world, preaching first in the synagogues and then, when rejected, moving into the streets, public places and homes. They also entered the Roman world which, like the Jewish world, had seemingly been prepared for the coming of the Messiah.

SHEEP AMONG WOLVES

They saw the remarkable work of the Holy Spirit as many became followers of Jesus Christ. "I am sending you out like sheep among wolves," the Lord had said to them earlier (Matthew 10:16). The words Jesus had spoken in His days on earth soon become a reality for them in their lives. Jesus had said that, because of Him, a family would turn against each other. Their ultimate faith and loyalty in Jesus Christ would bring conflict and division between close relatives (Matthew 10:34-35). Communities would be divided over Jesus. For Paul, the former zealous Pharisee, considered that everything was "rubbish" compared with "gaining Christ" and that rubbish included his heritage as a Jew (Philippians 3:4-9). Those who had asserted the Jewishness of their faith and their loyalty to the Jewish nation would have now let their loyalty to Jesus take precedence. Then there was the choice between Caesar and Christ (Matthew 22:21; Acts 4:19): while certain duties were owed to the state, ultimate loyalty must be to Christ.

The disciples were to learn that in triumph there would be pain. They would discover that now they had not only to embrace the cross but also to carry the marks of the cross in their bodies as a new community, the *ekklesia* of God (those called out of the world). As the Body of Christ, they would now share in the sufferings of Christ. And they would conquer the world, not with the sword but with the cross of shame and suffering. Jesus had rightly told them that if they were to be His disciples they had to deny themselves, take up their cross and follow Him, that to lose their life was to find it (Matthew 16:24-25). There was now no way back. This new expression of early Christianity was inextricably linked to suffering and persecution. They would be the hated minority, the scum of the earth, the refuse of the world (1 Corinthians 4:13). Weak and vulnerable, they succeeded against all the odds. But at a tremendous cost. For Christ's followers knew alienation and, as we have seen in chapter 3, all but one of the apostles followed Him in martyrdom.

GROWTH OF THE EARLY CHURCH

The conditions that, humanly speaking, encouraged Christianity and facilitated its rapid spread were:

1. **Pax Romana**
   The Roman Empire, which covered the known civilised world, was by now unified and at peace. Communications (often by letter) and travel (by road and sea) were easier than for many centuries before and after. The empire's political unity and single system of law made the concept of a worldwide Church easier to imagine.

2. **Greek language**
   Greek was the trade language used throughout the Roman Empire. The abiding Greek interest in philosophy meant that religious and philosophical subjects were commonly discussed.

3. **Jewish diaspora**
   Jews had settled all across the empire, bringing with them monotheism, morality and a simple style of worship. Judaism attracted a lot of attention and many Gentiles came to worship at the synagogues.

4. **Hungry souls**
   There seems to have been a great spiritual hunger at this time, as mystery religions came flooding in from the east.

And so the Church grew. But this growth was met with rejection and hostility. The fact of persecution of the early Christians is not in doubt, but its full extent is unknown. It appears that, on the whole, ordinary Christians were not harassed; it was the leaders and the most zealous and active believers who were the focus of persecution.

Jewish reaction

This was an implacable hostility. The four main stumbling blocks were:

- **The cross**, for a crucified Messiah was nonsensical to Jews who were waiting for a victorious political leader.
- **The resurrection**, which they could not accept as a fact, particularly because Sadducees did not believe in any kind of resurrection or afterlife.
- **The inclusion of the Gentiles** in the Church on equal terms with Jews. This was a very serious hindrance.
- **Jesus the Son of God**, a concept that was hard to accept for followers of a faith whose main distinctive had always been its monotheism.

The Jews circulated false accusations against Christians, and encouraged anti-Christian mob violence by the general population. They also made sure that the Roman bureaucracy penalised Christians instead of giving them the privileges that Jews enjoyed. They were able to inflict serious economic consequences on Christians from a Jewish background, who would also be cursed during synagogue prayers. There were also occasions when, according to Justin Martyr (died c. 165), "the Jews treat us as open enemies, putting us to death and torturing us".

Roman reaction

Religion was considered a state matter, and everyone in the empire was required to participate in the rituals of the Roman state religion. This religion was gradually evolving from worship of the various Roman gods of myth and legend to include worship of the living Roman emperor, whoever he might be at any given time. Following other religions was allowed, so long as people also observed the state religion and their other religious practices did not involve gross immorality. But anything that seemed to undermine the state religion or constitute a political threat to the empire was not permitted. Those who refused to sacrifice to the emperor were guilty of the serious crime of *majestas* (lese-majesty, or treason against the emperor).[25]

At first Christianity was tolerated by the authorities as it was considered to be a Jewish sect. Judaism was a religion favoured by the Roman state, partly because it was a national religion – a concept which Romans understood and often approved – and partly because Jews were a useful source of revenue for the state. Although hated by the general population, Jews (7% of the Roman Empire) were influential among the ruling classes, who protected them and gave them many privileges including exemption from making the mandatory sacrifices to the emperor.

But soon Christianity began to be viewed as a definite threat to the Roman state religion. For a start, Christian evangelists declared that all other religions were false. Worse still, they refused to worship the emperor. The apocalyptic hope that Christians spoke of as they longed for the return of Christ was interpreted by others as plotting a coup to overthrow the emperor and seize political power. The way in which some Christians – church leaders especially – renounced wealth and embraced poverty was completely baffling to onlookers, who accused the Christians of being anarchists.

Christians reacted to being considered traitors by withdrawing into what appeared to non-Christians to be anti-social and highly suspect secret societies, with no obvious organisational structure that might have made them seem more normal. No one knew what went on at the Christians' secret meetings, but it was rumoured to involve consuming human flesh and babies' blood. The "holy kiss" that Paul mentions at the end of several of his letters was assumed to be very far from holy, and the fact that Christians called their evening meetings *agapes* [loves] suggested to the non-Christians that they were wild nights of lust.

The Christian attitude to family life drew criticism too, apparently based mainly on the fact that they refused to marry non-Christians, some of them did not marry at all, and Jesus' words about setting members of a family against each other (Matthew 10:34-35). Another problem, especially in Gaul (modern France), was the Christian habit of using the word "family" to mean their fellow-believers rather than their blood-relatives. What happened after death was also an issue, as unbelieving families were distressed by Christians rejecting the normal pagan burial rites and wanting to be buried amongst other Christians. The family unit was, in Roman eyes, the foundation of the state and of morality, so these practices seemed not just bizarre but wrong and dangerous.

Christians were also seen as a threat to society because of their attitude to slaves. They treated them well and gave them leadership roles in the Church.

In about 218 AD a former slave even became bishop of Rome. Roman governors, conscious of the vast slave populations, dreaded a slave uprising. Tertullian tells us of a slave who became a Christian and was immediately sent by his fearful master to the dreaded *ergastulum* (slaves' work prison).

To sum up, the Christians were "hated for their abominations", as the historian Tacitus wrote in approximately 116 AD.

Thus the Christians found themselves facing a triple hatred. They were hated by the Gentile population at large (who hated all Jews including those who had become Christians), by the Roman authorities, and by the Jews themselves.

Christians were very vulnerable to being accused and brought to court by *delators* [denouncers]. These individuals were something like an informer and something like a private prosecutor; they played an important part in Roman society, which had no system of public prosecutions. "*Christianus sum* [I am a Christian]" was confession of a crime for which there could be no extenuating circumstances and no forgiveness. Judges did not investigate or call witnesses, as they did for other crimes which the accused admitted to. They simply announced the sentence. This neglect of normal judicial procedure, said Tertullian,[26] was because of "public hatred".

SPORADIC PERSECUTION (UNTIL 250 AD)

The emperor's whim

The first century was characterised by fitful bursts of persecution, at the whim of the emperor. Although short in duration, these periods of persecution could be very intense, and occurred chiefly on the instructions of two emperors: Nero (54-68 AD) and Domitian (81-96 AD).

When the 17-year-old Nero became emperor he ruled humanely for some years, but later became a deranged sadist. He blamed the Christians for Rome's Great Fire in 64 AD (which some Romans thought the emperor had started himself) and on this pretext had many Christians crucified, thrown to the wild beasts as crowd entertainment, or burned to death at night to illuminate his gardens. It is unclear whether Christians outside the city of Rome were persecuted.

Like Nero, Domitian was a cruel, ruthless tyrant. The records show that he was very active in religious persecution, including the persecution of Christians. He focused on those in the highest positions either in the Roman state or in the Church. According to tradition, the apostle John was persecuted by Domitian, but escaped. Under Domitian, there seems to have been persecution in Asia Minor as well as in Rome.

The emperor restrains persecution

The three emperors who reigned from 98 to 161 AD did not initiate persecution against Christians. Rather, they acted to restrain persecution that was initiated by others. Trajan (98-117) established some ground rules which helped to prevent malicious accusations and enabled kindly magistrates to be merciful in many cases:

- No hard and fast rule can be laid down about how to deal with alleged Christians e.g. whether to take into account other misdeeds or their youth.
- The authorities should not proactively seek out Christians or hunt them down; they should wait for an accusation to be made by a *delator.*
- If charges of being a Christian are proved, then the Christian is to be punished.
- If anyone denies he is a Christian and can prove it, he should be pardoned. This proof includes offering incense to the emperor's statue and cursing Christ.
- Accusations (of Christianity or any other crime) made in anonymous written notices should be ignored.

Hadrian (117-138) built on this with further regulations:

- If Christians are to be accused it should be done in a formal, legal way, not by baying mobs and public riots.
- Accusations must relate to the breaking of a specific law.
- *Delators* who bring deliberate false accusations must be punished severely.

Antoninus Pius (138-161) was the reigning emperor when the aged Polycarp, Bishop of Smyrna, was martyred in about 155, by burning at the stake followed by stabbing. This happened in the middle of a bout of persecution at Smyrna, which occurred despite the emperor's generally tolerant attitude.

The emperor permits persecution

Marcus Aurelius (161-180) ruled in a time of grave crisis for the Roman Empire. The year 166 was particularly afflicted by disasters. To superstitious Romans, it was natural to try to find a cause for the gods' evident displeasure; the strange and obnoxious Christians, who would not worship the emperor or the other gods and apparently rejoiced in being killed, seemed likely culprits. Furthermore, Christians were generally believed to practise magic arts. Augustine tells us there was a proverb in North Africa: "If there is no rain, blame the Christians."[27] Many Christians were martyred in Rome, Gaul and Carthage (in modern Tunisia), with the approval of Emperor Marcus Aurelius, who found the Christians an obstacle to his desire to promote Stoic philosophy

Justin Martyr

Justin, born around 100 AD to Greek parents, became a Christian in Ephesus after an elderly man spoke to him about how Jesus was the fulfilment of God's promises to the Jews. He was also inspired by the faithfulness of Christian martyrs. Justin taught, debated and wrote about the Christian faith.

> Though we are beheaded, and crucified, and exposed to beasts and chains and fire and all other forms of torture, it is plain that we do not forsake the confession of our faith, but the more things of this kind which happen to us the more are there others who become believers and truly religious through the name of Jesus.[28]

Justin's own turn for martyrdom came in about 165, when he was arrested after a debate in Rome with the celebrated Cynic philosopher, Crescens. It is thought that Crescens had lost the debate and denounced Justin to the authorities out of spite. Justin was charged with practising an unauthorised religion. He refused to renounce Christ and was executed, along with six of his students.

as the national religion. In Lyon there were wholesale slaughters of Christians in the amphitheatre while others were martyred in cruelly ingenious ways, such as being roasted to death in an iron chair.[29] Many others, including Callistus, the former slave who had become Bishop of Rome, were sent to work in the mines of Sardinia.

The next bout of persecution occurred under Emperor Septimius Severus (193-211) though it is unclear how much he was responsible for it. He was certainly struggling to contain internal dissension and deal with external military threats to the empire, and therefore sought to promote religious harmony. He may have issued a decree in 201 to punish conversion to Judaism and Christianity (the latter rather a superfluous piece of legislation as it was still illegal to be a Christian). One of the focuses of his persecution was Alexandria in Egypt, a major centre of Christian scholarship at this time.

SYSTEMATIC PERSECUTION (250–312 AD)

The emperor initiates persecution

After four decades of rest, persecution began again, around the year 250. There were three significant differences now. Firstly, the Church was no longer small and weak, but had grown dramatically in the previous half century and now included many wealthy believers. Secondly, Christians were no longer universally unpopular, and many people and officials were sympathetic towards them. Thirdly, the persecution was clearly initiated by the emperor and had the aim of destroying the Church.

The concerns that may have prompted Emperor Septimius Severus to clamp down on Christians were even more alarming now. The empire was sick, beset with economic and social instability. Seventeen successive emperors ruled an average of four years each. The Persians and Goths threatened the frontiers. Christians were still of doubtful loyalty in the eyes of many, and were viewed as a kind of treacherous fifth column, partly because of the cautious Christian attitude to war. At the same time there was a revival of the old Roman religion.

Emperor Decius (249-251) issued an edict in 250 that on certain days all men must sacrifice to the emperor and the other gods. Certificates were issued to those who complied; those who did not were in serious trouble. This posed a

Perpetua and Felicitas (Felicity)

Perpetua and Felicitas were arrested in Carthage in 203 for the crime of converting to Christianity. Felicitas, a slave, was eight months' pregnant, and Perpetua, a well-educated noblewoman aged 22, had a baby whom she was allowed to keep with her in prison. Both the judge and Perpetua's father begged her to renounce her faith, but she held firm. Felicitas gave birth to a baby girl and two days later the women were executed by being thrown to the wild beasts for the entertainment of the crowds at the Roman circus. After being gored by a bull, they were finally killed by the sword. Perpetua's last words were: "Stand fast in the faith and love one another."

major problem for Christians. Some went into hiding. Some bribed officials to get a certificate without sacrificing to the emperor. Some tried to find a compromise – an action acceptable both to the authorities and to their own consciences, such as offering incense instead of a proper sacrifice. Some did indeed sacrifice to the emperor. Great pressure was put upon bishops and other church leaders; many were imprisoned, tortured or banished, and some were eventually executed. Persian and Armenian Christians were amongst those martyred in Rome. Old men and young boys alike were tortured. Many Christian women were also persecuted at this time and some were martyred in Carthage. The way in which the edict was enforced varied from place to place, and Alexandria was again a main focus of the persecutors. But before long Decius' attention turned to the Goths who were threatening his empire, the pressure on the Christians therefore began to ease, and when Decius died in battle in August 251 it ceased.

The next year, persecution began again, under Emperor Gallus (251-253). He was attempting to restore the faltering empire to "the good old days" by purging it of all the newer religions which he believed were sapping its morals and strength. The trigger was a plague which swept across the whole empire. Sacrifices were ordered to avert the wrath of the gods. "We see," wrote the North African bishops, "that a second season of attack is drawing near." But Gallus was a less effective persecutor than Decius had been and the Church, purified by its trials in 250-251, was stronger than before and Christians did not backslide as they had then.

Before long another anti-Christian imperial edict was issued, this time by Emperor Valerian in 257. It banned Christians, on pain of death, from meeting together and from using their cemeteries. It also directed that bishops and priests must be seized and forced to sacrifice to the emperor, with banishment the penalty for those who refused. Although many Christians were killed, banished or sent to the mines for disobeying this edict, the next year Valerian felt that a more severe edict was required to suppress them more firmly and issued a follow-up which specified further punishments for those who disobeyed the edict of 257. The focus was on leaders of the Church and Christians prominent in society. Xystus, Bishop of Rome, was the first to be martyred under the edict of 258, soon followed by many other clergy.

Respite from persecution

After this Christians had a long period of respite from persecution. Emperor Gallienus (260-268 and previously co-emperor with his father Valerian) even issued an edict of toleration in 260, restoring to the Church its confiscated buildings, re-opening the Christian cemeteries, and granting Christians freedom to gather for worship.

Emperor Aurelian (270-275) wanted to create a new religion for the empire, a kind of sun worship, and made plans to persecute Christians but they were not implemented.

During this time the Church was afflicted with divisions and schisms, partly because of the different ways in which Christians had responded to the edicts of Decius and Valerian. Was it legitimate to have fled/hidden, or should all have boldly refused? In particular there was the issue of apostate Christians, who had avoided persecution by sacrificing to the emperor, wanting to return to the Christian faith now that this was no longer dangerous. Many leaders, who might have been able to hold the Church together, had been martyred.

The Theban legion

In the days of the Roman Emperor Maximian,[30] there was a legion of the Roman army composed entirely of Christians from upper Egypt. It was known as the Theban legion[31] after the city of Thebes (now called Luxor). "They were good men and soldiers who, even under arms, did not forget to render to God the things of God, and to Caesar the things of Caesar," commented Bishop Eucher of Lyon when he recorded their story in the following century.[32] Their home town Thebes has been described by a modern writer as "a hotbed of Christianity" at the time.[33]

Around the year 286, the Theban and some other legions were sent to quell a rebellion in Gaul. After this task had been achieved, Emperor Maximian ordered that his victorious troops should kill some Christians and sacrifice to the Roman gods in gratitude for the successful completion of their mission.

The other legions followed their orders, but the Theban legion refused and withdrew, setting up camp near a town called Aguanum (now St-Maurice in southern Switzerland). According to Bishop Eucher, the Theban legion numbered around 6,600 men, meaning that it was several times larger than most legions in the late third century.

Encouraged by their officers, the Thebans sent to Maximian the following message:

> Emperor, we are your soldiers but also the soldiers of the true God. We owe you military service and obedience, but we cannot renounce Him who is our Creator and Master, and also yours even though you reject Him. In all things which are not against His law, we most willingly obey you, as we have done hitherto. We readily oppose your enemies whoever they are, but we cannot stain our hands with the blood of innocent people (Christians). We have taken an oath to God before we took one to you, you cannot place any confidence in our second oath if we violate the other (the first). You commanded us to execute Christians, behold we are such. We confess God the Father the creator of all things and His Son Jesus Christ, God. We have seen our comrades slain with the sword, we do not weep for them but rather rejoice at their honour. Neither

this, nor any other provocation have tempted us to revolt. Behold, we have arms in our hands, but we do not resist, because we would rather die innocent than live by any sin.

When Maximian, who was resting in nearby Octodurum, heard of the Thebans' unanimous refusal, he ordered that the legion should be decimated. Accordingly, every tenth man was put to death, and an announcement made that unless they obeyed their orders they would be decimated a second time. But the Thebans were resolute. They stoutly declared that they would never carry out such a sacrilegious order. They said they had a horror of idolatry, having been brought up as Christians and taught to worship the One Eternal God, and they were willing to suffer extreme penalties rather than do anything against their religion.

Infuriated, Maximian gave the go ahead for the second decimation and after it had been done warned the remainder (still about 4,200 men) that if they persisted in their disobedience every one of them would die – they should not trust in their large numbers to think that some would be spared.

The legionaries were inspired in their faith by their officers, especially their commander Maurice, who had exhorted the survivors of the first round of decimation to stand firm, reminding them of other soldiers who had become Christian martyrs, and urged them to be ready to die for Christ. He reminded them also of their baptismal vows to renounce Satan and worship only the Lord. He reminded them of their newly murdered comrades in the legion who had gone to heaven before them.

Maximian realised he would never persuade the Thebans to go against their Christian faith and ordered that the whole legion be slaughtered. Laying down their weapons, the Christian troops offered their necks to their executioners.

Some of the members of the legion were not present at Aguanum at the time of this massacre, because they had been posted to various other places (in modern Switzerland, Germany and Italy). These men, who may have numbered about 1,400, were methodically sought out and killed in ones, twos, handfuls or hundreds in 14 different locations.

More persecution by edict

Diocletian (284-305) was determined, like so many of his predecessors on the imperial throne, to save the tottering Roman Empire. He initiated a drastic reorganisation, including dividing the vast territory into two more governable and defensible halves, east and west. Each half was led by an Augustus, assisted by a Caesar (responsible for military affairs). Diocletian himself was Augustus of the eastern half, with a man called Galerius as his Caesar.

Galerius had a longstanding hostility to Christians. Egged on by others, he persuaded Diocletian (who had favoured Christians when he first came to power) that he should clamp down on Christians. As a result, Diocletian issued a series of edicts which ruthlessly suppressed Christianity. This period became known as "The Great Persecution".

- **First edict** (23 February 303) – This repealed Gallienus' edict of toleration and re-enacted Valerian's laws. All church buildings were to be destroyed, all Christian Scriptures burned, and Christian worship forbidden. Christian officials were to be deprived of civil rights, and lower ranking Christians demoted to slaves (which made it legal to torture them). No penalties were specified, so local magistrates could be as harsh or lenient as they chose in punishing transgressors.
- **Second edict** (March 303) – All Christian clergy to be imprisoned.
- **Third edict** (December 303) – Clergy to be released from prison if they would sacrifice to the emperor, but those who refused were to be tortured.
- **Fourth edict** (April 304) – All Christian believers to sacrifice to the emperor. The punishment for those who refused was death and the confiscation of their property.

These edicts were zealously enforced in the eastern part of the empire, but much less so in the western part, especially Britain and Gaul. In Asia Minor a Christian-majority town was completely wiped out. Many churches managed to hide their Scriptures and thus preserve them. When Diocletian abdicated in 305, the persecution ceased altogether in the west. In the east, by contrast, Galerius was still there to enforce the edicts for another six years, sometimes even more severely than under Diocletian.

In 308 Galerius issued a fifth and even stricter edict, which included the command that everything on sale in markets should be sprinkled with offerings made to the gods, thus polluting it in the eyes of Christians. It seems that at times there were too many Christians to kill so they were maimed instead. Eusebius describes how, in about 309, a group of 97 Egyptian Christians – men, women and children – were sent to the copper mines in Palestine, which was then under the rule of an exceptionally ruthless governor called Firmillianus. Each of the 97 had their right eye blinded by sword and fire and their left leg disabled by hot irons. The same punishment was inflicted on other Christians, for example a group "in the city of Gaza, being in the habit of assembling themselves for prayer and being constant in reading the Holy Scriptures".[34]

On his painful, stinking and revolting deathbed, Galerius issued yet one more edict. This time it was an edict of toleration (30 April 311), reversing the earlier edicts and asking the Christians to pray for his healing. He died a few days later.

But persecution had not yet quite finished in the eastern half of the empire. Galerius was succeeded by Maximin, who had refused to sign Galerius' edict of toleration, even though Constantine and Licinius – the imperial heavyweights at this complicated time – had done so. However, Maximin seems to have indicated that the degree of pressure put on Christians could be decided locally. Thousands of Christians were released from mines and exile; new churches were built and ruined ones restored. But in Tyre – to Maximin's delight – the town council put up a brass plaque forbidding Christianity within the city. The citizens of Nicomedia (near Istanbul in modern Turkey) begged Maximin for permission to banish the "atheists" as Christians were often called. The martyrdoms continued. Armenia, whose king Trdat had become a Christian, bringing all his subjects to the faith as well in 301, came to the aid of his persecuted co-religionists and defeated Maximin in battle.

THE END OF STATE PERSECUTION (313 AD)

In March 313, Constantine and Licinius, the two remaining emperors, issued a joint edict in Milan setting out a religious liberty policy for the whole empire.

We have long seen that we have no business to refuse freedom of religion. The power of seeing to matters of belief must be left to the judgment and desire of each individual, according to the man's own free will.

The fact that Maximin did not support the Edict of Milan was a temporary obstacle to its implementation in the east. But Licinius defeated him in battle on 30 April. On 13 June the edict was read aloud to the remnant of the sorely tested church in Nicomedia. A few weeks later Maximin died, the last of the great Roman persecutors.

Chapter 5

PERSECUTION OUTSIDE THE ROMAN EMPIRE

Beyond the boundaries of the vast Roman Empire lay many other nations and empires to which the Christian faith spread in the first half millennium after Christ.

ARMENIA

In about 301 AD Armenia, neighbouring the Roman Empire on its northeast border, became the first Christian nation. Across the country, idols were destroyed, pagan temples cleansed and then consecrated as churches, and thousands of people were baptised. The conversion of the Armenian king, and hence the adoption of Christianity as the national religion, was brought about by a remarkable believer called Gregory. It followed three centuries of revival movements, particularly in Asia Minor (modern Turkey, where Gregory grew up) and in Armenia. For even in these early times, there were numerous groups of Christians distressed by the worldliness that was developing in the Church. At this period, Asia Minor and Armenia were "the refuge of churches that had from the first, in varying degree, maintained purity of doctrine and godliness of life".[35]

Although Christianity was by now spreading fast in the Roman Empire, a decade of severe persecution at the hands of a series of Roman emperors began in 303 as we saw in the previous chapter.[36] After only ten years as a Christian nation, the Armenians lost their long-term protector, the Roman Empire, when in 311 the Romans went to war against the Armenians because of their new Christian identity. This is recorded by Eusebius:

> They [the Armenians] were Christians and zealous adherents of the Deity; so the God-hater [Roman Emperor Maximin] attempted to force them to sacrifice to idols and demons, thereby turning them from friends into foes and from allies into enemies.[37]

Gregory – persecution by pagans

Gregory was an Armenian brought up as a Christian in Caesarea[38] in the Roman province of Cappadocia (modern Kayseri in Turkey). He had been carried off to Cappadocia as a child, when all the rest of his family were executed because his father had assassinated the king of Armenia as part of a Persian plot. The Persians seized the rest of the Armenian royal family but one son escaped, called Trdat.

In 286 AD, with the help of the Romans, Trdat regained his father's throne. Gregory, now aged about 30, returned to Armenia too, and became one of the most trusted officials of the new King Trdat (Tiridates III). But, as a Christian, Gregory refused to worship Armenia's guardian goddess, and spoke openly about his faith in Christ. To make matters worse, the king discovered that Gregory's father had murdered his father. He had Gregory tortured and thrown into a deep underground pit where he was expected to starve to death, but a Christian woman working at the palace dropped bread down to Gregory every day and enabled him to survive for 13 years.

During this time King Trdat persecuted the Christians of Armenia, and also became insane. Gregory was finally brought up from the pit again, after the king's sister had dreamed that Gregory was the only person who could bring healing. Gregory prayed for the king and healed him, the king became a Christian, and Christianity became the nation's official religion. King Trdat and Gregory worked together to make the Gospel known across the country.

GEORGIA

To the north of Armenia lies Georgia, which declared Christianity as its state religion in the early fourth century, soon after Armenia and the Roman Empire had done so. Tradition records that the faith was brought to Georgia in the first century by the residents of Pontus who were present on the Day of Pentecost (Acts 2:9). Pontus, an area to the south of the Black Sea, included parts of what is now Georgia.

But it was a young Christian woman from Cappadocia whose preaching led to Georgia becoming a Christian nation. Nino had a vision in which she was commanded to preach the Gospel in Georgia, so she set out with around 50 other Christian women to obey her calling. They travelled through Armenia at a time when its King Trdat was still violently persecuting Christians, and all of the women except Nino were executed on his command. Nino continued alone to Georgia, arriving in about 319 AD, where her preaching converted the royal family and the whole nation.

THE PARTHIAN EMPIRE

The Parthian homeland was south-east of the Caspian Sea, but by 225 AD, after nearly 500 years of conquests, the Parthians controlled a large empire whose most important religion was Zoroastrianism.

There were Christians in the Parthian Empire from the first century onwards, as recorded in the *Chronicle of Arbil*. Arbil (Erbil) is now the capital of Iraqi Kurdistan, but then it was the capital of a kingdom called Adiabene, which had been conquered by the Parthians and brought into their empire.

Persecution by Zoroastrians

One of the first converts was Paqida, the son of a slave belonging to a Zoroastrian priest. When he became a Christian in 99 AD he was severely persecuted by his family. Despite it all, he refused to deny Christ, so finally his parents imprisoned him in a dark room. He escaped and became a missionary amongst the mountain villages of Adiabene; later he was made a bishop.

The first martyr of the Parthian Empire was Paqida's successor as Bishop of Adiabene, called Samsun. He preached among the Zoroastrian villages, bringing many to Christ and baptising them. This infuriated the Zoroastrian priests (Magi) and the Adiabene nobility. Samsun was captured, tortured and beheaded in 123 AD.

Persecution of Christians by Zoroastrians continued for the next century. In 160 AD the Bishop of Arbil travelled to the Parthian winter capital, Ctesiphon (near modern Baghdad), hoping to get an edict from the emperor to protect the Christians from abuse by the Zoroastrian priests. But the Parthian Empire was preparing for imminent war with the Roman Empire, and there was no opportunity for the bishop to present his case.

THE PERSIAN EMPIRE

In 225 AD the Persian provinces of the Parthian Empire rebelled against their Parthian rulers and speedily overthrew them. So the Parthian Empire became the Persian Empire, with Ctesiphon as its capital, and a dynasty of emperors was established, called the Sassanids (after their family name). Zoroastrianism became the official religion of the empire. Rome became its permanent enemy, as the two empires vied with each other for territory.

By 225 there were 17 Christian dioceses, mostly within the area of modern Iraq but two of them in modern Iran. Even though Christians did not follow the official religion of the Persian Empire, they were well treated. Indeed, many Christians fled from persecution in the Roman Empire to safety in the Persian Empire.

Constantine's good intentions backfire

But all this changed in 312 AD when the Roman Emperor Constantine himself became a Christian. The next year he established religious liberty in his empire, and then increasingly favoured Christianity. This was to have disastrous consequences for the Christians in the Persian Empire, who were now co-religionists of Persia's arch-enemy. In about 315 the Roman Emperor Constantine wrote to the Persian Emperor Shapur II, telling his former enemy (who was now apparently reaching out to Rome offering peace and friendship) how the God of the Christians had helped him in all his enterprises. He went on:

> Imagine, then, with what joy I heard news, so much in line with my desire, that the fairest provinces of Persia are to a great extent adorned

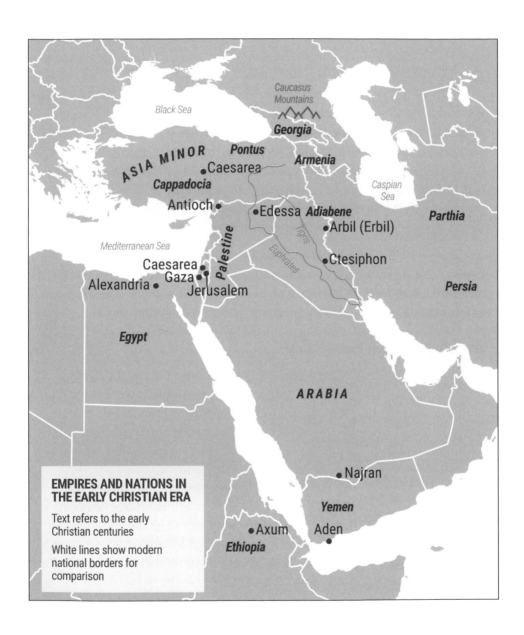

EMPIRES AND NATIONS IN
THE EARLY CHRISTIAN ERA

Text refers to the early
Christian centuries

White lines show modern
national borders for
comparison

by the presence of that class of men on whose behalf alone I am at present speaking – I mean the Christians. I pray, therefore, that both you and they may enjoy abundant prosperity, and that you and they may be equally blessed, for in this way you will experience the mercy and favour of that God who is the Lord and Father of us all. And now, because your power is great, I commend these people to your protection; because your piety is outstanding, I commit them to your care. Care for them with your accustomed humanity and kindness.[39]

Constantine's letter was surely well meant, encouraging Emperor Shapur to continue to care for the Christians in the Persian Empire. But to Shapur it seemed a threat, an indication of a possible "fifth column" in his empire. Even if it had not occurred to Shapur before, the letter must have now brought forcibly to his notice that that his empire was riddled with people identified with a foreign power, which was often an enemy power – Rome.

But still anti-Christian persecution did not begin in Persia. Then in 337 Constantine began to plan a great military campaign against the Persians. He died before it got underway, but the planning itself was enough to seal the fate of Christians in the Persian Empire and in 339 the persecution began.

The 40-year Great Persecution

Zoroastrian priests and Jewish leaders accused Shimun, Bishop of Ctesiphon, of spying for Rome. The emperor ordered him to be arrested and held until a double poll-tax had been paid by the Christians (or Nazarenes as he called them), "for our Divine Majesty has nothing but troubles of war, and they have nothing but rest and pleasure! They live in our territory, but their sympathies are with Caesar, our enemy." Shimun declared the Christians could not pay the extra tax because they were too poor, but it was extracted from them anyway, with great cruelty; many clergy were killed and church buildings destroyed. Emperor Shapur was enraged: "Shimun wants to arouse his disciples and his people to rebel against my Empire. He wants to make them slaves of Caesar, who has the same religion as they have; that is why he disobeys my order!"

Bishop Shimun was brought in chains before the emperor, who commanded him to worship the sun, saying that, if he did not, "I will destroy not only you but the whole body of Christians." Shimun refused and was led away to be tortured. The next day, Good Friday, Shimun was brought before the emperor again; he reasoned with the emperor on Christian doctrine and said he would never worship either the emperor or the sun. The same day, a hundred prisoners were ordered to be executed including many bishops and other clergy. Shimun was forced to watch and finally he himself was killed too.

Severe persecution continued for 40 years. The Gaza-born church historian Sozomen, writing in about 425, records the efforts of Christians in Syria, Persia and Edessa to calculate how many were killed during this period. He says that 16,000 had been listed by name but that in addition there was a multitude of other martyrs too great to be counted.

Another serious bout of persecution took place in 420-422. Then in 424 the Persian Church declared itself completely independent of any control from the bishops of the Roman Empire. This made Persia's Christian minority much less of a threat to the Persian authorities. The Christians were recognised as a community and achieved a settled position within society with minimal harassment.

ARABIA AND YEMEN

Christianity came early to the tribal mishmash that was Arabia, and by 364 was well enough established for a "Bishop of the Arabs" to attend the Synod of Antioch.

Down in the south of the Arabian peninsula was Yemen, known in ancient times as "Happy Arabia". Compared with the rest of Arabia, Yemen was wetter, more fertile, wealthier and more orderly, being ruled by a king. Christianity was bought to Yemen in 354 by the Roman ambassador, who was a bishop called "Theophilus the Indian" and probably grew up in the Maldives. Sent with lavish gifts from the Roman emperor, Theophilus' task was to ask the pagan king of Yemen for permission to build churches for Romans visiting Yemen and for any local people who wanted to become Christians. However, he went beyond this and managed to convert the king to Christianity. This development was strongly opposed by the Jewish community in Yemen. But the king was not dissuaded and went on to construct three church buildings, one in his capital, one in Aden and one in another port city, paid for by himself.

Persecution by Jews

Christians in Yemen later suffered fierce persecution at Jewish hands, especially those of King Dhu Nuwas (also called Masruq), who had seized the throne in a coup d'état. He was zealous in propagating Judaism and persecuting Christians. The worst single incident occurred in 523 when King Dhu Nuwas blockaded the oasis town of Najran, which finally surrendered after he promised that its inhabitants would be spared. But they were not spared. Instead, all the Christian men were killed and the church building burned. The king then ordered his general Zu-Yazan, who was also Jewish, to round up all the widows of the Christian men just killed, and tell them to deny Christ or they would die like their husbands. The troops (probably mainly pagans) found 177 wives and daughters of the martyred men, plus their many young children, who were all brought together to hear the general address them. Jesus had done their husbands no good and would do them no good either, Zu-Yazan told them, so "spit on his cross and become Jews with us."

The women replied, "God forbid that we should spit on His cross or that we should treat it with contempt for by it He has prepared for us redemption from all error. . . We pray that, as our husbands died, we may be deemed worthy to die, we also for the sake of Christ, God."

The women's prayer for martyrdom was granted. They and the children with them were taken to the place where their husbands had been killed and General Zu-Yazan ordered the Jews amongst the troops to start firing arrows at them. The women put their little children on the ground and covered them with their clothes, then stood with their hands lifted to heaven, praying, as the arrows showered down on them:

> Christ, God, come to our help! O, our Lord Jesus Christ, behold our oppression in this moment and turn not away from us, but grant in us the power to accomplish this our way by martyrdom for Thy sake, that we may also go and reach our brethren who died for Thy sake. And forgive us our sins and receive the sacrifice of our lives as acceptable before Thee.

One by one, the women fell to the ground, as their wounds overpowered them. The children too were wounded and crying out. When there was no woman left standing, General Zu-Yazan ordered his troops to take their swords and finish off the women and "their evil children". A sixth-century Syriac work called *The Book of the Himyarites*, which records the women's words, gives a partial list of the names of the martyrs that day; all the children mentioned are girls.

Chapter 6

WHEN CHRISTIANS BECAME THE PERSECUTORS

A dramatic shift in the history of the church in the Roman Empire occurred during the fourth century. This century began with "The Great Persecution"[40] of 303-305, a significant name given how severely Christians had already been persecuted at certain periods under Roman rule. But when the century drew to its close, Christianity was the official religion of the Roman Empire and non-Christians were being persecuted. Three key dates track this process of change.

WHAT HAPPENED IN 312 AD

The first key date was 27 October 312, when Emperor Constantine I, preparing for battle the following day, looked up to the sky and saw a cross of light with Greek words meaning "In this sign, conquer." He duly won a decisive and career-changing victory at the Battle of Milvian Bridge and decided to embrace Christianity. This did not, as it turned out, mean laying aside his previous pagan religion, and he retained the title of Pontifex Maximus (High Priest) of the Roman state cult until his death in 337. But he did order that Sunday and Christian holy days be given the same legal status as the pagan festivals, he put the Christian cross on his coins (along with pagan symbols and figures), and he forbade Jews from stoning to death those of their number who became Christians.[41] He banned the construction of new pagan temples and later in his reign began tearing down existing ones.

WHAT HAPPENED IN 313 AD

The second key date was just a few months later, in 313, when Emperors Constantine and Licinius jointly issued what is known as the Edict of Milan, to establish religious liberty in the Roman Empire.

Christians were at this time still a minority, but probably quite a decent-sized minority. Persecution had not prevented the faith from spreading, perhaps had even encouraged it. Tertullian, famous for the phrase usually misquoted as "the blood of martyrs is the seed of the Church",[42] also wrote:

> We are but of yesterday, and yet we have all the places that belong to you – cities, islands, fortresses, towns, market places, the military camps themselves, tribes, town councils, the palace, the senate, the forum – we have left you nothing but your temples.[43]

Tertullian died between 220 and 240, so the growing Christian presence in the Roman Empire that he describes was a century before religious liberty came.

After 312 the church, having both legal toleration and imperial approval, grew rapidly – too rapidly, according to some contemporary leaders. The church historian Eusebius, who had been Bishop of Caesarea Maritima in Palestine since about 313, wrote of "the hypocrisy of people who crept into the church" hoping for the emperor's favour.[44] Adopting the emperor's religion could do wonders for one's prospects in society, especially a society built on patronage as the Roman Empire was. As Robert Markus puts it:

> Eusebius put his finger on the radical novelty of the condition in which Christians now found themselves. There had been rich Christians before the time of Constantine, there had been educated or upper-class people to be found in Christian communities, and in growing numbers during the century before Constantine. But rarely can their Christianity have contributed to their standing in society, their wealth or power. But, from now on, their religion could itself become a source of prestige, and did so, to the dismay of bishops who, like Eusebius himself, were sometimes inclined to look for less worldly motives for conversion to Christianity.[45]

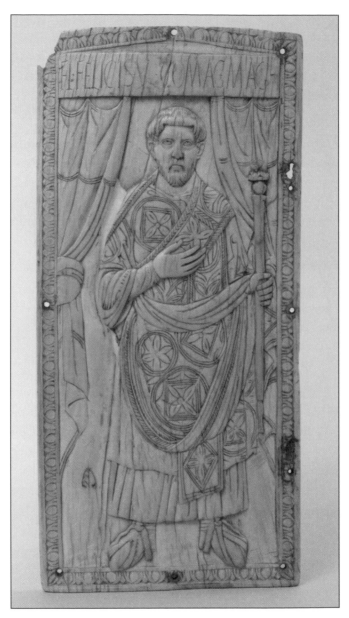

An ivory carving from 428 shows a consul from the Western Roman Empire. His clothes are remarkably similar to Christian liturgical vestments, showing how the Christian elite replicated the culture of the non-Christians around them (*Feuillet de diptyque du consul Flavius Felix*, 0428, source: gallica.bnf.fr/Bibliotheque nationale de France)

A hundred years later, bishops were still lamenting the conversions of convenience. Augustine of Hippo wrote of the "feigned" Christians who were joining the churches of his diocese (in modern Algeria). Within a few years of Augustine's death in 430, almost all educated Roman town-dwellers were Christians, and thus came to an end the "age of hypocrisy" which had begun in 313.

As it rose to dominance, Christianity had seamlessly absorbed Roman culture, and the lifestyle of these urban elite Christians was almost identical to that of their pagan peers except that the Christians went to church. The Church had never set up its own education system of education, so Christians who wanted to study shared the education of non-Christians and naturally embraced their arts, literature and intellectual thought.

Many Christians, at all levels of society, continued to participate in traditional Roman festivities, and some carried these practices over into their Christian worship. They shocked their bishops by dancing in church and getting drunk in cemeteries. When facing difficulties in their lives, they sought help from pagan charms and sorcerers just like the rest of society.

The lack of a distinctive Christian identity troubled many thoughtful believers in the late fourth century and early fifth century. Perplexed as to how they should live an authentic Christian life within a society of fashionable Christianity, committed Christians began to embrace asceticism, building on the traditional esteem for virginity, voluntary poverty and self-denial. Thus monastic communities came into being.[46]

WHAT HAPPENED IN 380 AD

The third key date was 27 February 380 when Emperor Theodosius I made Christianity the official religion of the Roman Empire by the so-called Edict of Thessalonica. More specifically, the empire's religion was to be Nicene Trinitarian Christianity.

Sadly and shamefully, the next two decades were marked by violent Christian riots in various cities across the empire, with the rioters set on destroying pagan temples and their idols. The persecuted had become the persecutors.

The pagans had already suffered legal pressure for a couple of generations, beginning, as we have seen, with Constantine himself targeting pagan places of worship. Constantine's son and successor, Emperor Constantius II, closed all pagan temples and introduced the death penalty for anyone caught performing a pagan sacrifice. During his reign (337-361), ordinary Christians began to vandalise pagan temples and tombs. After 361 the harassment of pagans waxed and waned until 381 when Emperor Theodosius issued the first of a series of 15 edicts against pagans, steadily increasing the pressure until his death in 395.

CHRISTIANS PERSECUTE EACH OTHER

Arianism

Theodosius targeted not only pagans but also those Christians whom he regarded as heretics. He defined heretics according to the findings of Council of Nicea (Iznik in modern Turkey), which had been convened by Constantine back in 325 to look at various issues of the day, including Christological questions. The Council affirmed that the three Persons of the Trinity, Father, Son and Holy Spirit, were co-equal and co-eternal, and specifically that Jesus was "of the same substance"[47] as the Father.[48] They rejected the viewpoint of a priest called Arius who held that Jesus had been created by the Father and therefore was not eternal and was of lower status than the Father.

Despite the council's decision, Arianism continued to thrive throughout most of the fourth century, along with a variant called Semi-Arianism. Even Emperor Constantius was an Arian. Arian Christians and orthodox (i.e. Nicene, Trinitarian) Christians persecuted each other alternately, according to the views of the emperor at the time.

By the end of the century, however, Arianism was declining within the Roman Empire, perhaps due to strenuous persecution by Emperor Theodosius especially after the Council of Constantinople (381 AD) which strongly condemned Arianism.[49]

But Arianism remained popular with the tribes surrounding and sometimes invading the empire. During the fifth century it thrived amongst certain Germanic tribes, such as the Vandals, Lombards and Goths (with their subgroups, the Visigoths and Ostrogoths).[50] The Vandals invaded Roman North Africa in 429 and occupied it until they were defeated by a Byzantine invasion force 534; they laboured for decades to convert the Nicene Christians there to Arianism. Arianism was also strong in southern Europe.

The Byzantine (or eastern Roman) Emperor Justinian I (ruled 527–565) was very active in fighting Arianism by military force. He attacked both the Vandal kingdom in North Africa and the Ostrogoth kingdom in Italy. Justinian also organised and codified the mass of pre-existing laws issued by himself and previous emperors going back about 400 years, to produce what is called the Codex Justinianus, competed in 529. Numerous laws in this Codex dealt with religious matters; in fact, the very first law required everyone under Byzantine rule to be an orthodox (i.e. non-Arian) Christian. Other laws secured a dominant status for orthodox Christianity, forbade certain pagan practices, and harshly discriminated against Jews and Samaritans.

By the eighth century, after many wars and laws, Arianism had been largely wiped out and all Christians were Trinitarian.

Other issues

The Arian/Nicene split was not the only internal division in Christianity that led to persecution and violence amongst Christians. In North Africa, a schism developed about clergy who had renounced their Christian faith during the dark days of persecution under Emperor Diocletian (284-305) while others had stood firm and been martyred. After the persecution had finished, the question arose of what to do with apostate clergy who now wanted to resume their ministries. When the Edict of Milan was passed, making it 100% safe to be a Christian, the question became even more marked. Donatus Magnus, bishop of Carthage from 315 to 355, led those who felt it would be offensive to the memory of the martyred faithful clergy to allow the apostates to officiate at church services again. This group became known as Donatists and were probably the numerical majority for a while. They were opposed by the pro-Roman group, who emphasised forgiveness and wanted to see the apostate clergy fully restored to their former roles in the church. The Donatists were persecuted by the Roman emperors in the fourth and fifth centuries, but they survived until Islam arrived and eliminated all forms of Christianity in the region.

In a similar way, a group of Christians who have sometimes been called "Nestorians" were driven out of the empire in the fifth century because of their Christological beliefs. They moved east to settle in Persia and beyond, where they became known as the "Church of the East".

In yet another Christological dispute, the Council of Chalcedon in 451 affirmed that Jesus had two natures (divine and human). But many Christians in North Africa and the Middle East believed He had only one nature (divine). These "monophysite" Christians suffered imperial persecution. The Syriac Orthodox Church, for example, had its Patriarch Mor Severius and many of its bishops sent into exile. The patriarch died in exile in 538 and by 544 the church had only three bishops left and was "in an abysmal situation".[51]

Similar persecution happened in the eighth and ninth centuries to Christians who venerated images.

After the Reformation

Doctrinal differences continued to fuel Christian-on-Christian persecution and violence through the centuries. Sadly, the examples are simply too many to list, but readers may be familiar with Protestants and Roman Catholics burning each other at the stake in sixteenth-century England, and the many wars of religion in various countries of northern Europe after the Reformation.

CHRISTIANS PERSECUTE NON-CHRISTIANS

We have already seen how this began as soon as religious liberty was granted in the Roman Empire and accelerated when Christianity became the empire's official religion. It is greatly to the dishonour of Christians that this continued.

Jewish people were a frequent target of unprovoked attacks by Christians. As far back as 613, the Visigoth king of Iberia (modern Spain and Portugal) ordered Jews to convert to Christianity or be expelled. Cruel persecution followed for those who remained. The Jews were expelled from France in 1182 and from England in 1290. Again, space does not permit further examples, although there are plenty.

CONCLUSION

The shattering impact of Emperor Constantine's public adoption of Christianity in 312 on church history, indeed on history in general, is ironic, given that his new "faith" appears to have had relatively little effect on him personally. It set in train a destructive struggle between orthodox Christians and heretics, and eventually created the new realities of sword-bearing believers and wars of theology.

It was Constantine's decision to say he was a Christian, even more than his introduction of religious liberty, that was the turning point which changed the Church from poor to rich, from despised to respectable, from shame to honour, from the cross to the sword, from weakness to earthly power, from Jesus in His humility to Christ triumphant, perceived as an emperor whose dominion is the earth and whose servants ruled as governors.

Accepting without demur the traditions and trappings of Roman culture, the Church seemed to have little trouble adapting to her new place in society. It was soon reflected in art and culture. Philippa Adrych and Dominic Dalglish point out that "Zeus on his throne was replaced by the new ruler of heaven and earth, and the emperor, long associated with a variety of divinities, now imparted his image onto the figure of Christ."[52]

In this way the Church and Christianity were transformed, reversing the New Testament principle of land as the commonwealth of Israel, people as the *ekklesia* of God, and the Temple as the inner shrine of our hearts filled with the Holy Spirit. Instead the Church embraced the Old Testament doctrine of physical land to be seized or kept by military force, of her people as a nation characterised by nationalism of the worst kind, and the construction of majestic buildings for earthly places of worship.

Thus Christianity created Christendom, an empire where every citizen must be subservient to a sovereign lord crowned as a Christian emperor, and where new laws were created to ostracise, torment or even kill all those who disagreed with the state orthodoxy, whether heretic, Jew or pagan.

The stage was set for internal schism and fragmentation. With this fragmentation came a new era of armed conflict, in which Christians fought each other, condemning their targets as pagan, heretical or demonic; the idea of viewing the other Christians as brethren with whom they disagreed on some theological points seems to have been rare.

As we have seen, centuries of warfare between Christians followed, particularly in North Africa and southern Europe, where the Vandals, Visigoths and Ostrogoths, who had embraced a Christianity based on Arianism, now found themselves in conflict with the Trinitarian Christians. It was a fight to the death, and finally Arianism was eliminated. The Angles, Saxons and Franks were spared this, never having been Arians.[53]

Christianity became firmly embedded in empire, nation and city-state, in the process becoming unrecognisable. What did it now have in common with those early believers, who had met in simplicity and faith, filled with the Holy Spirit of God and worshipping their crucified Lord? (Acts 2:42)

The internecine conflicts within the Church from the fourth century onwards, leaving Christians weak, self-absorbed and divided, paved the way for the rapid Islamic military conquest of the region in the seventh century.

Chapter 7

ISLAM

The devastating effect of the rise of Islam in the seventh century has been described as "greater than any other setback in Christianity's two thousand years of history".[54] After only a hundred years, the land where the Lord Jesus had spent His earthly life, and many other countries around the Mediterranean, including major centres of Christianity in North Africa where towering figures such as Tertullian and Augustine had lived, were all under Islamic rule.

The Christian presence then began to dwindle away, either swiftly or slowly. Within a few centuries some countries, such as modern Morocco, Algeria and Tunisia, had no indigenous Christians left at all; today's Christian communities in these countries are completely new, comprised mainly of first and second generation converts from Islam. In other countries, such as Syria and Iraq, historic Christian communities have clung on until the twenty-first century, albeit greatly reduced in size. But the rapid Christian exodus in response to the radical Islam and Islamist violence of our day means that these countries too may soon be emptied of all Christian witness.

All this began in Arabia, where the first Islamic state was established in 622 AD.

CHRISTIANITY IN PRE-ISLAMIC ARABIA

Arabia in the early seventh century was sandwiched between the two superpowers of the time, who were locked in a long-running conflict with each other. To the west lay the Byzantine Empire,[55] which was predominantly Christian. To the east lay the Persian Empire, which was predominantly Zoroastrian.

Arabia itself was largely pagan, inhabited by many tribes who worshipped numerous gods. Living amongst the pagan Arabs were communities of Jews who had settled in various trading cities, bringing with them their rabbis, Scriptures and synagogues. There were also a number of Christian communities. Christians from India and Persia seem to have played a major part in advancing their faith in Arabia, but some of the earliest Christian influence came from Christian ascetics living in the desert who had encounters with the desert-dwelling Arabs.

There were probably eight Christian dioceses (bishoprics) in pre-Islamic Arabia, showing the strength of the Christian presence. One of these was Najran, which, according to the Muslim historian Ibn Ishaq (died c. 761), was the first place that Christianity took root in southern Arabia. It was a Syrian builder and bricklayer called Phemion (also spelled Faymiyun), captured by the Arabs and sold as a slave, who brought Christianity to the people of Najran, around 500 AD. They had previously worshipped a tall date-palm tree. The first Najranite to decide to follow Christ was their chief, Abdullah ibn ath-Thamir, and his oasis town went on to become an important centre of Christianity in southern Arabia.[56] Another diocese in the south was Sanaa (the capital of modern Yemen) and a third was the island of Socotra, which is governed by Yemen.

The other five Arabian dioceses lay along the north-eastern coast. The furthest north were Dairin (in modern Saudi Arabia) and Mashmahig (modern Bahrain), both of which were in existence by 410 AD. By 424 there was a diocese called Beth Mazunaye or Mazon (modern Oman). The diocese of Hagar is mentioned in 576, from which the diocese of Hatta (modern United Arab Emirates) was later carved out, perhaps before the advent of Islam and certainly by the year 676. At some point these five northern dioceses were put

Archaeological evidence for Christianity in pre-Islamic Arabia

The island of Sir Bani Yas, just off the coast of Abu Dhabi, has archaeological remains of a Christian monastery dating from around the year 600. Some of the rooms were decorated with plaster crosses. This site was opened to the public in 2010.

The foundations of another ancient Christian monastery are to be found in the village of Samaheej in Bahrain.

In the 1980s the ruins of an ancient church building were discovered in Saudi Arabia, near to the town of Jubail and thought to date from the fourth century. No visitors are allowed. Crosses carved into the stone have been well preserved under the sand which covered the building for centuries.

Saudi Arabia: cross designs on a church probably dating from the fourth century. Source: Assyrian International News Agency (AINA) *4th Century Assyrian Church in Saudi Arabia*, http://www.aina.org/ata/20080828165925.htm

Entrance to fourth-century church near Jubail, Saudi Arabia. Source: *Jubail Church* by Harold Brockwell licensed under CC BY-SA 3.0

under the authority of a more senior bishop, the metropolitan of Beth Qatraye (modern Qatar).

Though structurally well established, even in Arabia, the Church at this time was already divided (1) Syrians versus Persians and (2) along bitterly contested theological lines.

MUHAMMAD

According to Islamic tradition, one of the pagan Arabs was a merchant called Muhammad, born in 570. Around the age of 40, he began to "receive" what he believed were messages from Allah for humankind brought to him by the angel Gabriel. These messages, which continued for more than two decades, were later collected by his followers and eventually written down to form the Quran.

Very few people in Muhammad's home town, Mecca, believed his teaching about the one true Allah. Rejection became hostility, and hostility became violence. Muhammad and his small band of followers fled from Mecca.

Many Jews and Christians at this time were sympathetic to Muhammad's teaching because of its emphasis on belief in one God and its condemnation of paganism. In any case Muhammad, at this period, was preaching only to the pagans, and accepted the validity of Judaism and Christianity. So there were good relations between the three monotheistic faiths. It is not surprising therefore that Muhammad sent some of his persecuted followers to the Christian kingdom of Abyssinia (Ethiopia) where they were welcomed and given refuge. But Muhammad himself and the other early Muslims went to another Arabian city, now called Medina.[57]

The people of Medina welcomed Muhammad and his teaching. After years of internal conflict they were pleased to have a strong leader to unite all the Arab tribes. Before long he was Medina's ruler, legislator, supreme judge and military commander. The first Islamic state had been born.

For ten years Muhammad ruled Medina. During this time, his Muslim armies spread out across the Arabian Peninsula to conquer, subdue and stamp on it the religion of Islam. This was jihad. Also during this time, friction developed between Muhammad and some Jewish tribes who refused to recognise his prophethood or to practise the customs of Islam. Muhammad responded by modifying his earlier teaching and told his followers to treat Jews and Christians as enemies not friends.

By the time Muhammad died in 632, all the tribes of Arabia, including those in Mecca, had submitted to him in some form or another.

MUHAMMAD'S SUCCESSORS

The series of caliphs who led the Arab Muslim community after Muhammad's death followed his example, and indeed his plans, and continued to seize territory and put it under Islamic rule. They began with the Christian Byzantine Empire: in 635 the Arab Muslim armies took Damascus, in 636 the rest of Syria, in 638 Jerusalem, in 642 Alexandria and all Egypt. In the year that Egypt fell, the Muslims launched an offensive against the Persian Empire and by 652 this too was conquered. At the same time they began conquering their way westwards from Egypt along North Africa, and in 711 crossed over to Spain by way of the rock now called Gibraltar. (This name is derived from Jabal-Tarik, meaning the mountain of Tarik. Tarik was the Muslim general who led this army.) From southern Spain the Muslims advanced northwards until they were well into the area of modern France (a name derived from the Franks who had settled there some 300 years earlier[58]).

Meanwhile another Muslim army was moving anti-clockwise round the Mediterranean and in 717 began besieging Constantinople, the Byzantine capital. Christendom was in danger of being completely encircled by Islam. This was only prevented by two military victories which halted the progress of both arms of the Muslim advance. Byzantine Emperor Leo III stood firm against the Arabs, who abandoned the siege of Constantinople after a year. Fighting continued to surge to and fro across Asia Minor but by 800 the Taurus Mountains had become established as the border between the Byzantine Empire and the Islamic Empire. In 732 Charles, the ruler of the Franks, defeated the Arabs at a battle fought between Tours and Poitiers, and drove them back south beyond the Pyrenees. Because of this victory he became known as Charles Martel, meaning Charles the hammer.

Islam, the rod of God's anger?

About 75 years after the Arab conquest of Christian Syria, the Syriac Orthodox Church, reflecting on the way in which Christian cities had toppled like nine-pins before the Muslim armies, came to the conclusion that Islam was God's judgment on the weak, immoral and corrupt Church. They believed that God was using Islam to discipline His wayward people, just as He had used Assyria in Old Testament times (Isaiah 10:5).

CHRISTIANS UNDER ISLAMIC RULE

Islamic law (sharia) – compiled over six centuries but based very strongly on Muhammad's "messages", his other teaching and his own example – lays down many detailed regulations for the everyday lives of Christians, Jews and other non-pagan non-Muslims living under Islamic rule.

The basic principle is that such people, called *dhimmi*, cannot be proper citizens of an Islamic state. They have a second-class status and are treated in a host of ways as inferior to Muslims. They also have to pay a special poll-tax called *jiyza* by which they acknowledge their inferiority and their submission to rule by Muslims.

Apostasy, flight or martyrdom?

To be treated as despised foreigners in one's own homeland, to struggle daily with the humiliating and disempowering *dhimmi* regulations and occasionally with outright persecution, was a test of faith which, sadly, many Christians failed. "Apostasy" is a harsh word, but that is what it was. For where Christianity disappeared it was mainly because Christians chose to convert to Islam for an easier life.

Patriarch Ishu'-Yab III wrote in anguished tones of the apostasy of Christians in Oman and the fact that Christian worship had ceased in that diocese, which he calls Mazon. The Omani Christians had given up their faith for purely material reasons.

They have not been compelled by sword, or fire, or torments, but merely seized with a desire for the half of their own possessions! Mad! – for apostasy has straightway swallowed them up, and they are destroyed for ever … Alas! Alas! From so many thousands of men called Christians, not one least offering is made to God as fitting sacrifice for our true Faith …

Why then, have your people of Mazon given up their faith because of them [the Muslim Arabs]? And that when the Arabs, as the people of Mazon themselves admit, did not compel them to give up their religion, but ordered them to give up merely half of their possessions in order to keep their Faith! But they have forsaken the Faith which brings eternal benefit, to keep half of the possessions of this transient age.[59]

A year or two later Ishuʻ-Yab wrote of the ineffectiveness of the bishops of Oman as the Christians abandoned their faith.

Out of the thousands and tens of thousands who belong to our God, two … who keep the empty title of bishops, simply sit idly by – sad objects, memorials now to move the Church of God to tears, after the likeness of the pillar of salt into which Lot's wife was turned, as a memorial of the burning of Sodom.[60]

Christians who were able – primarily the educated elite expatriates – tended to flee to countries that Islam had not reached. There was a huge exodus of such Christians from Carthage (in modern Tunisia) when it was captured by the Muslims in 698.

There were, however, also martyrs, sometimes many thousands killed together for Christ. Some endured terrible torture without denying Him.

Ultimately, each Christian made their own decision.

A Muslim historian, Ibn al-Athir (1160-1233) recorded what happened in Tunis after it was conquered by the Berber Caliph Abd al-Mumin on 14 July 1159. The Muslim inhabitants of Tunis were merely taxed by their conqueror, who was replacing one Muslim dynasty in North Africa with another. But the *dhimmi* were treated differently:

He remained for three days and he offered Islam to the Jews and Christians resident there. Those who converted were left in peace but those who refused were put to death.[61]

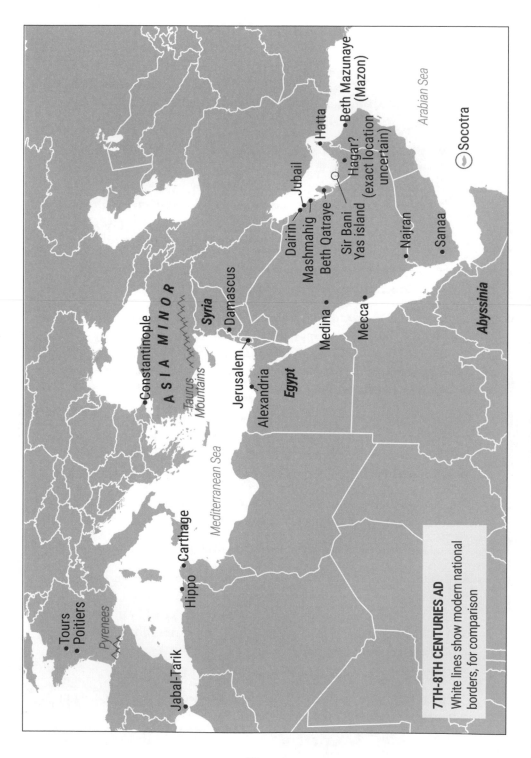

7TH-8TH CENTURIES AD
White lines show modern national borders, for comparison

Tours
Poitiers
Pyrenees
Jabal-Tarik
Hippo
Carthage
Constantinople
ASIA MINOR
Taurus Mountains
Syria
Damascus
Jerusalem
Alexandria
Egypt
Medina
Mecca
Mediterranean Sea
Jubail
Dairin
Mashmahig
Beth Qatraye
Sir Bani Yas island
Hagar? (exact location uncertain)
Hatta
Beth Mazunaye (Mazon)
Najran
Sanaa
Abyssinia
Arabian Sea
Socotra

The elimination of Christianity in North Africa

When Augustine of Hippo (in modern Algeria) died in 430 there were 700 bishoprics along the North African coast. By 1053 there were only five left (outside of Egypt) and by 1073 only two. Before long the entire Church in North Africa had disappeared, apart from in Egypt.

While the indigenous people of the rest of North Africa were mainly Berbers, in Egypt the people were descended from the ancient Pharaonic people and were called Copts. They had their own language, Coptic, still preserved in the liturgy of the Coptic Orthodox Church, but in other respects a long-dead language because Arabic, the language of the conquerors from the Arabian Peninsula, soon took its place in everyday life. Although many Egyptian Christians did convert to Islam, there were also many who did not. As a result the Egyptian Church today numbers around ten million, mainly families who have kept the faith despite nearly 15 centuries of pressure and persecution.

The elimination of Christianity in Arabia

What happened to the eight dioceses of Arabia? The metropolitan province of Beth Qatraye was a main target of the Islamic advance and Christianity declined rapidly. The last mention of the diocese of Mashmahig in the records

The remains of a church building at Suq, a few kilometres east of Hadiboh, the main town on Socotra. Source: Paul Dodson

is around 650. Dairin, Beth Mazunaye (Mazon), Hagar and Hatta survived until at least 676 and then are not heard of again. The monastery on Sir Bani Yas is thought to have continued until at least the early eighth century.

The three southern dioceses lasted longer. There was still a bishop of Sanaa round 840-850. (His name was Peter and it seems he had previously served as a bishop in China.) But after this the diocese of Sanaa disappears from the records.

The fate of the diocese of Najran is mysterious. According to Islamic sources, a delegation of Christians from Najran, including their bishop, travelled to Medina shortly before Muhammad's death and made a treaty with him. In return for an annual payment of 2,000 pieces of cloth, and a promise of supplying horses, camels and armour to the Muslims in time of war, they were allowed to stay in their homeland and continue as Christians under full Muslim protection.

However, Caliph Umar (ruled 634-644) considered that the Christians had violated the peace treaty and he therefore expelled them from Najran (also the Jews, whom he considered to be misbehaving too). Islamic sources praise Umar for removing all non-Muslims from the Arabian Peninsula. But there is evidence that a Christian and Jewish presence continued in or near Najran until around the year 1000, perhaps even until the thirteenth century.

In Socotra a Christian community remained for many centuries. A Muslim geographer in the tenth century noted that most of the island's inhabitants at that time were Christian. A Portuguese fleet arriving in 1507 found that the people worshipped at stone crosses. Francis Xavier, visiting in 1542, discovered Christians who told him they were descended from converts made by the Apostle Thomas when he came to Socotra on his way to India around 50 AD. In 1593, there were still two bishops (different denominations) resident on the island.[62] But by the time James Wellsted visited in 1834 only Muslims lived there. Wellsted wrote about the destruction of churches and graveyards by fanatical Wahhabi Muslims who arrived on Socotra in 1800, but he speculated that the disappearance of Christian people had already happened, by "a silent and gradual change, and not by any violent or exterminating measures".[63] So the Wahhabis destroyed the Christian monuments after Christianity itself had ceased to exist. The ruined buildings remain to this day.

Chapter 8

NORTH-WEST EUROPE IN THE FIRST MILLENNIUM

Pagan kings converted by Christian queens. Missionaries criss-crossing land and sea with the Gospel. Tribes whose names reverberate to this day, but whose distinctive ethnicity (if any) is now unknown. Dramatic mass conversions. Glorious martyrdoms. Battles and bloodshed.

The themes of this chapter are clear, but the details are few and the terminology can be confusing, not to mention the spelling. The Roman names "Britannia" and "Germania" are approximately the Britain and Germany of today.[64] But many other names of places, people and people-groups are hard to recognise. Contemporary sources are scarce. Much of the information comes from traditions, reverently recorded by believers in later centuries, which give scholars plenty of scope to quibble. Let us seek to be inspired by the cloud of witnesses, rather than confused by the mists of time.

The Roman Empire's "Wild West" was north-west Europe. For some centuries, this corner of the empire reached as far north as Hadrian's Wall and as far east as the river Rhine. Beyond these frontiers lived barbarians i.e. people who did not speak Latin or Greek. The Roman army was kept busy fighting off repeated raids by barbarians trying to get into Roman territory.

PERSECUTION BY PAGAN ROMANS

Within the Roman Empire lay Gaul (approximately modern France and Belgium), which had been conquered 58-51 BC, and the southern half of Britain, which was largely conquered by 51 AD. Undoubtedly, early Christians would have been present in both provinces, perhaps traders or soldiers from elsewhere in the empire and the local converts whom they had won. But they had to keep their heads down, as Christians in the Roman Empire were persecuted to a greater or lesser extent until the fourth century.

The first recorded mention of Christianity in Gaul was a great persecution in Lyon and nearby Vienne in 177 AD. Christians had already been forbidden to appear in the marketplace, forum, baths or any public place. If they did so, they were liable to be mocked, beaten and robbed by the populace. They were not safe at home either, for their houses were broken into and vandalised. Eventually the authorities rounded up 48 of the most zealous Christians, and gathered false accusations against them, for example, cannibalism and incest. They tortured and killed the Christians in a variety of ways, which included the use of red hot metal and wild beasts. The 48 martyrs – men, women and a boy of about 15 – came from every stratum of society, including an aristocrat, a doctor, a bishop (aged more than 90), a deacon and two slaves.

The earliest tales of Christianity in Britain also concern martyrs: Julius, Aaron and Alban. Julius and Aaron were executed, probably in the third century at Caerleon (near modern Newport, Wales). The much more famous Alban, who perhaps lived a little later, hid in his home a Christian priest who was fleeing during a time of "cruel persecution" to use the words of Bede, the eighth-century monk and scholar.[65] The faith of the priest so impressed Alban over a period of days that he himself believed too. When soldiers came to search the house, Alban put on the priest's cloak and let himself be arrested in place of his guest. Refusing to save himself from punishment by engaging in pagan rites, Alban declared, "I worship and adore the true and living God who created all things." He was severely whipped and then beheaded. The Roman town of Verulamium, where this happened, is now called St Albans.

During the fourth century, the status of Christianity in the Roman Empire moved from prohibited to permitted to compulsory. It is therefore little surprise that in this century Christians became more visible in both Britain and Gaul. In 314 AD three British bishops and 21 from Gaul attended a council in Arles called by Emperor Constantine.

PERSECUTION BY PAGAN BARBARIANS

So persecution and martyrdom at the hands of the Roman authorities came to an end, but the Christians of north-west Europe still faced opposition from pagans. For scarcely had Christianity established its dominance throughout the Roman Empire than the empire itself began to totter and fail. The Germanic tribes east of the Rhine, who had been pressing on the frontier for some time, started to actually break through and move into Roman territory.

These tribes had traditionally worshipped many gods, for example Tiu, Woden and Thor (whose names appear in Tuesday, Wednesday and Thursday). But the eastern Germanic tribes, such as the Goths and Vandals, became Christians in the fourth century, embracing the heretical Arian form of Christianity, rather than Biblical Trinitarian beliefs. It is recorded that, around the year 341, an Arian missionary translated the Bible into the Gothic language (which he wrote in Greek letters). He omitted the books of 1 and 2 Kings because he thought the war-loving Goths had better not hear too many battle stories.

Meanwhile the western Germanic tribes – the Franks, Angles and Saxons – retained their pagan religion (until they later became Trinitarian Christians).

The eastern Germanic tribes

The eastern tribes are not really part of our story, because they lived too far to the east to impinge much on north-west Europe. When they moved out of Germania, crossing the river Danube which was the Roman Empire's frontier, it was to eastern and southern Europe that they mainly went. In 410 the unthinkable happened and Rome itself fell to the army of Alaric the Goth. By the sixth century, as a church historian has said, "the future belonged to the Germans" at least as regards the empire that was centred on Rome.[66]

The Christian heresy of Arianism thrived amongst these tribes during the fifth century and there were many violent clashes between them and the Trinitarian Christians.[67] Arianism was more or less eradicated by the eighth century.

In 410 the phased withdrawal of Roman troops from Britain was completed, as Rome found it could no longer defend the whole of its empire. Once the Roman garrison had gone, there was nothing to stop the repeated raids on Britain, not only by Germanic tribes (Angles and Saxons) attacking from the south-east, but also by Irish from the west and Picts from the north. All the invading tribes were pagans.

Gaul was invaded by a succession of Germanic tribes including Vandals, Goths, Burgundians and finally the pagan Franks, whose young king Clovis led them to victory against a Roman army in 486. He chose Paris as his capital, from which he built up a strong kingdom. The name of his tribe eventually gave us the word "France". Later Clovis became a Christian, partly through the influence of his Trinitarian Christian wife, Clotilda, who was a Burgundian. Thus the Franks as a whole became Trinitarian Christians and later did much to facilitate Christian mission within their territories.

Meanwhile, in Britain, the newly arrived Angles and Saxons were eliminating the Christian presence and witness as they drove out the pre-existing population, the Celts. From about 450 onwards, Saxons settled in the south, eventually establishing three kingdoms: Essex. Sussex and Wessex. The Angles ventured much further and established three more kingdoms: Mercia (in the midlands), East Anglia and Northumbria. Through their wide geographical spread, they gave their name to Angle-land or England. A seventh kingdom existed in Kent, which Bede says was founded by another Germanic tribe called the Jutes who also settled in the Isle of Wight.

It looked for a while as if Germanic paganism might completely vanquish Christian faith in Britain. But Celtic Christianity clung on in the westernmost parts of Britain, where the invading tribes did not reach. Indeed, Christianity not only survived but also spread through deliberate missionary work.

IRELAND AND IRISH MISSIONARIES

One of the most famous of such missionaries was Maewyn Succat, the rebellious and impious son of a church deacon who farmed somewhere on the west coast of Britain. When he was 16, pagan Irish pirates kidnapped Maewyn and others, carrying them back to Ireland as slaves. His sufferings there drew the young man back to God. After six years he escaped and managed to get home again, but felt called by dreams and visions to share the Gospel with the Irish. Maewyn thoroughly prepared and trained himself for this task and then in 432 returned to Ireland as a missionary bishop with the name Patrick. For almost three decades he laboured in Ireland, sometimes imprisoned by pagan chiefs, sometimes in danger of his life, dying there at the age of about 75.

The Irish church, planted by Patrick in the face of persecution, became "the brightest spot culturally in northern Europe between 590 and 800".[68] Not only was it a centre of learning, but also a centre of mission, as Christians went out from Ireland to evangelise Switzerland, France, Italy, Scotland and northern England (to use the modern place-names).

ENGLAND AND ENGLISH MISSIONARIES

Meanwhile, the paganism of southern England was being tackled by Christians coming from the European mainland. In 597 Augustine landed in Kent with a band of 40 reluctant monks, sent by the mission-minded Pope Gregory. Ethelbert, the king of Kent, was a pagan, but his wife Bertha, was a Christian, and the great-granddaughter of Queen Clotilda who had led her husband Clovis to Christ. Bertha shared her faith with Ethelbert, worshipped in a little stone church that had survived from Roman times, and facilitated the mission of Augustine. Within months, many thousands had become Christians, including King Ethelbert.

Almost the same thing happened in northern England, where Bertha's daughter, Ethelburga, married the pagan king Edwin of Northumbria and led him to Christ. Thousands of people became Christians and were discipled and baptised by Paulinus, from Augustine's team. Even a pagan priest was converted and threw his spear at a temple to Woden, calling on the people to set it on fire. But Edwin was killed in battle against the pagan king of Mercia in 633 and Ethelburga fled back to Kent. The pagan invaders began to establish themselves and their religion but were driven out again in 635 by Oswald, who had become a Christian while in self-imposed exile amongst the Scots. Having got rid of the pagans, King Oswald sent to Iona, where he himself had been baptised, for a missionary to teach Christianity to his people. The man who came was Aidan, who, from his base on the island of Lindisfarne, worked tirelessly to restore Christianity to Northumbria.[69]

King Oswald died in 642 and his successor, the peace-loving King Oswine, continued to support Aidan's ministry until 651. In this tumultuous year, a pagan army attacked the Northumbrian capital, King Oswine was betrayed and assassinated, and Aidan himself fell ill during one of his missionary journeys and died leaning on the wall of a local church he had built.

Re-evangelised England was soon sending out missionaries elsewhere. Willibrord went to the Netherlands in 690. Boniface went to work amongst the German pagans in 718. He died a martyr in 754 while on a missionary preaching tour. Armed men descended on his camp, and Boniface (aged almost 80) held up the book he had been reading to try to protect his head from a sword-wielding attacker. This blood-stained book, with deep cuts into its parchment pages, still exists. It contains two essays by Ambrose, one on the Holy Spirit and the other called *How Good it is to Die*.

With this book the elderly Boniface, an English missionary who had served for years amongst the German pagans, tried to protect himself from a fatal sword blow in 754. Image used by permission of the Dommuseum (Cathedral Museum), Fulda, Germany

PERSECUTION BY PAGAN VIKINGS

The Scandinavian nations, and their territories even further to the north-west, retained their paganism considerably longer than Germany. There was little impact of Christianity on Scandinavian society almost until the end of the first millennium. The much-dreaded Vikings (also called Norsemen or Northmen) began their raids on Britain in 789 and on Ireland in 795. They focused especially on plundering the churches and monasteries, which were easy targets because they were undefended in Christian lands whose inhabitants would have never dreamed of stealing from such sacred places. Scholars debate whether the pagan Vikings picked these Christian targets for religious reasons or simply for financial gain. But, whatever their motive, the damage and destruction caused to these centres of Christian ministry and outreach was enormous.

The thriving Irish Church became so weakened by Viking invasions that, by the tenth century, the church authorities in Rome were seriously concerned that Ireland might have to be re-taught the faith.

NORWAY

In 994 one of the pagan Vikings, Olaf Trygveson, sailed to Britain for the usual robbery, arson and killing. But in the Scilly Isles he met a Christian hermit who prophesied that Olaf would become king of Norway and lead many to Christian faith. He also foretold that Olaf would first be severely wounded in battle, recover after seven days, and be baptised. All of this came to pass, and the following year Olaf became Norway's first Christian king, ruling also over Iceland and Greenland.

He made it a priority to convert his subjects to Christianity but, sad to say, his own conversion did not seem to have much impact on his violent lifestyle. On the one hand he brought over English missionaries, but on the other hand he sought to advance the Christian faith by torturing and killing pagans.

The Old Norse sagas of the twelfth to fourteenth centuries also credit him with establishing Christianity in the Orkney Islands, the Shetland Islands, the Faroe Islands, Iceland and Greenland, which all had Norse settlements.

DENMARK

Danish Vikings seem to have waited until well into the ninth century before starting to raid Britain. But through these raids they encountered Christians, some of whom were probably brought back to Denmark as slaves or wives. Many Danish Vikings settled in the Christian lands of England or Normandy.

There were Frankish Christian missionaries at work in Denmark from the early ninth century. An exiled Danish king was baptised in 826 but, without political power, he could do little to help the missionaries. His rival, King Horik I, who held the throne from 827 to 854, was strongly anti-Christian, no doubt at least in part because it was the faith of his enemies, the Frankish Empire. He not only rejected Christianity but also sought to hinder the work of the Frankish missionary Ansgar. A powerful preacher, but also a very humble and self-effacing man who cared for the poor and sick, Ansgar much later managed to establish good relations with King Horik who then gave him permission to build some churches in Denmark, where there was by that time a small Christian community. In 845 Horik's fleet attacked and sacked Hamburg and destroyed the treasures and books of the churches, leaving the diocese in ruins.

Missionaries to Denmark could also face opposition from other strata in society. Leofdag, a missionary bishop sent from Hamburg to evangelise the Danes, was martyred within months of his arrival in 948 when one of his own bodyguard speared him as he was fording a river.

Eventually, in about 960, another Danish king converted to Christianity. This was Harald Bluetooth, who energetically spread his new faith to his people. Fifteen years later he set up a large stone at Jelling, carved with runes stating (amongst other achievements) that he had "made the Danes Christian".

However, there was considerable syncretism amongst the first Danish Christians. Their pagan religion did not involve the worship of idols (as did the Germanic pagans) but focused on sacred springs, hilltops and groves of trees. Christian missionaries had much work to do in teaching and discipling these "Christians" in the following generations and this resulted in more martyrs.

SWEDEN

The first known missionaries to Sweden went at the invitation of the Swedish King Björn in about 829-30. The Swedes had already encountered Christianity through their Viking raids on Christian populations, and probably through trade.

One of the missionaries who went was Ansgar, who was finding the mission field in Denmark very hard because of hostility not only from King Horik I but also from the local people. The ship in which he and his companion sailed was attacked by pirates and they arrived destitute at the city-on-an-island Birka. But King Björn made them welcome and a prominent courtier called Hergeir built the first Christian chapel in Sweden. After two fruitful years, Ansgar was sent to Hamburg where he was appointed bishop of the newly formed missionary diocese, created to bring the Gospel to the north. His particular assignment was the evangelisation of Norway, Denmark and Sweden. He sent out other missionaries to continue the Swedish work, including Gautbert and Nithard. Gautbert also laboured with great success and built a church in Birka. But here, as in Denmark, the success of the Christian mission created jealousy and hatred amongst the pagans and eventually in 845 AD an angry mob broke into Gautbert's house, plundered it, killed Nithard and burnt the church. Gautbert either fled or was expelled from Sweden.

When news of this persecution reached Ansgar, he was himself fleeing from the furious Danish pagans who had attacked Hamburg, and could do nothing to help. Hergeir, however, managed for some years to keep the congregation at Birka together and to protect them from pagan attack. After Hergeir's death, the Swedish Christians were left defenceless.

Around 850 Ansgar travelled to Sweden again, and reached out to the then king, Olof I. According to one tradition, the king replied that he would ask the people whether they wanted to allow Christianity to be preached again in their country. The persuasive words of an old man that Christ was stronger than Thor convinced the assembly to say yes. According to another tradition, the king cast lots to decide whether or not to give permission for the Christian missionaries to return and the answer was "yes". Whatever really happened, the missionaries were allowed back to Sweden to share the Gospel without hindrance. Ansgar spent another two years in Sweden and rebuilt the church in Birka. Afterwards the work was continued by other missionaries, at least two of whom were Danish.

Although persecution had ceased in Sweden, the Christian faith did not take a firm hold. Many who believed later relapsed back into paganism. It was not until the early eleventh century that the Gospel began to make progress again in Sweden, after the arrival of English missionaries. One of them, Sigfrid, baptised the Swedish royal family in 1008, making King Olof Skötkonung the first Christian king of Sweden. Another, called Ulfrid, was martyred in 1028 in Uppsala, which was a major centre of pagan worship. Using an axe, he hacked to pieces an idol of Thor, and was killed on the spot by the outraged pagans. Sigfrid's three nephews, who had accompanied him on his mission, were beheaded at Växjö by pagans who also ransacked the church there.

Christianity became an officially recognised religion in Sweden, alongside paganism. Uppsala continued as a main centre of pagan worship and sacrifices; Christians had to pay to be exempted from participating. There was a time of terrible persecution of the Christians in Sweden around the year 1066, but gradually paganism faded from most of the south, but it lived on for longer in the wild and inaccessible north.

ICELAND

Iceland is generally thought to have been unpopulated until the Norsemen settled there in the 870s. But an ancient Icelandic source, the *Íslendingabók* (Book of the Icelanders), written between 1122 and 1133, records that the Norseman discovered "Christian men" already living in Iceland. There is also some archaeological evidence to indicate human habitation decades before the Norsemen arrived. An intriguing theory is that Celtic Christians, probably monks from Ireland, had selected this remote and lonely place to live out their calling to be hermits. They apparently left when the pagans from Norway arrived.

Christianity was reintroduced into Iceland in a more conventional way from 980 onwards, i.e. by missionaries. The first was Thorvald Konradsson, an Icelander who had travelled abroad, become a Christian and been baptised by a German bishop called Friedrich. The two travelled to Iceland together but the Icelanders did not respond to the Christian message. In 986 Thorvald was banished after he killed two men.

Another missionary was sent by King Olaf Trygveson when he himself had become a Christian. According to the *Íslendingabók* the Icelanders were again largely unmoved. But in the year 1000, the leading members of society assembled together to decide what to do about this religion that the Norwegian king was pressing on them. Iceland was not a monarchy but an oligarchy, ruled since 930 by a group of chieftains called the Althing. By a majority vote the Althing decided to adopt Christianity in Iceland, but to permit sacrifices to the pagan gods on condition they were done in private.

CONCLUSION

Our story has reached the end of the first millennium.[70] It was a turbulent time in north-west Europe, religiously and in many other ways as well. Christianity and paganism vied with each other and some pagan areas were evangelised, re-paganised and then re-evangelised. We may deplore the violence and apparently political motives of certain new "converts" but we must also recognise the unrecorded multitude of true believers.

We can rejoice in the great faith of the missionaries, who dedicated their lives to bringing salvation to those who had never heard the Gospel. Missionary work in those times was both dangerous and very sacrificial. Patrick, who spent almost 30 years in Ireland, described his yearning for what he had left behind:

> How I would have loved to go to my country [Britain] and my parents, and also to Gaul [where he had studied and trained] in order to visit the brethren and to see the face of the saints of my Lord! God knows it! that I much desired it; but I am bound by the Spirit.

Many believers bravely laid down their lives for Christ. Some have been remembered down the centuries; others are all but forgotten. There must be thousands more whose deaths were never recorded at all on earth, but are honoured in heaven with a martyr's crown.

Chapter 9

CHINA

East Asia has been evangelised over a period of more than 1300 years by the four major divisions of Christianity in turn: the Church of the East, Catholics, Protestants and Orthodox. Cruel persecution and courageous martyrs have been the recurring themes.

THE SYRIAN "LUMINOUS RELIGION"

The Gospel was first brought to China in 635 AD[71] by Syriac-speaking missionaries from the Church of the East, who travelled from Persia, where Christianity was a minority faith under Zoroastrian dominance. The leader of the missionary group was Alopen, who was received by the emperor at his capital, Chang'an (near modern Xi'an in Shaanxi province). The Christian Scriptures, brought by the missionaries, were translated in the Imperial Library, and their doctrine examined. The emperor then gave permission for Christianity to be propagated, and also provided a church in Chang'an.

Over the next two centuries, many communities of Chinese Christians sprang up, from the north-west to the south-east. The first century and a half is recorded in wonderful detail on a granite slab, carved in 781, headed with a cross and the words "Monument of the Syrian Luminous Religion's Coming to China".[72] It also records in detail the beliefs of the Christian missionaries, showing clearly their Trinitarian doctrine. For example,

There is none but our wondrous Three-One, the true Lord without beginning, Alaha.

Alaha means "God" in Syriac, a language derived from the Aramaic which Christ Himself spoke. Christ's incarnation, death on the cross for our salvation, resurrection and ascension are covered, as are Christ as the fulfilment of Old Testament prophecies and the work of the Holy Spirit. In a very Chinese style, the narrative tells us:

He determined the salvation of the Eight Stages,
Refining the earthly and perfecting the heavenly,
He revealed the gate of the Three Constants.
Unfolding life and destroying death.

The Eight Stages are probably the Beatitudes and the Three Constants may be faith, hope and love, which remain (1 Corinthians 13:13).

This is followed by information on the New Testament, baptism, daily worship and weekly Eucharist.

Persecution by Buddhists – and how the Church recovered

Problems began for the Christians in 683 when the emperor (son of the one who had welcomed Alopen) died and his widow, Wu Hou, seized political control of the country. She used her new power to promote Buddhism, which soon became the state religion. Buddhists attacked and tore down church buildings. Eventually, in 732 more missionary reinforcements came from Persia and before long the Christians were again enjoying the favour of the emperor, who gave them a hundred rolls of silk and portraits of himself and his four predecessors. Two years later, another missionary group arrived, who were "commanded to conduct worship in the palace".

Around this time the great ruling Tang dynasty of China was beginning to falter and weaken. There were military challenges from Turks (756), Tibetans (762) and Uighurs (765) but in each case the empire was saved by Duke Kuo, the commander-in-chief of the Chinese armies. Closely linked with the famous duke was a Christian called Izd-buzid, who was not only a mighty warrior but also a key gatherer of intelligence, thus earning honours and gifts from the grateful emperor. Many of these costly presents were passed on by Izd-buzid

Facsimile of the engraving on a granite stone carved in 781 AD, as it would have appeared originally. The stone, measuring approximately 3x1 metres tells the story of Christianity in China up to that date. The inset enlargement shows that the cross at the top has three dots at each of its extremities to signify the Trinity. It rises above lotus flowers (symbol of Buddhism) and clouds (symbol of Taoism).

to the Church, of which he was a great benefactor. After retiring from military service, he was ordained and eventually became a cor episcopos (rural bishop) near Chang'an. It is interesting to note that the home town of Izd-Buzid was in modern Afghanistan.

Persecution by Taoists: 20 months that were fatal to the Church?

In 845 China was ruled by a pro-Taoist emperor who decided to suppress all non-Chinese religions. His targets included Buddhism – which from a Chinese perspective comes from the west, as it began in India – and, of course, Zoroastrianism (originating further west in Persia) and Christianity (from still further west). The emperor's persecution policy lasted only 20 months, after which well-resourced Buddhism soon bounced back. However, it appears that Christianity, a much smaller community, was so damaged by this ordeal that it was unable to rally again.

After the previous bout of persecution in the late seventh and early eighth century, missionaries had come from Persia to strengthen the beleaguered Chinese Church. But this was not so easy in the second half of the ninth century, for China was by then wracked with disorder and civil wars. This chaos brought an end to the seaborne trade with south China and also to peaceful land communication across Central Asia. The weakened Church in China was cut off from its Mother Church.

The Christian presence dwindled to such an extent that an expedition sent in 980 from the Middle East to help the Chinese Christians reported that Christianity in China was extinct, the Christians had perished, their church had been destroyed and there was only one Christian left in the land.

THE "BLESSED PERSON" RELIGION

Thankfully, the situation was not quite that bad. A remnant of the East Syriac Church seems to have survived in China, and certainly it grew in neighbouring areas of Central Asia during the next four centuries. Thus, when the Mongols, led by Genghis Khan, conquered China in the thirteenth century, the Church began to flourish and grow again, enjoying first acceptance and then favour from the ruling powers. Some of the Mongol leaders became Christians. During the Mongol period, the East Syriac Church in China was called the

> "Faithful is the Lord. Your labours are not rejected, ye martyrs. King Christ has not passed by whom ye have loved in the land of China."

From a commemoration of "the martyrs of China" in a thirteenth-century Syriac book

Religion of Yelikewen, which is a transliteration of the Mongolian expression for "Blessed Person".

Persecution by Muslims

In the late thirteenth century, European Catholic missionaries arrived in China and soon won converts. The faith and courage of both the missionaries and the Chinese Christians in the face of persecution were remarkable. Space does not permit mention of more than a few examples, but one must be the massacre in Ili in 1342. Ili was a remote frontier town (now called Yining in Xinjiang province) to which criminals and persecuted Christians were banished. In 1342 a fanatical Muslim became the ruling khan (by poisoning his predecessor) and immediately ordered all Christians to convert to Islam or be killed. Neither the Europeans nor the Chinese took any notice, but continued to live and worship openly as Christians. The seven missionaries were arrested, tortured in front of a mob of angry Muslims and then beheaded. The local Christians, who included Uighurs, Kazakhs, Mongols, Russians and Han Chinese, refusing to flee, were imprisoned and savagely tortured. Many of them died.

Persecution by Chinese

In 1368 the Chinese rose against the Mongol Yuan dynasty who had ruled them for over a century. Hundreds of thousands of Mongols were slaughtered. Yelikewen Christians were targeted in the uprising because of their close association with the Mongols. The victorious Han Chinese established the Ming dynasty, which soon abolished all forms of Christianity in China.

The White Lotus persecution (1616-1617)

The White Lotus Society was a secret Buddhist sect that appears to have begun in the late thirteenth century and was very active against the hated Mongol rulers, soon moving into what might be called "organised crime".[73] In the 1610s it coordinated uprisings against the government of the day. By this time Christians were increasing in number once more. It was an easy matter for Shen Que, a government official who hated Christians, to order persecution of Christians along with reprisals against the White Lotus as they were all "secret societies". Foreign missionaries were to be expelled and Chinese Christians imprisoned for a month and tortured with the dreaded cangue, a small cage made of wood or bamboo in which a prisoner was enclosed with their head and hands protruding. Chinese Christians tried with enormous courage to defend and help the European missionaries who were tortured ruthlessly.

> Shen Que asked one missionary why he tried to convince people to follow a god who was a criminal sentenced to death by the Roman authorities.

MORE MISSIONARIES

A Russian Orthodox church was established in Beijing in 1683 and a mission in 1715. The first Protestant missionary arrived in 1807.

The Taiping Rebellion (1850-1864)

The Taiping Rebellion is better described as a civil war, in which Christians were pitted against the ruling Qing dynasty. It began as a response to the persecution of Christians by the Qing government and was initiated by a Christian called Hong Xiuquan. He hoped to overthrow the government and transform Chinese society spiritually and morally, resulting in a Christian China characterised by justice, equality and freedom.

Hong established himself in Tianjing (present-day Nanjing) and set up what he called the Taiping Heavenly Kingdom. His army gained control of a

> ### Rejoicing to suffer for Christ
>
> The two Zhong brothers were famed for their faithfulness to Christ through great suffering and for the joy shown on their faces because that suffering was for the sake of Christ, a joy which amazed non-Christians who saw it. The brothers were imprisoned in Nanjing and given 70 lashes each, leaving them half-dead. Then in March 1617 Zhong Ming-ren was sent to do hard manual labour strengthening the Great Wall, while Zhong Ming-Li was sent to haul imperial ships on the Grand Canal – work normally done by oxen or horses.

substantial amount of territory, so that at its height the Taiping Heavenly Kingdom had a population of almost 30 million people.

As the rebellion unfolded, Western interests became involved, principally the US, Britain and France. It developed into one of the bloodiest wars ever. Such grave atrocities were committed (by both sides) that the death toll is estimated at anywhere between 20 million and 100 million.

Hong's millenarian beliefs and the fact that he claimed to be the younger brother of Jesus have led some to disregard this 14-year conflict and downplay its importance in the history of Christian persecution in China. However, not only was the Taiping Rebellion very significant at the time, but also it was significant as a source of inspiration for Chinese communists in their early formative stage.[74]

Persecution by the Boxers

In the late nineteenth century a sub-group of the White Lotus Society had developed called the Righteous and Harmonious Fists, better known as the Boxers. At this time, China was humiliated by defeat in various wars. People were desperately poor and natural disasters had made their suffering worse. The Boxers blamed the blue-eyed "foreign devils" and also the Chinese Christians, who had offended the "gods of happiness and wealth" by deciding to follow Christ – hence the lack of rain, said the Boxers. In 1900 the Boxers rose in rebellion, their aim being to return Chinese culture to Confucian values such as respect for elders, ancestors, family and emperor. They wanted to rid

China of all Westerners and their "Western" religion, Christianity. They slaughtered 188 foreign missionaries and around 32,000 Chinese Christians.

PERSECUTION BY COMMUNISTS[75]

When communists gained control of mainland China in 1949, foreign missionaries left the country. Many Protestant churches, which were already well on the way to being self-supporting and self-governing, only had to add self-propagating to become "Three Self" churches i.e. fully independent of foreign missionary input.

Chinese Christians had to choose whether or not to submit to communist government control. Many Protestant churches did submit and are known as the Three Self Patriotic Movement. Others continued as unofficial churches, operating illegally, often called "house churches". Catholics divided in a similar way into the Chinese Patriotic Catholic Church, under Chinese government control, and an illegal Catholic Church under the authority of the Pope.

During the Cultural Revolution (1966-1976) no religious expression was allowed in China, not even the Three Self churches. All Christian activity had to be underground, and as a result the house churches grew.

Since then, persecution of Christians has waxed and waned, also varying between different parts of the country. The targets are normally Protestants. Arrest, imprisonment and sometimes torture are fairly common, but martyrdoms (e.g. death in custody) are relatively rare. Through it all, the house churches have continued to grow and Christians now greatly outnumber members of the Communist Party of China.

Chapter 10

JAPAN

EASTERN CHRISTIANITY?

At the time when the East Syriac Church was active in Chang'an, China, there were various distinguished Japanese Buddhist monks studying in the same area. Scholars have speculated that Christians and Buddhists could have had contact with each other in the multicultural, cosmopolitan Chinese capital, perhaps leading to the presence of an East Syriac Church in Japan as early as the eighth or ninth century. But, if so, it seems to have disappeared without trace.

THE "CHRISTIAN CENTURY"

Western Christianity was brought to Japan by the Portuguese. The Catholic missionary Francis Xavier arrived in 1549, a date which is considered to mark the beginning of Japan's "Christian century" during which many Japanese embraced the faith. By the early 1630s Japan had an estimated 760,000 Christians, or "Kirishitans" as they were called, making up 6% of the population.

Trading with Portuguese merchants was apparently a strong factor in the conversion of many *daimyos* (noblemen), followed by mass conversions of the populations they controlled. The port of Nagasaki became a Christian city. But many must have had a genuine faith, as shown by the unbelievable courage with which Kirishitans clung to Christ despite terrible persecution. No doubt the words of the Lord Jesus brought hope and comfort to the oppressed and poorest of this feudal society.

Persecution began abruptly in 1587 when the powerful *daimyo* Hideyoshi issued an order to expel all foreign missionaries. Most in fact remained, but worked more discreetly than before. Nine years later, when Hideyoshi needed to quarrel with Spain for economic reasons, he renewed his order, adding that all the Kirishitan leaders in Kyoto and Osaka should be executed. Twenty Japanese and six foreign Christians from various parts of Japan were crucified in Nagasaki on 5 February 1597.

Hideyoshi died the following year, but persecution did not die with him. In 1614 an order was issued to ban the Kirishitan religion throughout Japan and expel the missionaries and senior church leaders. Thirty years of savage persecution followed, producing many martyrs. The Japanese authorities soon found that "simple" execution methods like beheading, crucifixion and burning at the stake did not seem to instil fear in the onlookers but rather inspired them to greater faith. They therefore invented new methods involving prolonged suffering. The most agonising was to suspend the person upside down in a dark pit partly filled with excrement, with various precautions taken to avoid early death. Some Christians lingered for weeks before dying from this particular torture.

The third shogun, Iemitsu, who came to power in 1623, was very thorough in organising the oppression of the Kirishitans, through various new rules which remained in place for over 200 years. For example, those who denounced Kirishitans got a financial reward but, if anyone failed to denounce a Kirishitan, they and their five-family group[76] would all be executed. In 1633 he began a "closed country" policy to isolate Japan as much as possible from the rest of the world; this policy was maintained for 220 years.

THE UNDERGROUND CENTURIES

The ban on Kirishitans was not lifted until 1873. By that time there had been 4,045 martyrs whose names are known, but it has been estimated that the total number may have been as high as 40,000.

From 1644 until 1873 the Kirishitans were an underground church, who survived by pretending to be Buddhists. Even so, there were from time to time *kazure* (crumblings) i.e. large-scale round-ups of Kirishitans, when many would be imprisoned or executed.

As the generations passed for the underground church, the beliefs of the Kirishitans gradually shifted to embrace Japanese indigenous religions, but they still knew by heart long Christian prayers taught by the early Portuguese missionaries to their forefathers. They also had a special prayer of contrition which they recited at home after the annual treading on an engraved picture of Christ, in obedience to another of Iemitsu's anti-Kirishitan regulations.

Towards the end of this period, Protestant and Catholic missionaries arrived (1859), soon followed by Russian Orthodox (1861). These foreigners were apparently not considered to be Kirishitans and were therefore tolerated.

WHEN THE EMPEROR IS A GOD

In 1873 the wooden noticeboards banning the Kirishitan religion were taken down, the missionaries could evangelise openly, and many of the Kirishitans came out of hiding,[77] making it appear that there had suddenly been a huge wave of conversions. This unnerved the Japanese authorities, who tried to counteract a "Christianity once more on the loose"[78] by reinforcing the Emperor System. Before long, veneration of the emperor, the divine head of the state Shinto religion, had been made compulsory.

The days of torture and executions may have been past, but pressure still continued on Japanese Christians in the following decades. Protestants especially wanted to show that they were loyal citizens in the midst of various wars with which Japan was involved, yet found themselves struggling with issues such as bowing to the emperor. In 1891, during the annual rite of venerating the Emperor's Rescript on Education,[79] a Protestant Japanese school-teacher called Uchimura Kanzo hesitated momentarily. Then he bent his head but did not make a proper bow. The implied lack of respect in a society where the relative depth of a bow is all-important was taken very seriously. Uchimura was accused of blasphemy and lese-majesty,[80] and eventually had to resign from his teaching post. In later life he moved between various kinds of Christianity, striving to develop a specifically Japanese form of his faith.

The 1930s were a time of particular tension between Christianity and Shinto, with the military pressuring the Christians to participate in ceremonies at state Shinto shrines to venerate the war dead. The dilemma for Christians was whether or not this was worship. "Conformity and compromise were the order of the day"[81] as most Christians gladly clung to the argument that the rites were not religious but simply showed patriotism and loyalty. However, some of the smaller Protestant groups, such as the Holiness groups and the Brethren, began to be persecuted by the Tokko (Special Higher Police), who considered their views subversive.

BEFORE AND DURING WW2

International events were moving towards the Second World War. Western powers were seen to be taking an anti-Japanese stance, and it became increasingly urgent for Japanese Christianity to show itself to be truly Japanese i.e. without foreign influence or loyalties.

In 1940 a new Religious Bodies Law came into effect, imposing various restrictions and giving the government power to suppress religious organisations if their doctrine was not approved or they were too small. Only denominations with at least 50 church buildings and 5,000 members would have their charters renewed. This meant that more than 30 of the 44 Protestant denominations would not be legally recognised any more. Hastily the smaller ones began to amalgamate with each other. The Orthodox Church severed its ties with the Moscow Patriarchate in a bid to keep its charter. But the Roman Catholics, having removed Westerners from all senior leadership positions (as had Protestants), refused to cut their ties with the Pope in Rome. In the end the Japanese government backed down on the issue of the Pope.

In 1941 two pastors of the Holiness Church riled the authorities: one refused to do the daily pilgrimages to the local shrine for the war dead and the other preached a sermon which the authorities considered undermined the *kokutai* (national identity, sovereignty and system of government). In 1942 police arrested about a hundred members of the Holiness Church, accusing them of "denying the *kokutai*". Holiness teaching on the sinfulness of all people, including the emperor, and on Christ's Second Coming when Japan would become part of His Kingdom, were cited as incompatible with the *kokutai*. Several Holiness Church members were tortured and died in prison. The following year the government dismissed all Holiness pastors and banned the denomination.

Towards the end of the war, anti-Christian persecution increased further, with Anglican clergy and others imprisoned on suspicion of being spies or having a defeatist attitude. The harshest treatment was given to Korean and Taiwanese Christians.

POST-WAR FREEDOM OF RELIGION

After the war, the close relationship between the state and Shinto was unravelled, under the auspices of the Allied Occupation of Japan. In 1945 government funding for Shinto was banned, although shrines were allowed to continue. In 1946 the emperor issued a Rescript in which he appeared to renounce his divine status. In 1947 a new constitution guaranteed freedom of religion.

Article 20. Freedom of religion is guaranteed to all. No religious organization shall receive any privileges from the State, nor exercise any political authority. No person shall be compelled to take part in any religious act, celebration, rite or practice. The State and its organs shall refrain from religious education or any other religious activity.

From the Constitution of Japan, which came into effect on 3 May 1947

Chapter 11

KOREA

It is possible that the Gospel first reached Korea in the seventh to ninth centuries, thanks to the work of East Syriac missionaries who came along the Silk Road to China. Archaeologists have discovered the remains of seven bodies, each with a clay cross at its head, in a grave near Anshan, on the Liaodong peninsula (in modern China). Coins in the grave date the burials between 998 and 1006. In the seventh century this peninsula was part of the northernmost of three Korean kingdoms but by 1000 it had been conquered by a Manchurian tribe. Nevertheless, the burials indicate an East Syriac Christian community in an area that had recently been Korean.

Leaving aside those shadowy early centuries, for which no solid evidence exists, Christianity in Korea is remarkable for having developed entirely without foreign missionaries for perhaps 200 years. The only non-Korean Christians known to have set foot on Korean soil before 1794 were Christian troops amongst the Japanese military force that invaded Korea in the 1590s and the chaplains who accompanied them, one Spanish and one Japanese. It is not known whether they ever discussed their faith with the Korean population they were trying to conquer.

Koreans must have met Christians while travelling in other countries of East Asia, and brought the Gospel back to their homeland.

Koreans living in Japan in the second half of the sixteenth century may have met and discussed with Christians there, either foreign missionaries or members of the rapidly growing Japanese church. The first known Koreans to respond and believe were some of the prisoners of war brought back by the Japanese from Korea as slave labour in the 1590s. Over 2,000 of them became Christians in Japan, and at least 24 were martyred there.

Around the same time, educated Koreans visiting China encountered Christians and Christian literature there. Neo-Confucianism was the state religion of Korea and many Koreans viewed Christianity as a minor variant of Buddhism, a religion they despised. But some were drawn to study the monotheistic faith and, in a slow trickle, Koreans began to convert, most of them from the middle or upper classes.

A landmark occurred in 1777 when, for the first time, a group of Korean believers began to pray together and set aside every seventh day for rest. Very soon they were writing hymns. The Church gradually grew as Koreans shared the Gospel with each other.

In 1785, police caught some young men meeting for Christian worship in a clinic in Seoul belonging to Kim Beom-u. They were all arrested and Kim Beom-u was imprisoned. He was tortured but refused to deny Christ, so was banished. About a year later he died of his injuries, thus becoming the first martyr of the fledgling Church in Korea. In 1787 the king ordered that all Christian books be destroyed and no more imported. Some Christians hid their books, but many burnt them – after memorising the contents.

REVERENCE FOR PARENTS AND ANCESTORS – A CHALLENGE FOR CHRISTIANS

Traditional Confucian ancestral rituals posed an immediate problem for the young Korean Church. Were the rituals expressions of filial piety (which a Christian could perform with a clear conscience) or were they idolatrous worship (as most Christians thought)? In 1791 two cousins called Yun and Gwon were executed for burning their ancestral tablets and not performing ancestral rites. Their homes were destroyed, and their relatives banished or enslaved.[82] Church leaders and others deemed guilty by association were rounded up, beaten, tortured if necessary, and made to renounce their faith in Christ.

Filial piety was just one aspect of a serious tension between Christian doctrine and Korean culture. Koreans considered that social relationships (of which filial piety was the most important) were essential for a good and stable society. Christianity emphasised an individual's relationship with a transcendent God and their quest for their own personal salvation. This seemed irresponsibly selfish to the Korean neo-Confucians (who saw the same fault in Buddhism, with its focus on the next life instead of this one). In the Ten Commandments, filial piety was far down the list at number 5, instead of number 1. Loving your neighbour appeared a dubious way to organise a society in comparison with the tried and tested Korean emphasis on caring for your family. Christianity seemed like a recipe for anarchy.

FOREIGN MISSIONARIES AND PERSECUTION

In 1794 the first foreign missionary arrived. He was Chinese and had been sent in response to repeated requests from the Korean Christians. Over the next five years, the number of believers in Korea more than doubled to about 10,000 but the Korean authorities soon discovered the presence of the foreign missionary, an order was issued for his arrest (which he evaded), and moderate persecution began.

The first episode of severe persecution of Korean Christianity occurred in 1801. It was initiated by Dowager Queen Kim. Her late husband, the king, had received many complaints against Christianity, including that it was too class and gender inclusive, thus contradicting neo-Confucianism's belief in human inequality. Another complaint was that Christianity was causing the birth rate to fall. The queen banned Christianity, after which 672 Christians were arrested, mostly from the upper classes and a quarter of them women. They were tried in court (very unusual for women in Korean society at the time), beaten and tortured. Some 400 were exiled, 156 were beheaded and many others died in prison.

THE SILK LETTER

In October 1801 a Christian called Hwang Sa-yeong wrote a letter to the Bishop of Beijing on a piece of silk, to be hidden in the collar of a courier. (See appendix for an abridged translation.) In its 13,311 tiny Chinese characters, the Silk Letter described the persecution of the Christian community in Korea, requested financial support,[83] and asked the bishop to ask the Pope to ask the Chinese[84] emperor to decree that Western missionaries be allowed into Korea. Two other suggestions made in the Silk Letter for ending the Korean government's persecution of Christians were for China to take over part of Korea or for Western battleships to come and threaten Korea.

Unfortunately for Hwang, the courier betrayed him and the contents of the letter reached the Korean authorities. Hwang was arrested, tried and executed by the method reserved for the worst criminals – death by slow slicing. About a hundred alleged collaborators were executed too.

An edict was then issued that Christians should be treated as traitors and put to death so that they would have no descendants.

AFTER THE EDICT

After this persecution and edict, the Church in Korea was no longer a church of aristocratic scholars, for they had mostly been killed or had apostatised. It became an underground church, drawn mainly from the middle and lower classes of society, who endured a series of bouts of persecution.

Whole families were deprived of their livelihoods because one person was a Christian. Impoverished and ostracised, up to three-quarters of the Christian community fled to the remote and mountainous south-east. There they established Christian villages (*gyouchon*) with about 50 inhabitants each, and tried to survive by foraging, subsistence farming, growing tobacco, or making pottery and writing materials. Village leaders organised daily prayers and special meetings on Sundays. They read the Scriptures and other Christian literature. All social classes lived together communally and took joint responsibility for the care of children orphaned by persecution. Other social outcasts came to join the Christians in their villages.

The bravery with which Christian men and women had borne their sufferings in the 1801 persecution increased public curiosity about Christianity. Travelling around to sell pottery and literature, Christians were able to spread the faith and help to bind together the scattered Christian villages, without attracting hostile notice.

Some extracts from the Silk Letter, 1801

"The grace of our Lord in this country is special. From the beginning, Christian teaching came to us without an evangelist.[85] We cannot count all the special blessings we have received. The punishment this year was to root out our sinful shortcomings. But the Lord, in his grace, has not abandoned us..."

"I have heard that the blood of the martyrs becomes the seeds of the Church.[86] But unfortunately, our country is located next to Japan.[87] Those islanders are cruel and have forsaken the relationship with the Lord on their own. Our government approves of it and plans to imitate what they have done.[88] Is that not ridiculous?"

"Of course we should not just sit around and wait to die in this situation. But everything else can be discussed after we have had financial stability. We had no idea that the survival of the Church in a nation depended on that despicable mammon. If the Church were to die out just because of a lack in material wealth, how horrible would that be? That is why I dare to kneel before you in humble request. Please make a plea for us to other Western nations. If enough funding is provided to maintain the Church and save souls, I will ask your permission after every preparation has been made to manage it uprightly. Please have mercy on us and help us."

Translation by Alexander Y. Hwang and Lydia T. Kim, "The Silk Letter of Alexander Sayông Hwang: Introduction and Abridged Translation", *Missiology: An International Review*, Vol. 37, No. 2, April 2009, pp.165-179. The above extracts are from pages 174, 172 and 173, respectively.

The first European missionaries finally managed to get into the isolated "hermit kingdom" of Korea in 1831, and others soon followed. By this time, Korea's indigenous church structures were already well established. The atmosphere was hostile to Europeans and so missionaries tended to travel only at night and dressed as mourners i.e. with huge hats like upside down baskets, covering their faces. Another method was to be a "tentmaker" like the German Lutheran Karl Gützlaff who worked in Korea in 1832 as an interpreter for the East India Company and distributed Christian literature to Koreans he met. The Church grew,[89] but after a few years the Korean authorities discovered the missionaries, which triggered the fourth major persecution (1839).

The 1839 persecution was intended to exterminate the Church, and it began with arresting the leaders, many of whom were women because so many male leaders had already been martyred. Three French missionaries gave themselves up to the authorities, hoping to save their flock; their heads were hung up on public display near Seoul but it did not stop the persecution. At least 254 Christians were arrested, of whom 121 were either executed or died in prison. Whole families perished together. When the authorities realised that people were quite willing to die for Christ, they focused on encouraging apostasy. Believers aged from 13 to 79 were tortured to death.

Eventually a decree was issued which brought this bout of persecution to an end and simultaneously justified it with the following five criticisms of Christianity:

1. The Confucian way of praising heaven is better than the Christian way.
2. Jesus was executed as a criminal, so Christianity must be evil.
3. Christianity is popular with women and common people.
4. The incarnation is nonsensical.
5. Men and women mixing in church is immoral and celibacy is a threat to filial piety.

Many new hymns were written in a popular Korean style during the 70 years of persecution, bringing hope and comfort to suffering believers. For example,

> Let's go, let's go, let's go to Heaven!
> Where is Heaven?
> It's where there are ten thousand blessings.
> Heaven is high in the sky.
> The glory of God appears there.
> The Trinity is shining there,
> And the grace of the Holy Spirit is bestowed.
>
> by Choi Yang-eop (died 1861)[90]

THE GREAT PERSECUTION (1866-1871)

This period of persecution and martyrdom culminated with the Great Persecution when an estimated 8,000 Korean Christians died, that is, more than half the Christian community. Only about a tenth of the deaths were official executions; most died when they were unofficially killed by the authorities, lynched by their neighbours or starved to death in the mountains.

The first Protestant martyr of Korea?

European missionaries also died in the Great Persecution, including Welsh-born Robert Jermain Thomas, who is considered the first Protestant martyr of Korea. Thomas had set his heart on bringing the Bible to Korea and distributed some Bible portions and tracts along the coast in 1865.

In 1866 Thomas, presumably in an attempt to get into Korea, accepted the position of interpreter to the admiral of a French invasion fleet sent to avenge the deaths of nine French missionaries. But the French fleet was diverted to China, so Thomas transferred himself to an American merchant ship, the *General Sherman*.

Travelling upriver towards Pyongyang, the *General Sherman* was assumed by the Koreans to be part of an invading force. The ship ignored Korean warnings and commands to return to China. The Koreans then attacked the ship, which fired her cannon, killing a number of Koreans. Later the Koreans floated fire boats down the river and the ship caught alight. Thomas tried to distribute the Christian literature he had brought with him to Korean villagers who had gathered to watch. One account of his death states, "After he had distributed all the books but one, he left the schooner, when it was already in flames, with his last copy of the Bible. He humbly knelt down before the soldier waiting for him, begged him to accept the Bible, and shut his eyes to pray." Thomas was beheaded.

The Bibles he left in Korea had a considerable impact, even the one his executioner took from him, leading many souls to the Lord, after the soldier papered the walls of his house with the pages of the Bible. People read the Word of God on his walls and some became Christians.

But can Thomas' military involvement be truly separated from his mission? Was he executed as a Christian missionary or as a foreign invader?

109

The Great Persecution was worse than the other persecutions because it was targeted not only at leaders, but also at Christians of any position in society. The vast majority of those killed in the Great Persecution were ordinary believers, poor and uneducated, who could not defend themselves in court as had the scholarly church leaders in 1801.

The Great Persecution had been triggered by the threat of an attack on Korea by Russia and Korean Grand Prince Heungseon's idea of avoiding this by a French intervention with Korean Christian help. When the Russian threat receded, the Grand Prince, who had previously been sympathetic to Christians, turned against them. French warships, and a German adventurer who raided the tomb of the Grand Prince's father, only added to the problems of the Korean Christians, who became the scapegoats for all foreign aggression. After a couple of years the number of Christian arrests declined but the overall persecution situation got worse as the general population began to vent their anger on Christians.

In 1871, American warships came to retaliate against the destruction of the *General Sherman*. Hearing that Korean Christians had made secret contact with the Americans, the Grand Prince announced that any Korean who called for conciliation with the "Western barbarians" was betraying their country. He then intensified his efforts to persecute Christians, but by now they were so widely scattered that few were caught.

AFTER 70 YEARS OF PERSECUTION

The Korean Church emerged from 70 years of persecution poor, weakened and marginalised, but it began to grow again. Until this point it had been entirely Catholic, but now the influence of Protestant missionaries began to be felt. The Protestant missionaries operated in a very different way from the Catholics. The former brought their families with them, lived in American-style houses and wore Western suits. The latter lived in mission stations built in traditional Korean style, dressed either in Korean clothes or clergy robes, and lived on salaries a fraction of the size of the Protestants'. A Russian Orthodox mission to Korea was established in 1897.

John Ross, a Scottish Presbyterian missionary who supported the "Three Self" mission method,[91] wanted to facilitate the work of Korean evangelists.

Noticing how eagerly Koreans bought Christian books, he decided to translate the Bible into Korean. At first he struggled to find anyone willing to teach him written Korean because it was so dangerous for Koreans to associate with foreigners, but eventually he did and then built a translation team. In 1882 the first Korean Scripture portions (John and Luke) were published.

Church members would often prepare the way for missionaries by moving to live in non-Christian villages. After creating interest in the Gospel and buying property, they would then ask a missionary (foreign or Korean) to come and consolidate the work and establish a church. Many single and widowed women were very active in mission and ministry; they became known as "Bible women" and travelled widely in their evangelistic and pastoral work. Married Christian women had a significant role leading local prayer meetings or "family services" in the home. In 1891 the Presbyterian missions officially adopted the Three Self church-planting method, which John Ross had already been practising, and other missions soon followed suit.

During this period there were occasional episodes of persecution – mainly arrests and in 1888 one martyrdom. The isolated *gyouchon* villages were particularly vulnerable. When the anti-Western Boxer Rebellion[92] was raging in China, some Korean Christians and foreign missionaries were beaten and churches set on fire.

In addition to the spiritual ministry and outreach, there were other factors in late nineteenth-century Korea that promoted conversions to Christianity: Confucianism was losing its former grip on Korean society, the West was seen as an ally against Korea's traditional foe Japan, and a yearning for modernisation had begun – Protestantism was seen as attractively modern. Sometime before 1897, Protestant Christians developed a Christian ancestral memorial ritual, called *chudoyebae*, which must have made it much easier for Koreans struggling with the issue of ancestor veneration to make the decision to follow Christ.

In 1894 Korean men began to convert to Christianity in significant numbers, usually bringing their entire household to faith with them. If the new convert was a man of influence, his whole village might become Christians. It was characteristic of Koreans that they embraced a fresh loyalty with great enthusiasm and set themselves to achieving complete "mastery". Hence, for example, the dawn prayer meetings, which were started in Pyongyang by Gil Seon-ju who became a Christian in 1897 after reading *The Pilgrim's Progress.* Gil had previously followed a Taoism-influenced ascetic type of Buddhism and he carried this holistic and rigorous commitment into his new faith. He went on to become a key leader of the Korean Church, preaching sacrificial love, encouraging prayer meetings and supporting the self-reliant Three Self principle. For rural Christians who did not have cash to give, he suggested donating a day's labour to the church or setting aside a daily handful of rice.

It was during the 1890s that the north-western city of Pyongyang became the centre of Protestant Christianity in Korea. Many reasons have been suggested for this dramatic development, which led to Pyongyang being called "the Jerusalem of the East" because it had so many church buildings. Some of the 1890s converts said they had seen the martyrdom of Robert Jermain Thomas, three decades earlier, and still possessed the literature he had distributed.[93]

UNDER JAPANESE RULE

In 1905 Japan occupied Korea, describing it as their "protectorate". The harshness of Japanese rule and the humiliation of the situation caused a wave of Korean nationalism. In Pyongyang, Gil Seon-ju compared Korea to Israel in the Old Testament and called for personal repentance from sin as a necessary prelude to national recovery. More prayer meetings were set up. Tens of thousands of Koreans migrated to Manchuria, Russia and China because they did not want to live under Japanese rule, including some church communities which moved *en masse* and set up Christian villages in the countries where they settled.

Catholic church leaders in 1906 declared that the Japanese government was the lawful and God-appointed authority in Korea. They condemned the popular resistance movements which were developing, and said the Japanese would be a civilising influence on Korea. Running completely counter to popular feelings in Korea, this stance had a negative impact on the growth of the Catholic Church in Korea.

Meanwhile a great Protestant revival had begun, which peaked in Pyongyang in 1907.

In the same year, a mainly Christian campaign to collect money to pay off the Korean national debt was started. The thinking behind this was that, as most of the debt was owed to Japan, paying it off would help Korea to become independent again. There were many fund-raising activities, led mainly by women.

In 1910 Japan formally annexed Korea and continued to rule the peninsula until defeated in 1945 at the end of the Second World War. Thus, to the Korean mind, colonialism and imperialism were Japanese, not Western. This doubtless spared the Korean Christians some of the hostility that Christians in China and Japan faced due to their assumed links with the West.

Korea became like a giant prison camp, with intense surveillance. Korean language and culture were suppressed and Japanese people replaced Koreans in top jobs. Japanese teachers and civil servants wore swords.

THE CONSPIRACY TRIAL (ALSO CALLED THE 105-MAN INCIDENT)

At first the Japanese colonial rulers tried to win over the Christians, especially the powerful Western missionaries, arguing that they and the missionaries had a shared objective to uplift the Korean people.

But in 1911 several hundred men were arrested, mainly Christians, accused of plotting to assassinate the Japanese governor-general. Of these, 123 were brought to trial in February 1912. Most of them had been tortured and three had already died in custody. The trial was a farce, and no evidence was given except the men's own written confessions. Nevertheless 105 were convicted of treason and given prison sentences. Western nations protested (mainly because their missionaries were accused of encouraging the conspirators) and the sentences were reduced.

THE MARCH 1ST INDEPENDENCE MOVEMENT

In 1915 the Japanese colonial government banned religious instruction in private schools. They also ruled that on days when the emperor sacrificed at Shinto shrines, private schools must hold appropriate ceremonies. This was one of the main reasons why many Christians, concerned about the impact on Christian schools, got involved in the Korean independence movement.

A Declaration of Independence was drafted and signed by 33 religious leaders including 16 Christians, and huge pro-independence demonstrations were held on Saturday 1 March 1919. The Japanese banned church services the next day and began to arrest people. Orderly non-violent demonstrations continued for weeks, often on church property. The Japanese police with their swords and the army with their guns attacked the demonstrators. Sometimes riots ensued. Thousands were arrested, held without trial, and tortured, raped and flogged. Again, Christians were a main target, and virtually every pastor in Seoul and Pyongyang ended up in jail, as well as other church workers. Many Christians were killed and many church buildings burnt. In one case the Japanese herded about 30 villagers into a Methodist church before setting fire to it. Western "Christian" governments condemned the Japanese brutality. Thus Christianity became linked with Korean nationalism in the minds of both Koreans and Japanese.

SURVEILLANCE, SUPPRESSION AND CONTROL

After this, Japanese colonial policy became less military in style, swords were less in evidence, and some concessions were made to Korean language and culture. A new governor-general relaxed the rules regarding church ownership of property. But at the same time surveillance of Christian activities was increased. The 1920s also saw the rise of Communism, which, being inherently atheist, created anti-Christian feeling.

Christians living under such continuing pressure found comfort and strength in remembering the martyrs of long ago. It was at this time that Robert Jermain Thomas was hailed as the first Protestant martyr, for there had been no Korean Protestants during the terrible years of persecution between 1801 and 1871.

In 1925 the Japanese began to force Koreans to prove their loyalty to their Japanese colonial rulers by participating in rites at state Shinto shrines. Korean Christians resisted this, considering it idolatrous. In 1935 two American Presbyterian missionary teachers publicly refused to take part in the opening ceremonies of a provincial education centre at a state Shinto shrine. The result was widespread persecution of Korean Christians, with many pastors put in prison.

In 1937 the authorities ordered the churches themselves to conduct Shinto rites and visit shrines. The Korean Catholic leadership, accepting the regime's argument that the rites were not religious, had already ruled that Christians could participate in shrine worship. Soon the various Protestant denominations issued similar statements.

Some church members strongly disagreed with their leaders on this issue. Large numbers left the official churches, which they considered apostate, and emigrated, worshipped in private, moved to the mountains, or just waited for Christ's return. Many Christians were arrested for not participating in shrine worship, and some 50 died under torture or in prison. Around 200 Protestant churches were closed.

Further pressure was put on the Christians, especially the smaller Protestant denominations. The Korean authorities wanted the churches to cut their foreign links and for all the Protestant denominations to join together as one. By 1942 the churches were effectively under complete government control. Police permission had to be obtained for each church meeting, and police would always be present at the meetings. The content of the meetings was also strictly regulated. Christians were not allowed to preach or read Bible passages about judgment or the Second Coming. They were not allowed to sing or pray about the Kingdom of God or the Lordship of Christ.

But true faith survived. Catholics had a long history of being an underground church and Protestants had a tradition of self-support and family worship in the home.

1945 AND FREEDOM

The pressure came to a sudden end when Japan was defeated in 1945. It is a sad irony that it was the dropping of America's second atomic bomb on Nagasaki, which had once been a Christian city,[94] that finally caused Japan to surrender on 14 August. Soviet troops had moved into northern Korea on the day Nagasaki was bombed, and American troops moved into the south in September.

In 1945 the Korean Christian community was about 2-3% of the population overall, but a much higher percentage of the educated classes. Christians therefore played a significant part in the leadership of Korea after the Second World War. In fact, the interim governments set up in the north and south were both led by Christians.

Korean Christians gave thanks for religious liberty as well as political freedom. Churches and Christian institutions across the country reopened, and church building projects resumed. Believers who had been worshipping in private flocked back to the churches. Many hoped to establish a unified Christian nation.

However, the powerhouse of Korean Christianity in 1945 was in the north. Three-fifths of the Protestants (200,000 people) lived in the north and so did many of their best church leaders. There were also about 100,000 Catholics.

1946 AND KIM IL-SUNG

In January 1946, the pacifist Presbyterian leader of the interim northern government mysteriously disappeared and was never seen again. A young communist freedom fighter called Kim Il-sung seized power. He came from the Christian middle classes and his mother and maternal grandfather were staunch Presbyterians. Kim began a gradual suppression of Christianity. Although many Christians were leaving the north, those who remained strongly resisted Kim's actions against them. Indeed, church attendance in the north seems to have increased for the first few years, despite the growing persecution and the dwindling size of the Christian community.

1948 AND DIVISION

In 1948 Korea was divided into two nations. Northerners who wanted to leave at this point were allowed to do so, and amongst them were a large proportion of Christians, including many of the north-western elite.

The northern Christians were very much outsiders when they arrived in the south as refugees. They clung together and did not join the southern churches, instead starting nearly 2,000 churches of their own. The newly arrived northerners challenged the southern churches to a greater Christian commitment, in particular to be conservative, self-supporting, self-propagating, hardworking and anti-communist.

THE KOREAN WAR (1950-1953)

On Sunday 25 June 1950 North Korea launched an unexpected attack on South Korea. Most Protestant missionaries fled the country. Korean church leaders and foreign Catholic leaders were taken prisoner by the rapidly advancing communist army, and later carried back to the North when the communists retreated again. These Christian leaders were never to return to the South. An estimated 500 died in captivity, some executed and others perishing from cold or starvation.

Daddy! Say NO!

The normal method of execution of pastors captured by the North Korean communists was to shoot them. But in one case a large hole was dug, into which the pastor, his wife and several of their children were put. The pastor was asked to repent of having "misled" his people for many years by teaching them the Bible. If he refused, the whole family were to be buried alive. His children cried out, "O Daddy, Daddy! Think of us, Daddy!" The shaken father began to admit his guilt. But before he could finish, his wife nudged him, saying, "Daddy! Say NO!"

"Hush, children," she continued, "Tonight we are going to have supper with the King of kings and Lord of lords." She started to sing the old hymn *In the sweet by and by*, which begins,

> There's a land that is fairer than day,
> And by faith we can see it afar;
> For the Father waits over the way
> To prepare us a dwelling place there.

Her husband and children joined in. Meanwhile the soil was thrown back into the hole, and gradually the family was buried, each one singing until they had to fall silent when the soil reached their neck, the children first. Many people watched this execution, and almost all of them later became Christians.

Between the end of the Second World War and 1953, when a truce was agreed in the Korean War, an estimated 80,000 Protestants and up to 20,000 Catholics moved from North Korea to South Korea. This depleted the north of one third of its Christian population.

TWO OPPOSITE EXTREMES

In South Korea the Church has grown rapidly, becoming a dominant influence in society, and sending out missionaries all over the world. By contrast, North Korea, ruled by Kim Il-sung and his descendants, is a place of terrible persecution – probably the worst country in the world to be a Christian.

South Korea is now around 30% Christian, but only God knows how many faithful followers of Christ there are in North Korea.

Chapter 12

SOUTH ASIA

EARLY CHRISTIAN PRESENCE[95]

The Christians of South India have a strong and ancient tradition that the Gospel was brought to the Indian sub-continent by the apostle Thomas, who arrived in 50 or 52 AD. The Mar Thoma Christians of Kerala state believe that he founded churches in seven towns in south-west India, setting up a cross in each, and won thousands of converts from various castes, not so much by his verbal skills but because of his saintly life and miracles. Tradition also says that he suffered many false accusations and other kinds of opposition. Eventually, in about the year 72, he was martyred at Chennai where he was stabbed to death for refusing to worship the Hindu goddess Kali.[96] His tomb at nearby Mylapore became a place of pilgrimage; one notable pilgrim was Sighelm, an ambassador from the English kingdom of Wessex, who visited in 883 to present thank offerings from King Alfred the Great.[97]

The Thatta Nagar Fakirs of Sindh, in Pakistan, also believe themselves to be descended from converts baptised by Thomas at Thatta (near modern Karachi).[98] They claim to possess books and other artefacts that would prove this link but do not show these to outsiders.[99]

The earliest extant written source about Thomas in South Asia comes from the Syriac Church and was probably written faraway in the Church's ancient centre of learning Edessa (now Urfa, in south-east Turkey) between 180 and

230 AD. This describes Thomas preaching in the villages of the territory of King Gundapharos, a real historical figure who probably ruled from 21 to 50/60 AD. His capital was at Sirkap (near Taxila in modern Pakistan) and he also held court in Peshawar and Kabul. According to this document, both King Gundapharos and his brother became Christians, and Thomas later moved on to evangelise in another Indian kingdom where he was martyred.[100]

Early Christian writers record that the apostle Nathanael (Bartholomew) also visited India to preach, and left there a copy of the Gospel of Matthew in Hebrew. However, the word "India" in these records may refer to somewhere other than the sub-continent as it was a broad and vague term in those days.

Whatever the details of earlier times, there is strong documentary evidence that Christianity had reached parts of the sub-continent by the beginning of the third century. Certainly it appears that by this time there were Indian Christians and there were Christians in India (albeit the words "Indian and "India" had very broad meanings[101]). A document written around 196 AD mentions Christians amongst the Kaishans who were then ruling a territory equivalent to modern Afghanistan and most of Pakistan. By 225 there was a bishop of Baith Lapat (later Gundeshapur, now Shahabad, in north India) caring for Indian Christians who had been converted by missionaries from Persia and Mesopotamia. At this time there were also Christian communities with bishops in Afghanistan and Baluchistan (in modern Pakistan). The ancient *Chronicle of Seert* (or *Saard*) records that Bishop Dudi (i.e. David) of Basra "left his see and went to India, where he evangelised many people". This was probably in the last five years of the third century.

By the early fourth century, an Indian Church as such had come into existence, for John the Persian signed the Nicene Creed in 325 "on behalf of [the churches] in the whole of Persia, and in the great India…"

Twenty years later a group of 72 Christian families, around 400 people in total, travelled from Edessa to south-west India. The migration was a response to a dream by Bishop Joseph in which he saw that the Indian Christians were being humiliated and persecuted. With the blessing of his patriarch, who gave the group a copy of the Bible to take with them, Bishop Joseph, some clergy, men, women and children travelled to India under the leadership of a Christian businessman called Knai Thoma (Thomas of Cana). They settled in Kodungallur (Cranganore), which was one of the seven towns where the

The Taxila Cross was discovered near the site of the ancient city of Sirkap, near Taxila, in 1935. Probably dating from the second century AD, this small object is very precious to Pakistani Christians as a tangible sign of the long Christian heritage of their country

Apostle Thomas had built a church. The Middle Eastern newcomers taught, encouraged and built up the faith of the beleaguered Indian Christians, converted many other Indians to Christianity, and erected many church buildings. However, the Knananites, as they became called, never intermarried with Indian believers. Their community now numbers about 300,000 and continues to maintain its ethnic distinctiveness and also a consciousness of their Jewish origins. At a later date they were persecuted by Muslims and fled from Kodungallur further south. Still later they were persecuted by the Portuguese who tried to eradicate their Jewish customs and rituals.

In about 525 an Alexandrian merchant known as Cosmas Indicopleustes (Cosmas the India-Sailor) reported that there were churches in Malabar, in Kalyan (near Bombay), in the Ganges valley and amongst "the rest of the Indians". He also reported that there was a church in Sri Lanka, but that it was composed entirely of immigrant Christians from Persia, not indigenous Sri Lankans. Meanwhile the church in sixth century Afghanistan was flourishing, with bishops in nine cities.

Missionaries from the East Syriac Church in Persia were very active and effective in bringing the Gospel to South Asia. But in Hindu areas they faced a counter-offensive from Brahmins determined to halt the advance of Christianity, not by violence but by creating new Hindu legends and forging "ancient" pillar and rock inscriptions. Nevertheless, the East Syriac Church set up its ecclesiastical structures across the sub-continent.

ARABS, MONGOLS AND THE ELIMINATION OF THE CHURCH IN THE NORTH-WEST

According to some sources, the first battle between Muslims and South Asians occurred as early as 643, when an Arab army defeated the King of Zabulistan (in modern Afghanistan). The following year a similar clash occurred in Sindh – again the Muslims were victorious, but Caliph Umar soon ordered them home to Arabia again. This region was fought over for two centuries, until the Muslims established their rule.

When Genghis Khan (1162-1227) united various nomadic tribes from the region of modern-day Mongolia, he sowed the seeds for the growth of a vast empire, indeed the largest land empire there has ever been, which eventually stretched from eastern Europe to the Sea of Japan. What is now Afghanistan and part of Pakistan were conquered by the Mongols in the mid-thirteenth century but, before the end of that century, the Mongol Empire had split into four separate khanates or empires. In this new arrangement, Afghanistan and Pakistan fell into the territory of the Ilkhan Empire (Ilkhanate), which was the south-west portion of the old unified Mongol Empire. In 1282 Ahmed Tekuder became sultan of the Ilkhan Empire. He had been born into a Christian family and was originally called Nicholas Tekuder Khan. But he converted to Islam, changed his name, and – once on the throne – used his

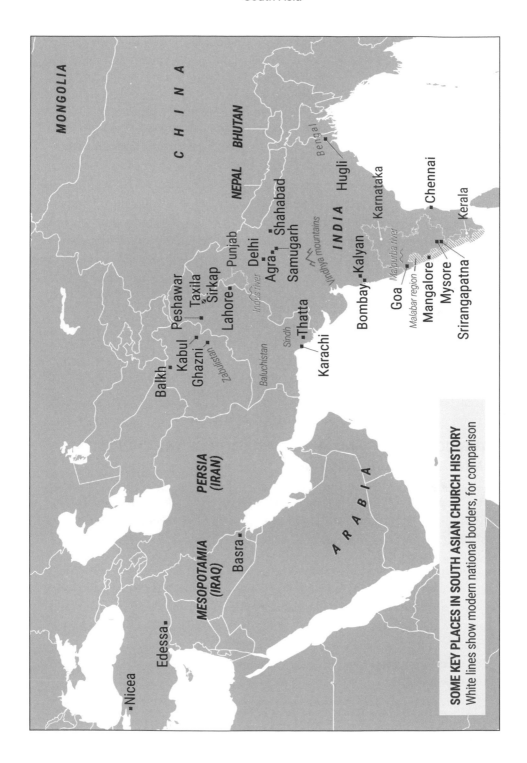

SOME KEY PLACES IN SOUTH ASIAN CHURCH HISTORY
White lines show modern national borders, for comparison

power to propagate his new religion vigorously, requiring all his officers to do the same. Tekuder's Islamisation efforts were not popular and he was overthrown in 1284.

In 1295, under Sultan Mahmood Ghazan, whose mother was a Christian, the Ilkhan Empire adopted Islam as its state religion. Ghazan, who had recently converted to Islam and even more recently seized the throne, began his reign by persecuting non-Muslims. Jews and Christians were forced to pay the classical Islamic *jizya* tax as a sign of subjugation and many were reportedly massacred. Two years later, an important Mongol ally, who had helped Ghazan gain his throne, was killed, after which Ghazan reversed his religious policies and began to punish religious intolerance and try to build good relations with non-Muslims.

But the period of respite for the Church in Afghanistan and Pakistan did not last long. By the end of the fourteenth century, Christians had been effectively eliminated by the fearsome Timur (also known by the names Timur Lenk, Tamerlane and numerous other variations). He was born a Muslim in what is now Uzbekistan, and during his life (1336-1405) reconquered much of the old Mongol empire and even beyond its frontiers to create the huge but short-lived Timurid Empire.

TURKIC MUSLIMS AND THE ELIMINATION OF THE CHURCH IN NORTH AND CENTRAL INDIA

A new phase of Muslim invasions began in the year 1001 when the Turkic Mamluk leader Mahmud of Ghazni (in modern Afghanistan) made the first of his many military incursions into north India. Seventeen of his invasions were east of the Indus river, where he plundered and conquered.

His successors continued to invade and conquer further and further eastwards across north India. A sultanate was set up in Delhi in the early thirteenth century. The sultans of Delhi governed their territory according to sharia: Hindus and Christians alike were subjugated as *dhimmi* (conquered non-Muslims in an Islamic state) and required to pay *jizya* in acknowledgement of their lowly status.

The Turkic Muslim dynasties of north India prevented the Mongols from penetrating further south into the sub-continent but continued to advance further south themselves, reaching the Vindhya mountains by 1330. In 1344 the southward advance of the Muslim armies was halted by an alliance of Hindu states, but by this time Christianity had in all likelihood been more or less eliminated from north and central India.

A Christian presence remained in south India and has continued unbroken until today.

EMPEROR AKBAR

For much of India and for many centuries, Muslim elites ruled over a population consisting mainly of Hindus, with a Christian minority embedded within it. The treatment of Christians (and Hindus) depended on the whim of the ruling emperor. The Mughal[102] Emperor Akbar (ruled 1556–1605) was an exceptional person, fascinated by religion of all kinds. He abolished the *jizya* tax on non-Muslims, thus creating equal status for all his subjects whatever their religion. In 1579 he sent to Goa, which was under Portuguese rule, asking "send me two learned priests who should bring with them the chief books of the Law and the Gospel, for I wish to study and learn the law and what is best and most perfect in it". Missionaries were duly sent and Akbar allowed them to preach and make converts; he even donated funds to build a church in Lahore in 1600.

EMPEROR JEHANGIR

Akbar was succeeded in 1605 by his son Salim, who changed his name to Jehangir when he became emperor. Jehangir wore a golden crucifix around his neck and began his reign by being even more favourable to Christians than his father had been. However, he was also more favourable to Muslims than his father had been, and sometimes tried to force Christians to apostatise. When the Portuguese Goans seized a Mughal ship in 1613, Jehangir's attitude to Christians took a sudden turn for the worse. He cut off his financial support for Christian clergy and closed the church buildings in Lahore and Agra that he had previously supported with generous financial and other gifts. Life became so difficult for Christians in Lahore that in 1614 they moved *en masse* to Agra. The next year good relations were restored between Emperor Jehangir and the Portuguese, and a few years later Jehangir stepped in to prevent

Muslims in Thatta burning down the new and beautiful church building there and murdering its priest. In 1624 the church in Lahore was reopened; however, it seems that the Lahore refugees in Agra never returned home.

EMPEROR SHAH JAHAN

Jehangir's son succeeded to the imperial throne in 1626, taking the title Shah Jahan (king of the world). He had tried to rebel against his father four years earlier and been disappointed that the Portuguese refused to support him. As soon as he was emperor he took his revenge by cutting off the funding that his father had paid to the Portuguese at the Mughal court. After ruthlessly dealing with various other enemies, he returned his focus to the Portuguese missionaries and in 1632 ordered the destruction of the Portuguese settlement at Hugli in Bengal. A Mughal army of 150,000 besieged Hugli, which was defended by just 700 Indian Christian troops and 300 European troops. After three months, Hugli fell and more than 4,000 Christians were captured and taken to Shah Jahan in Agra. Many of these Christian captives were killed, some were sold as slaves, some were forcibly converted to Islam and others converted voluntarily to save their lives.

In 1633 (or perhaps 1634) Shah Jahan ordered that all Christian places of worship should be closed and destroyed. Around this time he also issued a decree forbidding conversions from Islam, but this was not rigorously enforced. Christian worship was also banned. After a few years Shah Jahan partially relented and allowed some churches to be rebuilt and missions to be re-opened.

EMPEROR AURANGZEB

In 1658 Shah Jahan's third son Aurangzeb rebelled against his father and seized the empire from him, after a war against Shah Jahan's eldest son, Dara Shikoh, the heir-apparent. From his youth Aurangzeb had been a very devout and serious-minded Muslim. He embraced a classical form of Islam that was very conservative and extreme and in 1668 he began to issue a series of decrees enforcing a strict form of sharia, closing Hindu schools and destroying Hindu temples. All non-Muslim public religious displays were banned, but Christians suffered only scattered incidents of harassment, mainly focusing on foreign missionaries.

> ## Dara Shikoh – who never became emperor
>
> Shah Jehan's intended successor, Dara Shikoh, was a very different person from Aurangzeb. Dara Shikoh preferred a mystical type of Islam for himself but was keen for all the religions of India to coexist in harmony. He was a friend of the seventh Sikh guru and of European Christian missionaries, and he strove to find common ground between Islam and Hinduism. Not only was he favourable to non-Muslims but also he was also a patron of painting, music and dancing.
>
> All this of course horrified the strictly orthodox and puritanical Aurangzeb, who declared Dara Shikoh to be an apostate from Islam. According to sharia, an adult male apostate must die, and, after a sort of trial, Dara Shikoh was executed by Aurangzeb in 1659.
>
> It is interesting to speculate how different the history of India might have been if the tolerant Dara Shikoh – a very experienced military commander – had defeated his fanatical brother Aurangzeb at the Battle of Samugarh, near Agra, on 29 May 1658, instead of the other way round.

Indigenous Christians continued under Mughal rule, and the Mughals continued fighting other local rulers. In 1735 it was reported from Lahore that Christian officers formed the elite of the Mughal army and were famed for their loyalty and courage – and even more so for their Christian piety, which the enemy apparently found the most frightening thing of all.

SULTAN HYDER ALI

We must now take a jump forward in time and a jump southward geographically to look at persecution under the sultans of Mysore. This was far more lethal and bloody than anything the Mughals had done, for until now Indian Islam had generally been more lenient towards non-Muslims than Middle Eastern Islam was.

Hyder Ali (1722-1782) ruled Mysore, one of the kingdoms in south India. Also operating in the region were the Portuguese, whose strength was declining, and the British whose strength was increasing.

In 1748 Hyder Ali laid siege to the fort at Mangalore, in Portuguese territory. Inside the fort were around 80,000 Indian Christians[103] who were rightly doubtful that the Portuguese could defend them against Hyder Ali's Muslim forces. Hyder Ali offered to save the lives of the Christians if they would surrender to him, but they refused, choosing instead to trust in the British promise to come and rescue them. Unfortunately, the British never showed up, and the fort fell to Hyder Ali. Infuriated that the Christians had looked to British military help instead of surrendering to him, Hyder Ali sent 60,000 of the Christians to walk 202 miles to his capital Srirangapatna, near Mysore. Only 20,000 of them got there, 20,000 are known to have perished on the way and the other 20,000 remain unaccounted for.

TIPU SULTAN

Hyder Ali was succeeded by his son Tipu, usually referred to as Tipu Sultan, who continued killing non-Muslims on a similar scale to his father. In Mangalore, he killed about 25,000 Hindus and at least 25,000 Christians.

Tipu Sultan also tried to convert both Hindus and Christians to Islam. Some Christians he compelled to convert by threatening to cut off their ears and noses. Another of his methods was forced circumcision. In 1784 he circumcised 30,000 Christian men (some sources say 50,000) and deported them, presumably with their families, to another part of the country.

Despite this, Tipu Sultan is highly acclaimed in India, even today, for his military successes against the British. It was only when he was betrayed by a close aide, who had been bribed by the British, that Tipu was finally defeated and killed at Srirangapatna in 1799. The victorious British troops were commanded by Colonel Arthur Wellesley, later the Duke of Wellington.[104]

Sadly, the death of Tipu Sultan did not bring an end to the violence, as the British continued their efforts to subdue India. The following year, for example, Wellesley drowned 5,000 Indians in the Malpurba river when he attacked a military camp on 30 July 1800, with all the rest of the occupants of the camp either killed in other ways or taken prisoner. Those captured included women and children as well as men.[105]

More than three centuries later, Tipu Sultan is, in a sense, still responsible for ongoing violence in the area he ruled. His name reverberates powerfully in Karnataka, his native state, where Hindu protests and court cases have occurred every year since the state government decided in 2014 to mark Tipu Sultan's birthday on 10 November with an annual public celebration. Some people have even died in the Hindu-Muslim rioting.

Many of Tipu Sultan's military successes against the British are illustrated in detailed murals in the summer palace he built at Srirangapatna to commemorate his victory in 1784. Above is part of a large painting of a war procession, which showed Tipu's own troops and the French troops who fought alongside them. Tipu himself rides a white horse, under a royal umbrella, and is nonchalantly smelling a rose, thus showing how relaxed he feels about going to war. Opposite him, on a brown horse, under a less grand umbrella, is his trusted aide, Mir Sadiq. When Tipu was finally defeated and killed at Srirangapatna in 1799, it was due to the treachery of Mir Sadiq, who had been bribed by the British. Small wonder that his face has been scratched out in this painting.

BRITISH RULE

The defeat of Tipu Sultan in 1799 at Srirangapatna by British troops led by Wellesley was the beginning of the long process that eventually led to British government rule in India (as opposed to rule by Britain's East India Company). During the next century and a half British control largely prevented organised religious persecution in the sub-continent.

An exception to this was, of course, the persecution of individual converts by their families. European and American missionaries followed in the wake of British military conquests in India, but the foreigners saw little fruit from their evangelistic efforts. The isolated converts were mostly rejected by their families, meaning that they were dependent on the missionaries and often lived in the mission compound. Some were killed.

Another exception was the "Indian Mutiny" or "Indian Rebellion" of 1857. It has recently been shown that this uprising was strongly motivated by the concerns of both Hindu and Muslim Indians that the British were trying to impose Christianity on them. There were of course many other triggers, not least the racist treatment of Indian troops by their British officers, but the Indians' overriding desire to protect their religions has not been properly recognised until now. William Dalrymple, who looked at 20,000 rebel documents from the time to write his 2006 book *The Last Mughal*, concluded that the mutiny was basically a war of religion. "There were no doubt a multitude of private grievances, but it is now unambiguously clear that the rebels saw themselves as fighting a war to preserve their religion, and articulated it as such." When the rebel sepoys[106] entered Delhi, the ancient Mughal capital, on 11 May 1857 they hunted down and killed not only the British but also all the Indian Christians they could find, most of whom would have been recent converts from Hinduism or Islam. The first convert to be killed was Chiman Lal, who was pointed out to the rebel troops on the morning of 11 May. His conversion in 1852 had caused a huge scandal, because he was a high profile individual who used to run a hospital and was an official of the Mughal emperor.[107]

Given that the British (and all white people) were considered to be Christians, this was in effect an attempt to exterminate the Christian presence. The following year Rev William Owen published a book recording the courage and faithfulness of many Christians who were severely persecuted or killed during the uprising because they refused to deny Christ and convert to Islam or Hinduism. These Christians included Indians (from Muslim, Hindu and Sikh backgrounds) and British (Owen makes a careful distinction between those who were Christian believers and those who were not). He also points out that many Indian Christians, for example in South India, Bengal, and the north-west, responded to the outbreak of the mutiny by expressing their loyalty to the British and offering to help them in any way they could. There were also instances of non-Christian Indians protecting the Indian believers e.g. Hindus protecting Christians from attack by Muslims.[108] Owen also notes with sorrow that there were some Christians who saved their lives by apostatising, especially amongst the British.

> It is difficult, if not impracticable, to compare the number of apostates among the English with those from among the native converts. It does appear, however, from a careful examination of the various statements recently collected, that converted Hindoos and Mohamedans have been true to the standard of the cross in a larger proportion that those who were born and brought up in our Christian land ... it is most gratifying to know that among the native converts the lapsed are very few compared with those who have remained steadfast in the hour of trial. In some places there were two or three who apostatised where there were scores who remained steadfast.[109]

British people were greatly shocked by the "Indian Mutiny" and many saw it as divine punishment for the sins of Britain as a nation. A "day of national humiliation" was held in Britain on 7 October 1857 with special church services in every Anglican place of worship and in many Nonconformist ones too. Different preachers identified different national sins, but many mission-minded Christians considered that the foremost was the failure of Britain to evangelise India more effectively. Indeed, the East India Company had positively nurtured Hinduism.[110] It is interesting to contrast this with the Indian viewpoint that Indians had been subjected to aggressive state-sponsored conversion by the British.

After the 1857 uprising, the reputation of Western missionaries was seriously diminished. At the same time, British colonial government was formally instituted, taking the place of informal rule by the East India Company. A

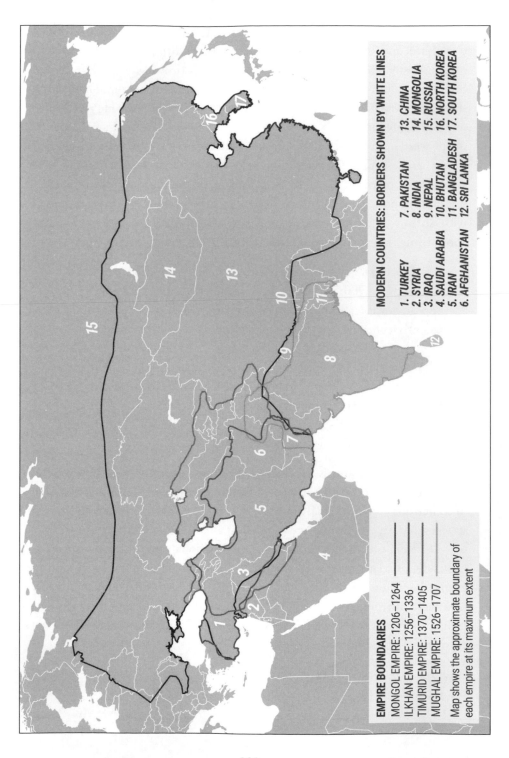

MODERN COUNTRIES: BORDERS SHOWN BY WHITE LINES

1. TURKEY
2. SYRIA
3. IRAQ
4. SAUDI ARABIA
5. IRAN
6. AFGHANISTAN
7. PAKISTAN
8. INDIA
9. NEPAL
10. BHUTAN
11. BANGLADESH
12. SRI LANKA
13. CHINA
14. MONGOLIA
15. RUSSIA
16. NORTH KOREA
17. SOUTH KOREA

EMPIRE BOUNDARIES

MONGOL EMPIRE: 1206–1264
ILKHAN EMPIRE: 1256–1336
TIMURID EMPIRE: 1370–1405
MUGHAL EMPIRE: 1526–1707

Map shows the approximate boundary of each empire at its maximum extent new way of governance was established, which involved local elected bodies and Indians participating in the administration of the country. The rule of law was very evident, with religious groups controlled by civil law – for example, preventing rival Hindu sects from engaging in violence against each other. This appears to have opened the way for greater indigenous leadership of Christian outreach in India. This in turn led to a focus on reaching the lowest strata of society, such as the "untouchables" and the tribal peoples. (Western missionaries had mainly evangelised the higher castes.)

In 1870 mass movements to Christianity began in south India, especially amongst the "untouchables" within the Telugu and Tamil peoples. In 1873 mass conversions began in the Punjab, again amongst the poorest people, through the witness of Indian evangelists.[111] Persecution was rare for these converts, who had been converted by other Indians, rather than by Westerners. After half a century the dramatic rate of church growth slowed down, which coincided with the beginning of Gandhi's activism around 1920.

AFTER INDEPENDENCE

India was given independence from British rule in 1947 and was simultaneously partitioned into a Hindu-majority state (India) and a Muslim-majority state (Pakistan). The latter comprised two separate territories lying to the east and west of India. In the panic and confusion that followed, as some 15 million people urgently uprooted themselves to move across the newly announced borders in one direction or the other, it is estimated that at least a million people died. Christians were seen as "neutral" and some Hindus and Muslims took to wearing crosses, hoping that they would not be attacked by followers of the other major religion. Many real Christians were killed.

Within six months Sri Lanka, too, was given independence from British rule. The independence of Afghanistan and Nepal had been recognised by Britain in 1919 and 1923 respectively, and Bhutan continued with the independence it had always had.

Pakistan[112]

In 1947, Indian Christians had to choose whether to live in a Hindu-majority state or a Muslim-majority one. Many Christians were more comfortable amongst Muslims, feeling that Islamic culture and religion were more similar to their own. They also wanted at all costs to escape from the Hindu caste system, which excluded and stigmatised the Christians, many of whom came from the lowliest backgrounds. They had every reason to believe that they would be treated as equal citizens in Pakistan because Muhammad Ali Jinnah, the founder of Pakistan, had made it very clear this was his intention:

> You may belong to any religion or caste or creed – that has nothing to do with the business of the State ... We are starting in days when there is no discrimination, no distinction between one community and another, no discrimination between one caste or creed and another. We are starting with the fundamental principle that we are all citizens and equal citizens of one State. [113]

Unfortunately for Pakistani Christians, Jinnah died in September 1948. Within months a process of Islamisation began, which gradually established Muslims as superior and favoured over Christians and Hindus. New laws introduced new forms of discrimination and vulnerability for the non-Muslim minorities.

For many years, Christians struggled against a system of separate electorates which ensured they had political representation but also ensured that their votes were of no value to the majority of members of the National Assembly, so their causes were neglected. The separate electorates system was eventually abolished in 2002.

Another legal issue was Section 295 of the Pakistan Penal Code, usually called the "blasphemy law". The mild and toothless law inherited from British Indian Penal Code was dramatically altered by amendments in 1982 and 1986 and then by a ruling of the Federal Shariat Court in 1990. The result was a fearsome legal instrument, which virtually invites false accusations, and lays down mandatory life imprisonment or death for various types of "blasphemy", defined so that it could include a Christian simply stating their personal beliefs. Non-Muslims are particularly vulnerable. Many Christians and others have been sentenced to death although no one has yet been executed. Several accused have been assassinated.

This is all in addition to Christians being considered contemptible (indeed "unclean") by many Muslims, resulting in discrimination at school and work, which creates a cycle of poverty, illiteracy and performing the dirtiest and most dangerous jobs. Christian girls and women are often kidnapped and forcibly converted to Islam, then forcibly married to their kidnapper; police tend to take the side of the kidnapper. In the last two decades, violent incidents against Christians have begun to become commonplace.

Bangladesh

Formerly East Pakistan, Bangladesh became a separate nation in 1971. It has taken a different path from West Pakistan (now Pakistan) and has not yielded so much to the Islamisation efforts of extremists. A tussle for influence continues, with secular groups trying to topple Islam from its position as state religion while Islamists press for greater Islamisation. Jamaat-e-Islami, the country's hardline Islamist party, has been banned from taking part in elections, but remains a powerful force.

Although Christians in Bangladesh are an even smaller percentage of the population (1%) than they are in Pakistan, they enjoy greater religious liberty and suffer less violence.

Afghanistan

Afghanistan is by far the most dangerous country in South Asia for Christians. Only God knows how many Afghan Christians there are in the country, but human estimates suggest around a thousand. All are believed to be converts from Islam or the children of converts. There are no church buildings.

For any crimes not covered by Afghan law, the authorities turn to sharia for guidance, and hence it is one of the modern nations with an official death sentence for apostasy from Islam. Part of the country is controlled not by the government but by the Taliban who ruthlessly enforce sharia and would therefore be more than likely to murder any convert from Islam they could find. Society in general is also vehemently opposed to converts from Islam and in favour of killing them, in line with sharia.

India

India is a secular state. This is affirmed in the preamble to the Indian constitution:

> WE, THE PEOPLE OF INDIA, having solemnly resolved to constitute India into a SOVEREIGN SOCIALIST SECULAR

DEMOCRATIC REPUBLIC and to secure to all its citizens: JUSTICE, social, economic and political; LIBERTY of thought, expression, belief, faith and worship; EQUALITY of status and of opportunity; and to promote among them all FRATERNITY assuring the dignity of the individual and the unity and integrity of the Nation; IN OUR CONSTITUENT ASSEMBLY this twenty-sixth day of November, 1949, do HEREBY ADOPT, ENACT AND GIVE TO OURSELVES THIS CONSTITUTION.

However an extremist form of Hinduism, called Hindutva,[114] has gradually gained influence in India, and is now very dominant politically. There are also militant Hindu organisations which often attack Christians, typically during a Sunday worship service. The normal result is damage to the building and injuries to the worshippers (deaths are rare). It is also normal that the police neither investigate nor seek to bring the perpetrators to justice. Worse still, the Christian victims are often arrested and their attackers allowed to go free. In 2014 Narendra Modi, leader of the Hindu nationalist Bharatiya Janata Party (BJP), became Prime Minister. This emboldened the Hindu militants and attacks on Christians increased.

Many of India's Christians are Dalits, at the bottom of the Indian caste structure and therefore traditionally discriminated against. A quota system now ensures that Dalits get access to jobs and education. However, these benefits do not apply to Christian or Muslim Dalits, only to those from religions which originated in India.

It is not illegal for Christians to share their faith, but false accusations that Christians have bribed, tricked or forced Hindus to convert are often used as excuses for anti-Christian violence. Several states also have laws against seeking to make converts by these methods, and there Christians can also be persecuted by the law.

Nepal

Nepal is another Hindu-majority nation. Until 2008 it was a Hindu kingdom, but then became a secular republic. The Church in Nepal has grown rapidly since the 1950s when Western mission efforts were established, but Christians are still less than 1.5% and feel themselves to be second-class citizens.

In 2015 a new clause was added to the constitution making it illegal to "convert another person from one religion to another". In August 2017 a law was passed which further restricted conversion and also criminalised "hurting religious sentiment". The law is worded so vaguely that any public Christian activity is potentially illegal. It came into effect in September 2018 and before long the arrests had started, the first being a Christian police officer who was arrested on 3 October for giving his testimony at a church conference.

Sri Lanka

Sri Lanka's population is predominantly ethnic Sinhalese Buddhists and the constitution gives Buddhism "the foremost place". There is also an ethnic Tamil minority, concentrated in the north and east, who are mainly Hindus. About 9% of the population are an ethnic group known as Moors, who are Muslims. The Tamils were defeated by the Sinhalese majority in 2009 after a civil war lasting 26 years, and they continue to be discriminated against. Many Sri Lankan Christians are Tamils, and they are doubly discriminated against, because of their faith and their ethnicity. Christians comprise around 8% of the population, with some Sinhalese and some Tamil.

Christians are often harassed by Buddhist mobs (sometimes led by Buddhist monks) and by the police, sometimes in collusion together. This typically takes the form of physical attacks on worship services or (false) claims that church buildings need to register in order to operate.

Bhutan

Like Sri Lanka, Bhutan is dominated by Buddhism with a Hindu minority of different ethnicity and Christians who have come from both backgrounds. The majority of citizens of this small Himalayan kingdom are the Drukpa, the royal Bhutanese, who view themselves as "sons of the soil". The Drukpas look down on the Nepali-speaking minority and consider them of little value so they do not mind if they convert from Buddhism to Christianity. If a Drukpa does the same thing, however, he or she is likely to be severely persecuted.

Chapter 13

THE LONG TWENTIETH CENTURY

It was often said in its latter years that the twentieth century was a century which had seen more Christian martyrs than any other. Is this true? It is hard to judge, given that many martyrdoms in the last 2,000 years must have been unnoticed (except in heaven), unrecorded or later forgotten. And what *proportion* of the Christian community were martyred? When and where Christians were few in number, martyrdoms had to be few as well, even if a large proportion of the community were killed. As we have already seen,[115] it is believed that more than half the Christians in Korea were martyred during the Great Persecution of 1866-71; yet this was "only" 8,000 deaths. And what is the definition of that rather flexible word "martyr"?

Be that as it may, the twentieth century can certainly be regarded as a century of global persecution of Christians. Huge numbers died because of their faithfulness to the Lord Jesus Christ.

FROM GENOCIDE TO GENOCIDE

For the sake of making historical sense, this chapter will extend the twentieth century back a couple of decades into the nineteenth century, and so include the full scope of the Armenian, Assyrian and Greek genocide. The chapter will also extend forward a couple of decades into the twenty-first century so as to make reference to the ongoing persecution of Christians today. This includes the anti-Christian persecution of the Syrian civil war, which has itself been termed a genocide,[116] and has severely affected the descendants of the survivors of that earlier genocide.

The forgotten genocide

In early 1915 a fatwa was issued against non-Muslims in the Ottoman Empire. Muslims were called to fight the Christian minorities with whom they had been living as neighbours, albeit not on equal or necessarily peaceful terms. Many refused to take part, but those who did participate inflicted colossal suffering and destruction on the Armenian, Greek and Assyrian Christians.

Over 1.5 million Armenians, up to 1.5 million Greeks and up to 750,000 Assyrians (including 250,000 Syriac Orthodox[117]) are thought to have died – men, women and children – in a state-sanctioned genocide over a period of 30 years. What led to such a horrifying death toll?

It began in 1839 with the best of European intentions

Armenians, Assyrians and Greek Christians had been treated as second-class citizens for centuries, in accordance with sharia (Islamic law) and had been given no protection from armed raids by Turks and Kurds. In 1839 the Ottomans were under pressure from the European powers to improve the situation of non-Muslims in their empire. The Ottoman authorities therefore introduced the first of the Tanzimat reforms (with more such reforms following until 1876).

This gradual improvement in their situation encouraged Armenians to request protection from the Ottoman government against the thefts, abductions, murders, fraud, punitive taxation etc. which they were suffering. The Ottomans viewed these pleas for help as rebellion and thought that the non-Muslim minorities wanted to secede from the empire.

Meanwhile three major massacres of Christians within the Ottoman Empire occurred. In 1843 at least 10,000 were killed in south-east

Anatolia after the British consuls in Van and Mosul had encouraged some Christians not to pay *jizya*, the classic Islamic tax on subjugated non-Muslims in return for which Muslims protect the Christians. When the Christians stopped paying, they were attacked and killed by Muslims, who considered the Christians had broken their contract. The Christians no doubt expected the British to come to their defence, but no military or other support was forthcoming. In 1860, another 10,000 Christians were killed in Lebanon, and in 1876 possibly as many as 25,000 were killed in Bulgaria.

The 1876 Bulgarian massacres led the British politician Gladstone to produce a pamphlet called *The Bulgarian horrors and the question of the East*. He fought the next general election (1880) on the issue of the need for British support for Christians in the Ottoman Empire. The government of the time, headed by Disraeli, recognised the plight of the Christians but did not want to intervene to help them because they feared that doing anything against the tottering Ottoman Empire might enable Russia to push through to the Mediterranean. Disraeli considered that British politico-economic interests took precedence over the suffering of the persecuted Christians.

In 1877-78, the Ottomans lost lands in the Balkans in a war with Russia. The war had started when Russia intervened to protect Slavic Christians from Ottoman brutality in Europe. This loss of territory led to a change in Ottoman tactics: violent suppression of the non-Muslim subjects who were campaigning for their rights. In 1877 Kurdish militias massacred 1400 Christian men and enslaved many women in four Armenian areas of south-east Anatolia.

In 1894-96 organised massacres of Christians took place, during which as many as 300,000 Armenians were killed. Sultan Abdul Hamid's agents would incite Turkish Muslims to rise up against their Armenian Christian neighbours, alleging that the Armenians were plotting to attack them. This procedure was repeated in 13 large towns. When 8,000 Armenians were killed in Urfa in December 1895, the young men were killed by the traditional Islamic method for slaughtering animals to eat: they were thrown on their backs, held by their hands and feet and then their throats were slit while a prayer was recited.

Many Christians believed their best chance of escaping Ottoman dominion was to appeal to the "Christian" powers in the West and Russia. The response to this appeal was minimal. Some aid was provided by Western missionaries and some warnings were issued at a diplomatic level, which the Ottomans ignored.

By 1913 the Young Turks had come to power in the Ottoman Empire and adopted a new policy whereby the empire no longer accepted multiple ethnicities and religions. The aim now was to create a purely Turkish and Muslim state.

Armenians

The Armenians were one of the biggest obstacles to this new policy. Their kingdom had been part of the Ottoman Empire since the sixteenth century and Armenian people, with their strongly Christian identity, now lived throughout the empire. In late 1914, extermination became the Ottoman authorities' answer to the "Armenian question".

In 1914 all able-bodied Armenian men aged between 18 and 60 were conscripted as part of a general mobilisation in preparation for the First World War. The new Armenian recruits to the Ottoman army served for a while as unarmed labour and then were executed by their Turkish officers and fellow soldiers.

In 1915 alone, approximately 800,000 Armenians were killed. Anyone who tried to protect Armenians often met the same end. Some 200,000 Armenians converted to Islam in order to be spared. On 24 April 1915 there was a big round up of thousands of Armenian intellectuals and leaders (who were later executed), thus "cutting off the head" of the Armenian community, as Armenians saw it.

Other Armenians – mainly women and children – were freighted by train or forced to walk hundreds of miles without provisions to concentration camps in the Syrian desert. Only one quarter of the deportees survived the exposure, starvation, violent attacks and other abuses to reach their destinations, which usually lacked any food, water or shelter. On arrival, many were systematically murdered. Killing units in Deir al-Zor smashed children against rocks, mutilated adults with swords, and burned people alive. In 1916 nearly 300,000 were massacred there. On 24 October that year the police chief in Deir al-Zor had 2,000 Armenian orphans tied together and thrown into the Euphrates river.

Assyrians

Assyrians, a much smaller minority in the Ottoman Empire comprising Assyrian, Syriac and Chaldean Christians, suffered the same experiences as the Armenians except that they were not deported. They call the genocide *Seyfo* (the Syriac word for "sword"). The attacks against the Assyrians were relatively small scale to begin with. But after the Assyrians had joined with the Russians in 1915 to try to liberate the Armenians in Van province of Turkey, the Assyrians were subjected to a level of violence that almost annihilated them. Many fled to Persia (Iran) where they were persecuted by the Persians and Kurds, forcing them to flee again to Hamadan in northern Persia in 1918. During this retreat, a third of their number were killed or kidnapped. The road to Hamadan was littered with the bodies of those who died of starvation, exhaustion, disease, or had been slaughtered by Turks, Persians and Kurds en route.

Further tragedy for the Assyrians of Iraq occurred over the following 15 years. In 1925 the Council of the League of Nations decided a border between Iraq and Turkey. Encouraged by "the Powers who had used them as soldiers and allies against the Turks", the Assyrians had hoped for their own independent country, but found that the homeland they had expected was shared out between Turkey and Iraq. In Iraq, no longer part of the Ottoman Empire but now a British Mandate, the Assyrians continued to fight loyally for the British, on the understanding that, when the UK granted independence to Iraq, the Assyrians would be given autonomy. However, when independence came in 1932, there was no separate state for the Assyrians. They found themselves a vulnerable minority, different in ethnicity and religion, from the majority Muslim Arabs. In August 1933 a terrible massacre of Assyrians occurred in and around Simele, northern Iraq, with something between 600 and 3,000 killed.[118]

Greeks

The Ottoman Empire also had a Greek Christian minority, who lived in Anatolia, most of them near the Black Sea. In 1914 plans were afoot to relocate them to the safety of Greece in exchange for Muslims from the Balkans. But the outbreak of the First World War prevented this from being accomplished. The Greek communities were forced on death marches to central Anatolia. Muslim boycotts of Greek businesses were authorised, and Christian properties seized and given to Muslims. Unlike most of the men, Greek women and children were often given the option of converting to Islam. Those who refused were treated very harshly or killed.

After the First World War, Ottoman Turkey continued to rid itself of all Christians, massacring or deporting those who did not flee. A particularly appalling event occurred in the predominantly Christian city of Smyrna (now called Izmir) in September 1922. The troops of Turkey's victorious revolutionary leader, Mustapha Kemal (later called Atatürk) indulged in an orgy of rape and slaughter and finally burnt down the Christian neighbourhoods of the city. Henry Morgenthau, America's former ambassador to Constantinople, had warned the powers in London and Washington that a massacre was likely: "Unless Britain asserts herself by showing that she, and somebody else, has an interest in protecting these Christians, the Turks will be as merciless as they were with the Armenians."[119]

The Greek Orthodox Metropolitan Bishop of Smyrna, Chrysostom, the most senior Christian cleric in the city and recognised by the Ottomans as the head of its Greek community, also realised what was about to happen to the city's Christian inhabitants. On 6 September 1922 he asked Charles Dobson, the Anglican vicar of

Smyrna, to send a telegram to the Archbishop of Canterbury, pleading for him to inform the British Prime Minister Lloyd George. The last line of the telegram read: "For Christ's sake, hasten to avoid the calamity which we feel is approaching."

Four days later Metropolitan Chrysostom was dead. After a formal visit to the office of the Turkish General Noureddin, the general handed him over to the mob, who beat him, spat on him, stabbed him repeatedly, tore out his beard, gouged out his eyes and cut off his nose and ears. He died of his wounds in a back street of the city. French soldiers, watching this, wanted to intervene, but their officer, following his orders to remain neutral, forbade his men, at the point of a revolver, from saving the metropolitan's life.[120]

Meanwhile a flotilla of more than 20 European and American warships, looked on from the Aegean Sea. Many had made their way to Smyrna from other parts of the Mediterranean, after hearing of the massive defeat of the Greek army by Turkish troops at the Battle of Dumlupinar (26-30 August 1922). The following day, Mustafa Kemal ordered his armies to advance to the Mediterranean. So the Turks began pushing the remains of the Greek army back to the sea at Smyrna. But the ships only watched; they did nothing to assist the hundreds of thousands of Greek and Armenian Christians crowding on to the waterfront as their homes blazed and the flames came ever nearer to the sea. After a week, the British admiral decided to start rescuing the Christians, and so did many other ships.

However, Admiral Mark Bristol, the American High Commissioner in Constantinople, only cared about American business interests. He did not want to jeopardise his hopes of US access to Turkish oil by assisting those whom the Turks were persecuting. "I am for the US, first, last and always," he said. His only concern, as the Ottoman Empire disintegrated, was what would bring profit to his country, and therefore he was resolutely pro-Turkish. He had opposed a suggestion that the US take a mandate over Armenia at the end of the First World War on the grounds that Armenia lacked natural resources and was therefore of no use to America. He had ordered the crews of the three American destroyers to assist only in protecting American lives and property. He warned the two American journalists he had allowed to sail to Smyrna on the USS *Lawrence* that they must report events from his own (pro-Turkish) perspective.[121]

Despite this, many thousands of Greeks and Armenians were eventually rescued by the ships which had gathered in Smyrna harbour, even by some American vessels. The total death toll in Smyrna during those few days was estimated by Edward Hale Bierstadt, executive of the United States Emergency Committee, at 100,000. At least 25,000 (Greek sources suggest more than 100,000 and Bierstadt says 160,000) adult male survivors of this event were afterwards deported to the interior of Turkey, where many died from the harsh conditions.[122]

In 1900, Christians had constituted around 32% of Ottoman Turkey's population. It is easy to understand why the figure had dropped by 1927 to about 1.8%. Today it is thought to be less than 0.2%.

STATISTICS OF THE TWENTIETH-CENTURY CHURCH

In 1900 there were an estimated 558 million Christians in the world, out of a total population of 1.619 billion. Christians therefore made up 34.5% of the world's population.[123] By 2000, the figures were 1.973 billion Christians in a world population of 6.063 billion, making the Christians 32.5% of the total.[124] It is striking that, despite Christians almost tripling in numbers during the twentieth century, their proportion in the world population slightly dropped.

In 2017, the Christian population had grown to 2.446 billion while the world population had expanded to 7.432 billion.[125] So numbers of Christians had increased by nearly half a billion, but as a proportion of the world's population Christianity was barely holding its own at 32.9%.

What these figures do not show is the geographical shift in Christian faith during the course of the twentieth century. In 1900, the West was undoubtedly the stronghold of Christianity and the Western missionary movement was bringing the Gospel worldwide. Many people of many religions were becoming Christians, but not necessarily directly because of Western mission work. For example, we have already seen in chapter 12 how the mass conversions that began in the Punjab and South India in the 1870s were mainly the fruit of the ministry of indigenous Indian evangelists.

Also in 1900, the Church was still a significant presence numerically in its birthplace, the Middle East, although the great missionary movement of the East Syriac Church had faded away many centuries earlier and Christians had become used to living submissively as a minority under Islamic rule.

In 2000, Western Christianity was reeling under the onslaught of secular humanism, which had succeeded in making the Christian faith a subject of general contempt and mockery as well as undermining its influence on Western culture and values. The proportion of people identifying as Christians, let alone going to church, was declining year by year, and many sections of the Church seemed scarcely to know what they believed.

Christianity in the Middle East was only a remnant of what it had been a hundred years earlier, with millions killed for their faith and millions more emigrating to safer places. Numbers have continued to drop in the new millennium. But in places as widely different as Uganda, India, China and Iran, the twentieth century had been a story of church growth. By 2000, there were national Christians in every country of the world.

UGANDA, AN EXAMPLE OF CHURCH GROWTH AND PERSECUTION

Persecution and martyrdoms often accompanied twentieth-century church growth. Uganda is an example of dramatic church growth. Although Christianity did not arrive until 1877, the country was 7% Christian by 1900,[126] 55% Christian in 1969[127] and almost 90% Christian in 2000.[128]

Martyrdoms began in 1885, due to the hostility of King Mwanga II who ruled over the kingdom of Buganda (now part of modern Uganda). King Mwanga noticed that Christians were putting their loyalty to Christ before their traditional loyalty to the monarch, and in 1885 killed three young African Christians and a group of British missionaries. The following year he burnt alive a group of at least 26 page boys who had decided to follow Christ and therefore refused to sleep with the king. The youths walked to their deaths singing hymns and praying for their enemies, thus inspiring many bystanders to find out more about Christianity.

Further martyrdoms under King Mwanga followed. Ninety years later, thousands more Christians were being martyred under the military dictator Idi Amin in the 1970s, including Archbishop Janani Luwum, who had eventually begun to protest against the injustice and violence of the regime.

Other Ugandan Christians have died at the hands of Muslim extremists. Some are individual converts from Islam, such as 16-year-old Shamimu Muteteri Hassan, killed by her father with a large hammer in July 2007, just two months after her conversion, because she refused his demands to return to Islam. Other targets are those who are active in evangelising Muslims. Francis Namukubalo, the son of a Muslim sheikh who became a Christian, was very active in sharing his faith with Muslims in Mbale District where he lived. He was used to getting threats, but on 21 September 2016 he was lured by two friends into an ambush where around 20 Muslims set on him and stabbed him to death. Christians who express disagreement with Islam are also targeted. Islamic militants were suspected by Ugandan police of perpetrating an attack on an open-air Christian prayer meeting in Kampala in January 1997, where some speakers had criticised the Quran. Six people died and around 40 were injured in that incident.

CAUSES OF PERSECUTION

Persecution of Christians in the "long twentieth century" is very well documented, and many volumes could be written about it. In a book of this length we can only try to survey the main distinctives.

Seven key ideologies that arose during this period have been the main drivers of anti-Christian persecution. Some of these ideologies have fed off each other in a remarkable way. Hitler was aware that the Muslim Ottoman Empire had "got away with" a genocide of millions of Christians, which gave him confidence to try the same with Poles and Jews. Later the Hindutva leaders referenced the Nazi treatment of Jews with regard to their own "problem" with Muslims in India.

We will look at these seven ideologies in turn, remembering that many other examples of persecution and martyrdom in the "long twentieth century", such as killing converts from other religions, do not fall into these categories and cannot be mentioned simply due to lack of space.

It was not a coincidence that so many new ideologies came to the fore in such a short period. David Reynolds argues[129] that the collapse of many European monarchies during World War One (Austro-Hungarian, German, Russian) led to mass movements of "guided democracy" which supported communism, voted in fascism and, many decades later, voted in Islamism. Some of the twentieth-century British viceroys of India, reflecting on the collapse of monarchies in Europe, warned that an independent India, with its complex and diverse society, would give rise to ideologies that could be very violent and destabilise the country. They held that, to ensure future stability as the UK withdrew from India, it would be better not to create one vast republic but to distribute the Indian territories among the various Indian princely states, to be governed by Indian monarchs as in the time before the British Raj.

It is also important to remember that many citizens, and sometimes the vast majority, do not accept the ideologies of those who rule them, or not to any extreme degree. Thus, for example, in Buddhist-majority countries, it is only a small minority of Buddhists who take their Buddhist nationalism to such an extreme as to attack or oppress Christians and other non-Buddhists. Most Buddhists do not.

But before turning to the seven ideologies, we will first consider some other factors that have contributed to the persecution of Christians in the "long twentieth century" either by contributing to the rise of the ideologies or more directly.

In Western colonial times

The nineteenth century saw Western colonialist powers conquering vast swathes of the world, accompanied by Western missionaries bringing Christianity. For many, both in the West and in the conquered regions, the West's civilisation and political, military and economic power was inextricably linked with Christianity. This was humiliating for long-established religions such as Islam, Hinduism, Buddhism and Confucianism. Worse, it was dangerous, because the growth of Christianity looked set to destroy their ancient religions and societies.

In China, as the colonialist powers sought to divide and rule, a massive reaction occurred. The Boxer Rebellion was launched, not only to rid the country of European powers but also to destroy Christianity.[130] In Hinduism, Buddhism and Islam, leading thinkers returned back to their historic religions with renewed vigour and utilised the philosophy and methodology of Christian missions to relaunch them, revitalise their religion in the hearts and minds of their followers, and undo the work of the Christian missionaries.

British colonial policies sometimes facilitated the persecution of Christians in a more direct way. A clear example is Lugard's policy of indirect rule in Nigeria, where he was Governor and then Governor-General (1912-1919). By this policy, the British governed through existing Islamic religious structures. This meant that the Christians were discriminated against and marginalised. It also led to problems for Christians post-independence.

In post-colonial times

Post-independence problems were also created for Christians in some former British colonies because of the arrangements made when the British handed over control, for example, in Sudan and Malaysia. In both these countries, it was agreed that Christian-majority areas were to be joined with larger Muslim-majority areas as a single sovereign state. The result was predictable: sooner or later the Christian minority in the independent country began to be oppressed and subjugated by the Muslim majority.

Sudan and Malaysia were just two of a huge number of new nation-states which emerged after the Second World War as, one by one, they gained independence. A number, rejecting the capitalism of their former colonial masters, experimented with socialism in the early years of independence. But economic failure and continued Western domination by other methods, caused many to turn away from socialism to religion. The result was often the creation of a link between religion, ethnicity and land i.e. religious territoriality, which produced a quest for a new national identity in the new nation-states. Christian minorities were not considered part of this new national identity, no matter how hard the Christians tried to affirm their loyalty and belonging. During this period, there was a rise of American political and economic power worldwide, the launch of new American missionary movements, and the advent of Pax Americana, as the US military assumed the role of the world's policeman.

These factors had a profound effect on Christian communities in the newly independent countries. The historic Christian communities found themselves under pressure. The newer Christian communities, who were the fruits of Western missionary work, were increasingly regarded as aliens. Thus the stage was set for great waves of persecution that, to a degree, have their origins in both the colonial and post-colonial contexts. Religions that had been humiliated and shamed, had seen their lands taken, and had found themselves under Western (which in their eyes meant Christian) colonial rule, threw off the yoke of colonialism only to find themselves now required to submit to American and other Western domination. Many reacted by attacking, harassing and subjugating the non-Western Christians within their borders or sought to rid their countries of any Christian presence.

The Cold War (1945-1991) between the West, under America's leadership, and the communist bloc, led by the Soviet Union, was viewed by some as Christians versus communists or even Christians versus socialists. Emerging nations like Ethiopia and South Africa found themselves choosing between socialist doctrines and Western democracy. So the tensions of the Cold War were also played out on the ground in hostility towards local Christians.

The first two decades of the twenty-first century have been increasingly marked by conflict, in particular in the Islamic world. Following the tragic events of the 9/11 Islamist attack on American targets in 2001, the US, UK and other Western countries launched what America's President Bush called a global "war on terror" which was perceived by many Muslims as a "war on Islam". The "war on terror" designation thus turned what had been a territorial dispute into an ideological one. It was hard for Muslims to retaliate against mighty America and its Western supporters, but easy to attack Christian minority communities in Muslim-majority countries, who – most Muslims felt sure – must be on the side of their co-religionists in the West. This was another reason why persecution of Christians by Muslims escalated.

We will now consider the seven ideologies which have dominated the twentieth century and how they have led to Christian persecution.

COMMUNISM

In 1917 Lenin and his Bolshevik party took control of the Russian state. For the next 70 years, through civil and other wars, famine, dictatorship, purges and industrialisation, their communist ideology dominated. A key part of this ideology was militant atheism. Although atheism was played down at certain times and places, for example in order to include the Muslim areas of Central Asia, it continued as part of the Communist Party's basic aims.[131]

Religion was famously viewed by Karl Marx, author of the *Communist Manifesto*, as like opium for the oppressed masses. By this he meant that it gave them pleasant illusions which prevented them from rising up in revolution to demand the things that would, in his view, bring them true happiness.

By contrast, Lenin viewed religion as an illness from which people might be cured – an infectious illness that believers could pass to others. Soviet law reflected these concepts and strove to remove any possible influence of religious people on society. The first Soviet Constitution (1918) even-handedly gave all citizens "the right to religious and anti-religious propaganda" (Article 124). But in 1929 Stalin introduced the very restrictive "Law on Religious Associations" and amended Article 124 of the constitution to "the right of religious profession and the right to anti-religious propaganda". So atheism could be spread but not religion. Later this imbalance was made even more extreme when Article 124 was amended again to "freedom of religious worship and freedom of anti-religious propaganda". In this way the rights of believers had been whittled away to nothing more than meeting together in certain buildings ("special premises" in the language of the 1929 law) for worship services ("to satisfy their religious needs" said the 1929 law).

Individuals "infected" with religion were thus isolated from the rest of society. At the same time, they were given various treatments to try to cure and restore them to a "healthy" atheistic materialism.

These "cures" began for the children of Christian families with the atheism they encountered when they first went to kindergarten, and continued throughout their school years. The 1929 law forbade any religious instruction for children (and also for young people and women) or any kind of religious activity or meetings at all, even for handicraft work. Parents were not

Solzhenitsyn on the persecution of Christians in the early years of the Soviet Union

It was Dostoevsky, once again, who drew from the French Revolution and its seeming hatred of the Church the lesson that "revolution must necessarily begin with atheism." That is absolutely true. But the world had never before known a godlessness as organized, militarized, and tenaciously malevolent as that practiced by Marxism. Within the philosophical system of Marx and Lenin, and at the heart of their psychology, hatred of God is the principal driving force, more fundamental than all their political and economic pretensions. Militant atheism is not merely incidental or marginal to Communist policy; it is not a side effect, but the central pivot. To achieve its diabolical ends. Communism needs to control a population devoid of religious and national feeling, and this entails the destruction of faith and nationhood. Communists proclaim both of these objectives openly, and just as openly go about carrying them out. The degree to which the atheistic world longs to annihilate religion, the extent to which religion sticks in its throat, was demonstrated by the web of intrigue surrounding the recent attempts on the life of the Pope.

The 1920's in the USSR witnessed an uninterrupted procession of victims and martyrs amongst the Orthodox clergy. Two metropolitans were shot, one of whom, Veniamin of Petrograd, had been elected by the popular vote of his diocese. Patriarch Tikhon himself passed through the hands of the Cheka-GPU[132] and then died under suspicious circumstances. Scores of archbishops and bishops perished. Tens of thousands of priests, monks, and nuns, pressured by the Chekists to renounce the Word of God, were tortured, shot in cellars, sent to camps, exiled to the desolate tundra of the far North, or turned out into the streets in their old age without food or shelter. All these Christian martyrs went unswervingly to their deaths for the faith; instances of apostasy were few and far between.

For tens of millions of laymen access to the Church was blocked, and they were forbidden to bring up their children in the Faith: religious parents were wrenched from their children and thrown into prison, while the children were turned from the faith by threats and lies.

From Aleksandr Solzhenitsyn's address "Men have forgotten God", on the occasion of his acceptance of the 1983 Templeton Prize for Progress in Religion, at the Guildhall, London, 10 May 1983.[133]

specifically forbidden to teach their own children their own religion but, according to Article 52 of the Russian Code on Marriage and Family, they were supposed to bring their children up "in the spirit of the Moral Code of the builder of Communism". Since this included atheism there was a severe conflict between the two principles. Children of Christian parents had terrible struggles at school. They were often traumatised by the conflicting information they received at home and at school, and often suffered lower marks or fails unless they pretended to be atheists.

Christians typically found themselves excluded from higher education. Either they could not get on the course in the first place, or they were expelled before they had completed it. They experienced the same problems getting and keeping jobs. Without qualifications, they were in any case limited to rather lowly types of employment and thus appeared, as a group, to lack intelligence. Some moved from place to place (in line with Matthew 10:23) hoping to start afresh where they were not known and thus be able to keep a job. Others who had managed somehow to get training or qualifications would find themselves repeatedly dismissed from the kind of work they had the skills for, and might eventually resort to the most humdrum roles in the hope that they would be left alone.

Young Christian men were obliged to do compulsory military service where, isolated and far from home, many were severely punished for their faith. The issue would often arise over the Christian's refusal on religious grounds to take the oath, although willing to serve in the army. Some were sentenced to years in corrective labour camps. Viktor Nikolayevich Montik, born in Belorussia in 1952, was sent to a camp for this reason. For the first year and a half the camp administration tried to flatter him into abandoning his faith. Then they deprived him of letters, banned him from using the camp shop for months at a time, deprived him of visitors, and repeatedly put him in solitary confinement for 15-day periods, but still he was faithful. When two criminal prisoners became Christians, the authorities fabricated a new criminal case against Viktor.

An important part of communist ideology is that work gives dignity. The very phrase "corrective labour camps" indicates that these places of degrading punishment were seen as a means of correcting the wrong thinking of those sentenced to serve in them. Most women in the Soviet Union worked – hence small Christian children spent their days in atheistic kindergartens. But for

Christian women with husbands in prison, it was even harder than normal to keep a job. To make matters considerably worse, it was illegal for friends to help them materially. Women with ten or more children were honoured in the Soviet Union as "heroine mothers" but many Christian mothers of ten did not receive this honour or the financial help that went to non-Christian mothers of large families.

One of the aspects of Christianity which irritated the Soviet authorities was how Christians would help other citizens in material need. This was very embarrassing for the authorities as it showed up the failure of communism to meet those needs. According to the 1974 book, *State and Religion*, "Socialist society thus creates all the necessary conditions so that Soviet people should have no need to lower their human dignity in turning to religious charity." But it was not true. It was not the communist collective which saw to the welfare of those struggling with misfortune; it was the Christians.

It was also the Christians who maintained some kind of morality, honesty and decency in societies, as atheism gradually took its toll on ethical behaviour. After less than 30 years of Soviet rule in Lithuania, Christians described the situation as follows:

> While before the introduction of atheist education in Lithuania juvenile thieving, robber, homicide attempts, sexual profligacy were very rare, now they are constant phenomena. Special children's rooms have been set up in police stations to combat juvenile delinquency. Alcoholism, crimes against property, murders, lies, dishonesty and the absence of a sense of duty were never before so widespread in Lithuania as in recent years. We meet with callous consciences wherever we meet workers and officials: in shops, factories, offices, clinics, everywhere. Practice has demonstrated that atheist education is incapable of fostering strong moral principles among the young and that atheist propaganda is unable to alter the society's moral level.[134]

Church leaders were, of course, a special target of persecution, and congregations were, of course, likely to have infiltrators and informers. The principal method used on the leaders was "divide and rule". Disinformation and rumours were circulated. Individuals were pressurised and intimidated in an effort to compromise them or persuade them to collaborate secretly with the authorities. Some pastors became informers against their ministry colleagues, for example in Romania. Most Christians in the Soviet Union and eastern Europe took seriously the Bible's teaching on obedience and submission to civil authorities; this doubtless contributed to the agonised debates amongst Christians on how to respond to these situations. Unofficial congregations faced more direct persecution, in that their meetings were broken up by police, and worshippers were beaten, fined or sometimes jailed.

Despite or perhaps because of this persecution, the Christian faith was not destroyed. Many families and individuals kept the faith, and many other people were drawn to Christ, perhaps by the very harshness and barrenness of the communist ideology. In Romania it was from faithful Christians, meeting together (in small groups because of the danger of infiltrators) to pray and study the Bible, that the movement came which led to the overthrow of Ceausescu in 1989.

In considering communism, we have focused on the Soviet Union where this ideology was first put into effect. Although both the Soviet Union and the countries of eastern Europe under its control have been free for a generation now, there are other countries in the world where communism dominates or has done until much more recently. These include China, North Korea, Laos, Vietnam, Eritrea and Cuba. In all of them, Christians suffer oppression and persecution to varying degrees. North Korea is probably the worst country in the world to be a Christian, and Eritrea comes a close second regarding evangelical believers.

We will now look at China, by far the largest of these countries, and with its own special spiritual brand of Marxism as established by Mao Zedong.

MAOISM

Mao Zedong (also written in English as Mao Tse Tung or Mao Tse-tung) was the dominant figure of Chinese communism for many decades of the twentieth century. He developed a type of communism which did not focus on economic doctrine as in classical Marxism, nor on the political strategies of Leninism and Stalinism. Maoism is primarily spiritual and, as such, a potentially greater challenge to Christianity, which it mimics in many ways, and indeed to all religions.

Maoism seeks a total change of individual hearts and minds. The 27-year-old Mao was a founder member of the Chinese Communist Party in 1921, when its total membership was not more than 70 people. In the previous four years he had been deeply influenced by Li Dazhao (also known as Li Ta-chao), the head of the Beijing University Library, where Mao worked as an assistant librarian. Li Dazhao, whom the Chinese Communist Party now honours as its first true leader, believed in revolution by transforming the thought of individuals. This was a very different concept or "revolution" from that of Lenin who had so recently won power in the Russian Revolution of 1917.

Li sought to adapt Marxism for the Chinese environment, recognising that China was so underdeveloped that Marx's economic principles would not have the same effect there as in the West. But, as a historian, he saw that the Bolshevik victory in Russia was the beginning of the "mass movement of the twentieth century". For Li, "the roots of all forms of socialism are purely ethical. Cooperation and friendship are the general principles of the social life of man..."[135] Mao followed Li in believing that (1) the human mind is infinitely malleable and able to expand spiritually, and (2) the human will (when it has been corrected and set on the right path) is all-powerful, so that "the subjective creates the objective" i.e. the mind and spirit can make material changes.

So Maoism is about the transformation of the individual and society, changing society's external conditions by means of individuals' inward beliefs, and all of it rooted in selfless love (or at least in cooperation and friendship, to use Li Dazhao's words). Readers will realise at once the resemblance to Christianity.

In 1935 the de facto leadership of the Chinese Communist Party passed to Mao Zedong. Although he did not yet hold a key position, "his power derived from his unique and successful ideology, his personal charisma and his popular support."[136]

On 1 October 1949 Mao proclaimed the founding of the People's Republic of China. He was by now chairman of the Communist Party of China and continued in this post until his death in 1976.

After 1949 huge efforts went into bringing about the spiritual transformation of every Chinese citizen (700 million at that time), with different methods used for different strata of society and levels of education. The aim was to instil correct thinking (*szu-hsiang*) in every mind. The result was to be new people who were 100% dedicated to serving others, willing to lay aside all their personal desires, even in matters of sex, marriage and children, for the sake of the collective. "Fight self: serve the people" was the fundamental principle.

The Chinese understanding of "thought" is that it determines all actions – much more so than any ideology ending in "ism". The thought of Mao Zedong was therefore considered to be a very real force, making real and relevant all that Marxism and Leninism held. So Mao's *szu-hsiang* bears a striking resemblance to the *logos* of the Bible, the Word of God by which He created the world and which became incarnate in the Lord Jesus Christ (John 1:1-14).

The People's Republic of China was seen as the spiritual centre for liberation movements worldwide. Maoism saw a global moral battle between the forces of good and evil, with the same moral struggle going on in the life of every individual. It was missionary, messianic and eschatological.

Before long the religion-like ideology of Maoism had effectively made a god of Mao himself. His deification had begun in 1945 at the Seventh Congress of the Community Party of China. At this meeting a new Party Constitution was launched with a preamble which enshrined "The Thought of Mao Zedong" as necessary to "guide the entire work of the Party". By the early 1960s, his image was in every home, school, office and factory. Hymn-like songs described him as the great saviour of the people. He was compared to the sun in its life-giving character, and looked to as the guide for every aspect of life.

The emphasis on inner spiritual transformation did not preclude the use of violence. Mao said that "a revolution is not a dinner party... a revolution is an act of violence by which one class overthrows another... it is necessary to create terror in every rural area... proper limits have to be exceeded in order to right a wrong..."[137] The physical cost of Mao's spiritual transformation was to be the loss of so many millions of lives that no one can be sure of the real total.

While senior colleagues in the Communist Party of China did not always agree with Mao, and at times sidelined him, his popularity with the Chinese masses continued undimmed. Despite the terrible years of the Cultural Revolution, he emerged

> not only as victor, but as Prophet, Priest and King – and Messiah. As prophet, because of his inspired revelation and his charisma as priest, because he was the interpreter of the doctrine and the representative of the people; as king, because he was the acclaimed and enthroned leader. He now took his place by right in the Communist 'Trinity' of Marx, Lenin and himself – the father of the Marxist revolution; the son who performed the father's will; and Mao who was the people's *parakletos*, advocate or holy spirit.
>
> Every day throughout China, a great paean of worship and love flowed upwards to Mao – Great Teacher, Great Leader, Great Helmsman, Great Commander – for the revelation which he had brought to the people; not just revolution, but the revelation behind it. [138]

The "little red book" containing selected quotations from Mao's writings, first produced in 1964, was seen to bring miraculous healing, help young people excel at sport, help peasants grow better crops and drove many to weep in repentance for their evil deeds. Even more influential was an even smaller book, barely a pamphlet, called *The Three Greats* or *The Three Constantly Read Articles of Chairman Mao*. These articles are stories, like some of the stories told by Jesus, and encourage readers to self-sacrificial service of others.

Chinese families would gather in the home for rituals before a table piled with Mao's books, his portrait hanging above. They would seek his guidance in the morning, thank him for his kindness at midday, and in the evening report back to him what had happened that day. Huge and fervent public rallies were held, like Christian evangelistic meetings but focused on Mao instead of Jesus. Smaller, more local rallies, were like church services, with readings from Scripture, songs, sermon and a benediction at the end.

Mao hoped and expected to be remembered above all as the "Teacher", that is, Marxist word made flesh. It is easy to understand why Maoism and Christianity clash head on and why the Church has been persecuted to a greater or lesser degree ever since Mao and the Communist Party gained control of China in 1949. It can be seen as Maoism's great rival for the hearts and minds of the Chinese population.

We have already seen in chapter 9 a little of the way in which this plays out for Chinese Christians today. The unofficial churches, often called "house churches", can be considered the one part of Chinese society which the Communist Party of China does not control. Chinese Christians believe that the total number of Christians in China is now at least 150 million and could be as many as 200 million and increasing at the rate of about 1.2 million a year. (The official government figure remains at 38 million Christians – just below the 40 million members of the Communist Party of China.)

The current approach of the Chinese government has been described as an "accelerated brake". The rules and restrictions vary in every province, city and village. The government constructs church buildings in some places and demolishes them in others. They allow an annual quota of Bibles to be printed but have restricted the sale of online Bibles. In some places, church buildings are forbidden to display a cross on the outside. In some they can have a cross on the front wall but not on top of the roof. In some the church buildings (even some of those built by the government) carry crosses high above the roof.

In October 2017 a new ideology known as "Xi Jinping Thought" was launched at the 19th National Congress of the Communist Party of China. Officially named "Xi Jinping Thought on Socialism with Chinese Characteristics for a New Era", it was to be incorporated into the constitution of the Communist Party of China. Xi Jinping at the time was not only president of China, with an indefinite term of power ahead of him, but also Party chairman. Xi Jinping Thought has been described as essentially "a blueprint for consolidating and strengthening power at three levels: the nation, the party and Mr Xi himself".[139] Under President Xi, persecution of "house church" Christians has greatly increased. His intention seems to be to bring the house churches under his control, or weaken them so much they become ineffective, or destroy them.

Despite the danger to themselves, Chinese Christians are boldly standing up and asking their government for freedom. On 12 September 2018 a group of 279 Chinese pastors bravely issued a public declaration calling on the government to allow full religious freedom. They were responding to the escalating persecution of Christians in their country in the previous few years. The declaration concluded, "For the sake of the gospel, we are prepared to bear all losses – even the loss of our freedom and of our lives."

However, the persecution continued. Less than three months later a large scale incident occurred, when Pastor Wang Yi of the Early Rain Covenant Church in Chengdu, Sichuan province, was arrested on 9 December 2018, along with his wife and about a hundred of his church members. Eighty of the church members were released after some weeks, and then another 30 were arrested. Meanwhile Pastor Wang Yi had issued a letter from jail, making clear that all he wanted was to be able to worship Christ freely, but that he was willing to suffer anything rather than deny Him. "Separate me from my wife and children, ruin my reputation, destroy my life and my family – the authorities are capable of doing all of these things. However, no one in this world can force me to renounce my faith."

FASCISM

The definition of fascism seems quite a puzzle to scholars, but its origins are clear. The Italian word *fascio*, literally meaning a bundle or sheaf, began to be used during the 1870s to mean a political group made up of people holding many different (even contradictory) political viewpoints. The idea was that while each separate rod in the bundle might be fragile on its own, together they were strong. So a *fascio* was a group or league – with revolutionary tendencies. There were many *fasci* scattered across Italy, and one of them had Benito Mussolini as a member. The movement known as fascism evolved in the early twentieth century from some of the more nationalist of these *fasci*.

Given these origins, it is perhaps not so surprising that fascism is a complex ideology, with myriad different definitions. Most definitions agree that it is authoritarian and ultranationalist. Robert Paxton defines it as "a form of political practice distinctive to the 20th century that arouses popular enthusiasm by sophisticated propaganda techniques for an anti-liberal, anti-socialist, violently exclusionary, expansionist nationalist agenda".

Fascism exalts nation and often race above the individual and stands for a centralised government, headed by a dictatorial leader, which forcibly suppresses all opposition and aims for a strongly regimented society and economy. It takes a positive view of violence, and promotes masculinity and youth. There is an emphasis on mass mobilisation, romantic symbolism and the idea of national rebirth out of dangerous decadence or collapse.

Before long, fascism had moved to the political right and embraced a racist goal of empowering the supposedly superior people and ridding society of the supposedly inferior ones.

Italy

In the early 1920s an ideology known as clerical fascism emerged, which combined fascism with religion. In the case of Italy this meant fascism combined with Roman Catholicism.

When Mussolini became Prime Minister in 1922, the Pope had for more than half a century been without any temporal powers, for the Kingdom of Italy had annexed the remaining Papal states in 1870. In 1929 Mussolini (who had by now abandoned any pretence of democracy and was ruling Italy as a dictator) signed an agreement known as the Lateran Treaty which restored to the Pope some Italian lands to rule as a state, albeit a greatly reduced area – only the Vatican City. Soon after this, relations between Mussolini and the Catholic Church soured.

However, Catholics were back in favour with Mussolini by 1935 when his government issued the Buffarini Guidi circular, banning all religious activities of Pentecostal Christians. According to this circular, Pentecostals were "developing religious practices contrary to the social order and harmful to the psychological and physical integrity of the race".[140] The Italian Assemblies of

Mussolini said

"Fascism is a religion."

"The twentieth century will be known in history as the Century of Fascism."

Both statements quoted in *Fortune* magazine, July 1934

God describe how they had to become an underground church. Those discovered meeting together for worship, even in private homes or in the countryside, were arrested en masse, imprisoned and subjected to special surveillance.[141] The Salvation Army was also targeted. Persecution was severe until 1943 and then continued at a lower level until the circular was abolished in 1955. The Catholic Church was widely believed to have supported the persecution of non-Catholic Christians during fascist times. In 2014 Pope Francis, at a meeting with 350 evangelicals, asked forgiveness for what Catholics had done to Pentecostal Christians in the 1930s.[142]

Mussolini never adopted Hitler's genocidal policies towards Jews, and refused to round up and deport Italian Jews. But he did introduce some strongly anti-Jewish laws in 1938. Vatican Radio made known the Pope's condemnation of anti-Semitism and the murder of Jews in Germany. After Mussolini was overthrown in July 1943, the Nazis occupied northern Italy and were at last free to implement Hitler's "Final Solution" there; thousands of Italian Jews died in Nazi concentration camps.[143]

Germany

The most famous, or infamous, type of twentieth-century fascism was the ideology of the National Socialist German Workers' Party, usually called the Nazi Party. The special characteristic of this version of fascism was its racism, and the special characteristics of Nazi-style racism were a virulent anti-Semitism, a quest to find a scientific basis for racism, and a programme of eugenics to put the theories into practice.

The National Socialist German Workers' Party was founded in 1919 as the German Workers' Party. The following year it added "National Socialist" to its name, and the year after that Adolf Hitler became its leader. It believed in a racial hierarchy, with what they called Aryans at the top, as the "master race". (The Nazi use of the term "Aryan" for a non-Jewish Caucasian, preferably with blonde hair and blue eyes, was a completely new meaning of the word.) The Nazis aimed to create a racially pure society of Aryans, not only in historically German territory but also elsewhere.

On 30 January 1933 Hitler was appointed Chancellor of Germany. The Nazis did not gain an outright majority in the elections the previous year, but they had won more votes than any other party. Before long, he was head of state as well as head of government – the undisputed *Führer* (leader) of Germany, which was now a one-party dictatorship. Germany and the lands it was about to conquer were called the Third Reich (Third Empire[144]). "Undesirable" people were dealt with ruthlessly. Draconian restrictions, loss of civil rights, and imprisonment (often in a concentration camp) were just the start. All too often this was followed by murder. The "undesirables" included Jews, Roma (Gypsies), black people, homosexuals and Jehovah's Witnesses.

Even Aryans suffering from mental or physical disabilities were "undesirable"; around 350,000 were sterilised and at least 100,000 were murdered in their residential institutions by doctors and medical staff.

Six million Jews were murdered in a deliberate genocidal attempt at complete extermination, often called the Holocaust. Hitler had also planned the destruction of the Polish people (mainly Roman Catholics). He reminded his generals that history overlooked the fact that Genghis Khan had deliberately slaughtered millions of women and children, and, similarly, "Who, after all, speaks today of the annihilation of the Armenians?"[145] He was right in his analysis. Anguished diplomats and journalists had reported to the West about the genocide of Armenian and other Christians during the First World War, even with photographic evidence, but no one in power seemed to care even at the time, let alone three decades later. So Hitler was able to repeat the process with the Jews during the Second World War, and few believed the reports that came out of Germany until the war was over and the terrible truth of the gas chambers was undeniably revealed.

Nazi persecution of Jehovah's Witnesses

There were only about 15,000 Jehovah's Witnesses in Germany in 1933. But they were perhaps conspicuous as they would not raise their arms in the *Heil Hitler* salute because they believed it was wrong to submit to any government or secular power. By April 1933 their buildings were being closed, and by the summer their religion had been banned in most parts of Germany. Individual Jehovah's Witnesses were sacked from their jobs and refused pensions. Between 1938 and 1945 around 10,000 were held in concentration camps, of whom 25% did not survive.

How did the German Church respond to the rise of Nazism in the 1920s and 1930s? Two-thirds of the population were Protestants and most of these belonged to the German Evangelical Church (*Landeskirchen*, literally the "church of the country"), whose theology included loyalty to the state, and which saw itself as a pillar of German society. It comprised 28 regional churches, some Lutheran, some Reformed and some United (Prussian Union). Two movements emerged in this Church Federation, taking opposite positions.

During the 1920s the self-styled "German Christians" (*Deutsche Christen*) embraced many of the nationalist and even racist aspects of Nazi ideology. Many Christians had been beguiled by Article 24 of the 25-point programme published by the Nazi Party in 1920 which said, "The Party as such upholds the point of view of a positive Christianity…" This sentence was sandwiched between others saying that nothing must conflict with the "manners and moral sentiments of the Germanic race" and that the Party sought to combat "the Jewish-materialistic spirit at home and abroad". The nationalism, racism and anti-Semitism of the beginning and end of Article 24 apparently did not trouble them, as they focused on the comforting middle.

When the Nazis gained political power, the "German Christians" grouping continued to support Hitler and his ideology. They managed to dominate decision-making in the synods of the various regional *Landeskirchen* and created the so called "Reich Church". This was a national body unifying all the different Protestant denominations to showcase a Christianity that conformed with state policies – which historians have described as a "Nazified Christianity". The leadership of the Reich Church were all Nazis, and they rid the Church of all things Jewish, including Jewish-background Christians and the Old Testament.

The Confessing Church (*Bekennende Kirche*) developed in opposition to the "German Christians" and aimed to resist the "Nazification" of the Church. Their founding document, the Barmen Declaration (1934), set out basic Biblical Christian doctrines and stated that the head of the Church was Christ (i.e. not the *Führer*). The main concern of the Confessing Church was to prevent the state interfering with church affairs, but there were individuals within the movement who also spoke out to oppose other things the Nazi regime were doing, especially what they were doing to Jews. Of course, the

And when the cup you give is filled to brimming
With bitter suffering, hard to understand,
We take it gladly, trusting though with trembling,
Out of so good and so beloved a hand.

From a hymn *By gracious powers so wonderfully sheltered* by Dietrich Bonhoeffer (1906-1945) translated by Fred Pratt Green and Keith Clements as. Bonhoeffer was a German pastor and theologian who strongly opposed the Nazi regime and helped to establish the Confessing Church, which insisted that Jesus Christ was its head, not Adolf Hitler.

many Christians who spoke out were persecuted. The famous pastor Martin Niemöller spent seven years in concentration camps for criticising Hitler and his policies. Many less well known pastors were also imprisoned or banned from preaching. Some endured show trials and some were killed.

The Roman Catholic Church in Germany, which accounted for about a third of the population, grew suspicious of Nazi ideology long before the Protestants. Not being the dominant "church of the country", Catholics tended to find the nationalism of National Socialism less palatable than did leading Christians within the *Landeskirche*. Furthermore, some of the early Nazi leaders were vehemently anti-Catholic and there was a Catholic political party called the Centre Party, which naturally could not find much to agree with in the far right Nazi Party. Some Catholic bishops banned their flock from joining the Nazi Party but this ban was lifted after Hitler's speech on 23 March 1933 in which he described Christianity as the "foundation" for German values.

The following month the Nazis began negotiating with the Catholics, the stated aim being to establish a concordat to guarantee the rights and religious liberty of the Catholics, who were eager for such protection because they had experienced marginalisation and harassment in the last decades of the nineteenth century. While the negotiations were in progress, the Nazis began a campaign of intimidating Catholics, shutting down their publications, breaking up meetings of the Centre Party, and putting the most vocal individuals in concentration camps. In spite of this, a concordat was somehow agreed and signed on 20 July 1933. It gave the Catholic Church the right to continue to exist in Nazi Germany, to continue to have contact with the Vatican and to continue running its charities, schools, youth groups and other Catholic organisations. In return, bishops had to swear an oath to "honour" the government, and the Church and its representatives were banned from participating in politics. The Centre Party was dissolved.

As Cardinal Pacelli, the chief negotiator for the Catholics, had feared, the Nazis were soon flouting the terms of the concordat. In December of the same year, a rule was made that all editors and publishers must belong to a Nazi "literary society". This effectively gagged Catholic publications and stifled any Catholic protests. Catholic schools were closed and replaced with "community schools", which were of course run by Nazi sympathisers. In 1934 several Catholics who had been leaders of the now defunct Centre Party were murdered in the "Night of the Long Knives" when at least 85, but probably hundreds, of Hitler's political opponents died in extrajudicial killings over a three-day period. Anti-Catholic persecution intensified in 1936 when dozens of priests were arrested by the Gestapo, accused of corruption, prostitution, homosexuality and paedophilia, and given show trials. Anti-Catholic propaganda appeared in newspapers and on billboards.

The Nazi regime saw the churches as a source of potential dissent (as indeed they were) and began to put pressure on them. Between 1934 and 1936 the Nazis shut down a number of church youth groups, both Catholic and Lutheran. As Nazi pressure on the churches increased, anti-Nazi feeling grew amongst both Catholics and Protestants. This included a concern to protect church members who were from a Jewish background, and therefore a target of the Nazi persecution and extermination programme. In March 1935 a statement of protest was read from the pulpits of Confessing churches. The Nazi authorities reacted by briefly arresting more than 700 pastors.

Two years later a papal encyclical entitled *With Burning Concern* (*Mit brennender Sorge*) was smuggled into Germany. Over 250,000 copies were secretly printed, and it was read from the pulpits of every Catholic church in Germany on Palm Sunday, 21 March 1937. Without naming Hitler, National Socialism or Nazis, the encyclical strongly condemned the idolising of race or the people or the state, the breaking of the terms of concordat, and much else besides of what the Nazis believed and did.

> ... despite many and grave misgivings, We then decided not to withhold Our consent [to the concordat of 1933] for We wished to spare the Faithful of Germany, as far as it was humanly possible, the trials and difficulties they would have had to face, given the circumstances, had the negotiations fallen through. It was by acts that We wished to make it plain, Christ's interests being Our sole object, that the pacific and maternal hand of the Church would be extended to anyone who did not actually refuse it.

> ... The experiences of these last years have fixed responsibilities and laid bare intrigues, which from the outset only aimed at a war of extermination. In the furrows, where We tried to sow the seed of a sincere peace, other men – the "enemy" of Holy Scripture – oversowed the cockle of distrust, unrest, hatred, defamation, of a determined hostility overt or veiled, fed from many sources and wielding many tools, against Christ and His Church. They, and they alone with their accomplices, silent or vociferous, are today responsible, should the storm of religious war, instead of the rainbow of peace, blacken the German skies. [146]

The next day the Gestapo raided Catholic churches across the country to confiscate as many copies of the encyclical as they could find, and closed down the presses on which it had been printed. The level of persecution of the churches was soon ratcheted up higher. There was more anti-Catholic propaganda in 1938-39 and more show trials of Catholic priests, some of whom ended up in concentration camps.

It may seem remarkable that Protestant Christians were not more rigorously persecuted by the Nazis. Compare, for example, the short and mild Nazi response when the Confessing pastors read their protest sermon in Confessing churches in 1935 with the sustained and severe treatment of Catholic priests after they read the papal encyclical in Catholic churches in 1937. But this is at least partly a reflection of the equally remarkable fact that so many Protestants did not actively oppose the Nazis or their anti-Semitism, but either supported them or looked for a compromise and a way to live together. Persecution was directed only at the people who did resist the regime, who were relatively few in number. Some also were not openly persecuted but silenced in other ways. For example, certain Confessing Church pastors, less outspoken than their leaders, were conscripted into the army and sent to serve in the most dangerous places, with the result that many of them died. The Nazis had managed to infiltrate and control the Protestant Church, so only "needed" to deal with individual Protestants who opposed them. By contrast, the Catholic Church had no "Nazified" wing, stood firmly to its doctrinal beliefs, and therefore was persecuted as a whole. (After the war, however, some in the Catholic hierarchy enabled some senior Nazis to escape to South America.)

It is interesting to note that the fascist government of Italy mainly persecuted Protestants, effectively in alliance with the dominant Catholic Church, but the fascist government of Germany appeared to concentrate more on persecuting Catholics while managing to form a strong alliance with leading elements of the dominant Protestant Church.

When the Second World War was over, Germany had been conquered and Hitler was dead, the Council of the Protestant Church in Germany issued "The Stuttgart Declaration of Guilt" (19 October 1945) to express their regret for complicity in the crimes of the Nazi era. Written by Niemöller and others, the Declaration includes the following passage:

> With great pain we say: By us infinite wrong was brought over many peoples and countries. That which we often testified to in our communities, we express now in the name of the whole church: We did fight for long years in the name of Jesus Christ against the mentality that found its awful expression in the National Socialist regime of violence; but we accuse ourselves for not standing to our beliefs more courageously, for not praying more faithfully, for not believing more joyously, and for not loving more ardently.

British Anglican reactions

The Anglican Church in the UK was divided in its attitude to Nazism (with a large number who were indifferent) – just as was the German Evangelical Church. The de facto leaders of the two groupings were George Bell, Bishop of Chichester, and Arthur Headlam, Bishop of Gloucester. Bishop Bell strongly and actively supported the Confessing Church. He also advocated on behalf of persecuted Christians in Germany for which he was much criticised.

Bishop Headlam was the first chairman of the Archbishop of Canterbury's Council on Foreign Relations, which met for the first time in February 1933. Headlam saw himself as taking a cautious, objective and balanced view of events in Germany, but was seen by others as giving credibility to the "German Christians", the Reich Church and the Nazis. He was apparently persuaded by the sincerity of devout Germans who believed that National Socialism was sympathetic to Christianity. On 16 April 1937 Headlam wrote to the Archbishop of Canterbury, criticising the theology of the Confessing Church and calling Martin Niemöller "a truculent sailor" who, he suspected, had a nationalism just as aggressive as Hitler's. He finished his letter:

> I think the partisan character of the interest people seem to take in foreign countries is often rather dangerous. After all Hitler is a person with great power, and I do not think that a policy of gratuitously insulting him is likely to work for the peace of Europe. [147]

HINDUTVA

Another ideology that emerged in the 1920s was Hindutva, meaning "Hindu-ness". Like Nazism, it aimed to create a pure nation and had an aggressively expansionist foreign policy, although in this case the nation was to be Greater India (*Akhand Bharat*), not Greater Germany, and the goal was religious purity, not racial purity. While Nazi ideology emphasised Germany as the fatherland, Hindutva ideology emphasised India as not only the fatherland (*pitrubhumi*) and motherland (*matrubhumi*) but also the holy land (*punyabhumi*). Another difference was that while Nazism had its time of political power in the 1930s and 1940s, Hindutva only began to be influential in Indian politics in the 1980s and did not gain full power in India until 2014.

This time lag has meant that leaders of Hindutva have been able to look back to the Nazis for role models and inspiration. Vinayak Damodar Savarkar (1883-1966), who coined the term "Hindutva", admired fascism and Nazism. He saw Germany's Jewish minority as akin to India's Muslim minority.

Madhav Sadashiv Golwalkar (1906-1973) was the second person to hold the office of supreme leader of the Rashtriya Swayamsevak Sangh (RSS), a paramilitary organisation founded in 1925 to mobilise support for Hindutva ideology. He wrote:

> To keep up the purity of the Race and its culture, Germany shocked the world by her purging the country of the Semitic Races – the Jews. Race pride at its highest has been manifested here. Germany has also shown how well nigh impossible it is for Races and cultures, having differences going to the root, to be assimilated into one united whole, a good lesson for us in Hindusthan to learn and profit by. [148]

The power of a song

A Bengali poem called *Vande Mataram* beautifully describes India as the motherland of Hindus. The poem became famous when Bankimcandra Chatterji included it in his 1882 novel *Anandamath*,[149] and even more famous after it was set to music. Then in 1937 it was adopted by the Congress Party as India's National Song, with enthusiastic support from Gandhi and Nehru. This decision was strongly opposed by Indian Muslims, because the song had by now gained the nuance of being not just pro-Hindu but also anti-Muslim, for *Anandamath* depicted Muslims in a very negative light. The book had been written at a time when Hindus were periodically massacring Muslims, the British doing little to stop it or punish the attackers.

Vande Mataram has remained far more popular in India than the official Indian national anthem. With a line about "swords flash out in seventy million hands" the poem/song has also inspired attempts at Hindu nationalist violence. As part of the Hindutva agenda, children in most Indian schools are now required to sing *Vande Mataram* every day, with its message that India is the land of the Hindus and everyone else is a foreigner. Thus it sends the message that Indian Christians are unwelcome foreigners who, like Muslims, must be removed from the soil of India. The music of the 2008 British film *Slumdog Millionaire* includes the words of *Vande Mataram* with a modern arrangement of the tune, and so the message has gone out to the Indian diaspora too.

Hindutva began as a movement seeking Indian independence from British rule. Gandhi was seeking the same goal at the same time by non-violent methods according to his interpretation of the Hindu scriptures. By contrast, Hindutva, from the beginning, had interpreted the Hindu scriptures, like the *Bhagavad Gita*, as teaching a "warrior morality" and a "warrior religion" justifying a violent approach to non-Hindus and to Hindus who disagreed with Hindutva. It was a member of the RSS who murdered Gandhi in 1948, blaming him for being pro-Muslim and thus causing the partition of India and all the suffering to Hindus which that had entailed at independence the year before.

Other drivers of the development of Hindutva ideology included a feeling of humiliation and offence because of those who looked down on Hindu culture or even blasphemed it. Globalisation caused non-Hindu cultures to grow in influence, especially in the cities to which India's rural population were increasingly moving. Hindutva sought to return India to the golden age of Hindu culture, and to cleanse it of other cultural influences.

A network of Hindutva organisations developed from the RSS during the twentieth century, some violent, some political. Chief amongst the latter is the Bharatiya Janata Party (BJP), which has a fascist wing called Shiv Sena. The BJP won political power in various Indian states, and then in 2014 swept to power in the country as a whole, by winning a general election with an unexpectedly large margin.

By repeated physical attacks against non-Hindus in recent decades, these organisations have managed to normalise the idea of such violence. Followers of other religions which originated in India (Sikhism, Buddhism and Jainism) are generally not targeted. Some notorious incidents of anti-Muslim violence have occurred. The worst was in Gujarat in 2002 when over 800 Muslims were killed and 205 mosques destroyed.

Anti-Christian attacks are less deadly but far more frequent. Typically a mob of Hindu extremists will burst into a Sunday worship service or prayer meeting, damaging or destroying the building and its contents, injuring some Christians but not usually killing anyone. Particular targets are pastors and Christian converts from Hinduism.

Believers in the Hindutva ideology have successfully infiltrated the armed forces and police. This may be one reason why police rarely do anything against the perpetrators of such violence, but do quite often arrest the Christian victims of such attacks. It has also been suggested that Hindutva militants often choose Christian targets rather than Muslim ones because, as a general rule, Christians do not retaliate and Muslims do.

Hindutva activists have other ways of putting pressure on non-Hindus, especially Christians. One is through the legal process. Seven Indian states[150] have what are in effect anti-conversion laws, although actually called "Freedom of Religion" laws. These laws forbid the use of force, fraud or allurement to gain converts. They are a great hazard to Christians sharing their faith in these Indian states because it is so easy to falsely accuse a Christian of using these methods. Another kind of pressure is to restrict the access of Christians (and Muslims) to higher education, employment and public roles.

Another major problem for Indian Christians today are the Ghar Wapsi (Coming Back Home) activities designed to make the Christians "reconvert" to Hinduism. This phrase is used whether or not the Christians being pressured to become Hindus have ever been Hindu before. The Hindutva reasoning is that as Indians, the ancestors of the Christians, whether recent or remote, must have once been Hindus.

The Hindutva movement is rejected by the majority of tolerant Hindus who have seen their religion "hijacked" by a minority whom they consider to be extremists; they believe that in no way does Hindutva represent the history and culture of authentic Hinduism.

BUDDHIST NATIONALISM

Buddhism, the traditional and dominant religion in large parts of East Asia, South Asia and South-East Asia, has played a crucial role in arousing nationalist feelings against occupying colonial powers, just as Hinduism did in India. If the colonising power was Western, as in Sri Lanka and Burma (now Myanmar), this immediately set Buddhists against Christians, because Christianity was identified with the West. In Korea, under Japanese rule from 1905 until 1945, a Buddhist nationalism developed which was distinct from Japanese Buddhism. In Tibet, under Chinese rule from 1720 to 1912 and again from 1950 until today, a Buddhist nationalism developed which was distinct from Chinese Buddhism.

Buddhist nationalism has also developed in times and places where colonisation was not an issue, the religion being strongly identified with the history and heritage of the nation. In uncolonised Thailand, Buddhism became an important part of the state's official nationalism in the late nineteenth century and remains so today. The twentieth century has seen Chinese Buddhists look to their religion to counteract Western cultural influence in their country. In Japan, which actively embraced many aspects of Western culture, Buddhists emphasised that their religion was essential to Japanese cultural identity. In the post-colonial period, Buddhism has contributed to new forms of national integration. But Buddhist nationalism is not merely seeking to defend traditional values; it is often embraced in the pursuit of modernity in the social and economic spheres. It continues to be a source of national identity in several Asian countries, in the increasingly globalised twenty-first century, with the result that non-Buddhist minorities such as Christians, Muslims and Hindus tend to be perceived as threats to the nation-state.

Sri Lanka

Buddhism has two major branches, the older and more conservative of which is called Theravada, meaning "the doctrine of the elders" i.e. the doctrine of senior Buddhist monks. Theravada Buddhism is dominant in Sri Lanka (also in Myanmar, Thailand, Laos and Cambodia).

Theravada Buddhism is closely combined with Sinhalese culture and ethnicity to create a political ideology which can be called Sinhalese Buddhist nationalism. It came into being in the late nineteenth century, primarily as a reaction to British colonisation, but became increasingly assertive after Sri Lanka gained independence in 1948.

One of the founders of Sinhalese Buddhist nationalism was Anagarika Dharmapala (1864-1933). He was a leading light in the Buddhist revival and key in bringing Buddhism to the West. Educated at Christian missionary schools, he created Buddhist schools and other Buddhist institutions to match those of the Christians. In 1902 he wrote of Sri Lanka:

This bright, beautiful island was made into a Paradise by the Aryan[151] Sinhalese before its destruction was brought about by the barbaric vandals. Its people did not know irreligion... Christianity and polytheism are responsible for the vulgar practices of killing animals, stealing, prostitution, licentiousness, lying and drunkenness... The ancient, historic, refined people, under the diabolism of vicious paganism, introduced by the British administrators, are now declining slowly away. [152]

Such a close linkage between the "British administrators" and the destruction that he sees caused by their "irreligion", "Christianity", "polytheism" and "paganism" puts religion centre stage in the struggle for independence and in the Sri Lankan identity. It is hardly surprising that Sinhalese Buddhist nationalism continues hostile to Sri Lankan Christians, as we have already seen in chapter 12. In addition to the violence and spurious legal claims against churches, there is Buddhist nationalist pressure against Christian individuals having any involvement in governance in Sri Lanka.

Myanmar (Burma)

Myanmar is about 88% Theravada Buddhist and this religion has long been an important part of national identity, especially amongst the Burman (Bama) ethnic majority. "To be a Burman is to be a Buddhist" runs a popular saying.[153] Theravada Buddhism came to Myanmar a thousand years ago, displacing another form of Buddhism which had probably been there for about a thousand years already. In 1961 a law was passed to make Buddhism the state religion, but before it could be enacted it was repealed in 1962 after a military coup brought General Ne Win to power. Under his military regime, a secular ideology called the "Burmese Way to Socialism" was introduced, which remained the government ideology until 1988. Although never the official religion of Myanmar, Theravada Buddhism is now effectively a political as well as a spiritual institution. The Buddhist monastic communities (*sanghas*) have an important role in the state.

Many of the other ethnic groups never converted to Buddhism but continued with the animism and ancestor worship of pre-Buddhist times. Western missionaries found it very hard to convert Buddhists, but their work amongst animists was much more fruitful.

The first Western missionaries to Burma were Catholics who came in 1554-57 and then re-started the work in 1720. It is estimated that, after about half a century, there were approximately 2,000 Christians scattered across the country. Protestant missions began in 1807 when British Baptists arrived,[154] followed in 1813 by the American Baptists, Adoniram and Ann Judson. It was Judson who led the first Burmese to Christ – a Buddhist called U Naw, who was baptised in 1819. Anglican missionaries arrived in 1825, and other Protestants in the early twentieth century, but Baptists saw most fruit, after they had switched their focus to the non-Buddhist ethnic minorities. It is interesting to note that there was a very positive response to the Gospel amongst the animistic Kachin people, whereas Christian mission work made slow progress amongst the Shan people, who had been considerably influenced by Buddhism.[155] The Baptist Church is very strong in Myanmar today.

While this missionary work was progressing, three wars were fought between Britain and Burma (1824-26, 1852 and 1885) during which Britain gradually took control of more and more Burmese territory. The Buddhist monk Ledi Sayadaw (1846-1923) feared that the British colonial presence would eliminate Buddhism in Burma and therefore started to popularise meditation amongst lay people. But since the 1960s the main method of maintaining the dominance of Buddhism in the country has not been meditation but violent attacks by the armed forces on non-Buddhists, i.e. Christians and Muslims.

Ethnic factors complicate the situation, as most of the non-Buddhists are also non-Burmans, and therefore it can be argued that they are being targeted partly for their ethnicity. But there are aspects of persecution which clearly show pressure being used to advance Buddhism and hinder Christianity. It is interesting to consider how different things might have been for the mainly Christian ethnic minorities if the British had exerted themselves to ensure that the 1947 Panglong Agreement was implemented. This agreement, made less than a year before independence, gave "full autonomy in administration" to the areas where the minorities lived. Representatives from the Executive Council of the British Governor of Burma attended the conference at which the agreement was made and signed by representatives of the Shan, Kachin and Chin, and by Aung San on behalf of the Burmese Government. The autonomy, which had been promised by the British to the ethnic minorities, never happened.[156]

The horrific military attacks on Rohingya Muslims in Myanmar in 2017 received much international attention. But appalling violence has also been dealt out by the army on mainly Christian ethnic groups such as the Karen, Chin and Kachin. Beginning under the former military regime, the violence has continued under the democratically elected government of Aung San Suu Kyi. Typically, villages are attacked and all who do not escape into the jungle are killed. Sometimes the troops plant landmines around the village to maim and kill survivors who later try to return to their homes. Some years ago, troops had a habit of using captured civilians to walk ahead of them as human minesweepers. Men were also used as army porters, carrying such enormous loads that in some cases they were literally worked to death.

Christian cemeteries are desecrated and church buildings are attacked. The publication of Christian literature is strictly controlled, with the result that a whole church or a whole village may have to share a single copy of the Bible. Conversion to Buddhism is actively promoted. Children from poor Christian families in remote areas are offered free food and education in Na Ta La Buddhist schools where they are prevented from attending church and must learn and practise Buddhism. When they complete their studies they are guaranteed a government job on condition they officially convert to Buddhism. Buddhists who choose to follow Christ are persecuted.

An ultra-nationalist Buddhist organisation, generally known by its Burmese abbreviation Ma Ba Tha, was founded in Mandalay on 15 January 2014 at a large conference of Buddhist monks. The purpose of the new body was to defend Theravada Buddhism in Myanmar. Its name is translated into English in various ways, for example, "Association for the Protection of Race and Religion" and their main target was Muslims. Ma Ba Tha managed to get four "Race and Religion Protection Laws" passed in 2015. One banned polygamy, one required anyone changing their religion to get official approval, one placed a lot of restrictions on Buddhist women marrying non-Buddhist men, and one ruled that in certain parts of the country women must space the birth of the children at least three years apart. Ma Ba Tha were so extreme in their hostility that the government banned them in 2017. However, the organisation simply rebranded itself under the name The Buddha Dhamma Charity Foundation.

ISLAMISM[157]

Islamism is an ideology with a multitude of names, which embraces a multitude of movements and discourses, seeing Islam as a political ideology, a total system and way of life, not separating sacred from secular. Based on classical Islam and the early Islamic sources, it sees Islamic states ruled by Islamic law (sharia) as a viable and desirable alternative to any other form of governance. Islamism is also called political Islam, radical Islam or Islamic fundamentalism. This ideology seeks political dominance for Islam across the whole globe, sees the state as the best tool for implementing sharia, and believes peace is only possible under Islamic rule. It is not content with a society composed of Muslim people but requires society to be Islamic in its basic structures. Many ordinary and peaceful Muslims do not adhere to the ideology of Islamism and therefore it is important to draw a distinction between Muslims as fellow human beings and Islam as a political ideology.

Like the equivalent movements in Hinduism and Buddhism, this ideology began largely as a reaction against colonial rule. At the beginning of the twentieth century, Islam was experiencing chronic decline, and thinking Muslims were thoroughly alarmed. In 1910, an estimated 215 million of the world's 250 million Muslims were under Christian rule. Britain's King George V alone had 80 million Muslim subjects. By 1920 almost the whole Muslim world was under Western colonial rule. In 1924 the last vestige of the old Islamic political powers vanished when the Ottoman Caliphate was abolished. This kind of situation was, in a sense, more humiliating for Muslims than for any other people because their religion so clearly taught that they should rule and not be ruled.

Three key Islamists of the twentieth century: al-Banna, Qutb and Mawdudi

Three Sunni[158] Muslims born in the first decade of the twentieth century were greatly influential in establishing Islamism. In Egypt in 1928, Hassan al-Banna (1906-1949) founded the Muslim Brotherhood, the first grassroots Islamist movement in modern times. Its basic aim was to create an Islamic state under sharia in Egypt and then in the rest of the world too. The main ideologue of the Muslim Brotherhood was Sayyid Qutb (1906-1966), who was greatly influenced by Abul Ala Mawdudi (1903-1979) in the Indian subcontinent.

Mawdudi in his turn was inspired by al-Banna's example, with the result that he founded the Jamaat-i-Islami organisation in 1941. Its goal was the complete transformation of individuals, societies and politics in line with Islamist ideology.

The perceived weakness of the Muslim world created a longing for a return to the golden age of Islam, when it had been politically and militarily dominant. Islamism looked to the sources of classical Islam, not just the Quran but also Muhammad's own example and words (as handed down in traditions called *hadith)* which had together been developed by Islamic scholars long ago into the detailed laws of the sharia. They recalled with satisfaction the early Islamic conquests and the dramatically rapid expansion of Islamic rule as lands fell one by one to the Muslim armies.

Islamists looked also to Islamic scholars of the past, such as Abd al-Wahhab in eighteenth-century Arabia, the founder of the very rigid and "puritanical" form of Islam, known as Wahhabism or Salafism,[159] which predominates in Saudi Arabia today. Christians and other non-Muslims visiting or living in Saudi Arabia are forbidden to make any public display of their faith. Even meeting together to pray in a private home can result in arrest. There is a death sentence for leaving Islam. Funded by oil money, Saudi Arabia is very active in spreading Wahhabism, which has resulted in the radicalisation of many mosques around the world. Saudi Arabia has also been very active in financially supporting Al-Qaeda and Islamic State, who share its ideology.

Saudi Arabia's tiny but immensely rich and influential neighbour Qatar is doing exactly the same thing but on behalf of the Muslim Brotherhood. Together Saudi Arabia and Qatar have been very successful over recent decades in promoting the Islamist ideology amongst Sunni Muslims worldwide. The difference between them is that the Wahhabism/Salafism promoted by Saudi Arabia is working at the grassroots, through the mosques and *dawa*[160] (Muslim mission) organisations. The Muslim Brotherhood aims to work through political processes to take control of society and impose sharia. One result is a greatly increased hostility towards Christians, which is showing itself in increased violence and other kinds of persecution in almost every Muslim-majority context. Even Indonesia, for many generations a model of peaceful and mutually respectful Muslim-Christian coexistence as equals, was affected, and by the last years of the twentieth century, serious anti-Christian violence was occurring, for example in the Maluku Islands, with many thousands killed.

Three key words of the Islamist discourse: jihad, jahiliyya and takfir

Another Islamic scholar from whom the early twentieth-century Islamists took inspiration is Ibn Taymiyya (1263-1328), a prolific author who lived in Damascus and spent several years in prison because his views were so extreme. Ibn Taymiyya exalted military jihad as the best religious act a man can perform – better than pilgrimage, prayer or fasting as a way of showing love and devotion to Allah. He advocated a permanent physical struggle between Islam and non-Muslims. Wherever Muslims are a weak minority, he said, they must endeavour by all possible means to become powerful, dominate the non-Muslims and take control of the state. He taught that when non-Muslims were conquered by Muslims, their territory was being restored by Allah to its rightful owners, the Muslims.

Qutb's writings became the primary ideological source not only of the Muslim Brotherhood but of all contemporary Islamist movements. He taught an idea, first put forward by Mawdudi, to expand the scope of the Islamic term *jahiliyya* (times of ignorance and immorality) from pagan pre-Islamic Arabia to refer to all societies that were not living properly according to sharia. The worst examples of *jahiliyya*, according to Qutb, were the Christian West, the Marxists and the Jews, who he believed were all plotting together against true Islam. But he also considered that many Muslim-majority countries of the time were in a state of *jahiliyya*. The way to eradicate the evil of *jahiliyya*, said Qutb, was physical, forceful jihad.

Qutb also promoted the doctrine of *takfir*, the process of judging Muslims (individuals, regimes, societies and states) to be apostates or infidels if they fail to conform 100% to sharia. According to classical Islam, apostates from Islam and infidels (pagans) should be killed. So this doctrine gave licence to Islamists to kill their fellow Muslims who did not agree with the Islamists' own extreme views.

With these re-definitions of old vocabulary, revivals of old concepts, and a return to Muhammad's emphasis on the violent aspects of jihad, Islamism was ready to fight in any way – but especially literally – against the vast range of people its ideology said should be viewed as enemies. Christians, of course, were included in those considered to be enemies.

During the course of the twentieth century, Islamism spread out from Egypt and India to the rest of the "House of Islam". Although this ideology remains a minority viewpoint, the doctrine of *takfir* makes it very dangerous for the more moderate Muslim majority to speak against it.

A key twentieth-century date for Islamists

A key date for Islamists was 20 November 1979 AD. In the Islamic calendar (a lunar calendar starting from the *hijra*, the migration of Muslims from Mecca to Medina in 622 AD) this date was 1 Muharram 1400 AH (after *hijra*), that is, the first day of the Islamic fifteenth century. Many Islamists believed a prophecy that Islam would rise for 700 years, then decline for 700 years (and this is roughly what had happened in history), then start to rise again. So there was great expectation around this time that Islam would begin to regain its former power and glory.

It is surely no coincidence that 1979 was the year of the Islamic revolution in Iran. A series of events during this year ousted the Shah and made the country into an Islamic Republic with Ayatollah Khomeini as its supreme leader i.e. shifting it from a pro-Western monarchy to an anti-Western theocracy. Since then Iran has moved into the position of leader and defender of Shia[161] Muslims worldwide. It has also become a major persecutor of Christians, especially those who are converts from Islam rather than members of the historic Christian communities such as Armenians, Assyrians and Catholics. There has been one execution for apostasy (in 1990) and a handful of other martyrdoms at the hands of state officials, but on the whole it has been a case of closing churches; arresting, beating up (or sometimes torturing) and imprisoning believers; restricting access to literature; and other measures. Iranian Christians are even tracked and monitored outside of Iran. If the Iranian authorities intended to suppress the Iranian Church, their persecution programme has failed. The Church has grown extraordinarily rapidly since the Iranian Revolution, as many hundreds of thousands of Muslims have turned to Christ.

The four decades since 1979 have seen Islamist violence steadily rise round the world. The shifting networks of Islamist organisations have grown ever more complex, as groups pledge allegiance to each other or splinter into more groups. Some are more militant than others, some have more extreme views than others, some have more ambitious aims than others (creating a new caliphate, for example), but all are utterly intolerant of anyone who does not share their own beliefs.

A few of these organisations have become household names – the Taliban which held power in most of Afghanistan from 1996 to 2001, ruling it with a ferocious strictness that went well beyond the requirements of sharia; Al-Qaeda, responsible for the 9/11 atrocity in America in 2001; and Islamic State (IS, often called ISIL, ISIS or Daesh), which spread so rapidly across Syria and Iraq in 2014 and 2015.

It is sobering to consider how Western democratic countries contributed to the rise of Islamist forces that have caused untold suffering to vulnerable Christian minorities. The Taliban, which all but destroyed the Church in Afghanistan, and Al-Qaeda, whose vast network of affiliated organisations has targeted Christians worldwide, both developed from the Mujahideen insurgents in Afghanistan. The Mujahideen, who fought against the Soviet invaders of Afghanistan from 1979 to 1989, had been armed, trained and funded (to the tune of about three billion dollars) by the CIA, as a policy of American President Jimmy Carter and his National Security Adviser Zbigniew Brzezinski. The American hope was to draw the Soviet Union into a long, costly and draining conflict in Afghanistan. Not only the CIA but also Britain's MI6, Pakistan's ISI and Saudi Arabia were all involved.[162]

The US's ally Pakistan was at this time led by President Zia-ul-Haq, a hardline Islamist who did much to Islamise his country, thus making the situation of its Christian and Hindu minorities much more difficult. Under Zia the "blasphemy law" (Section 295 of the Pakistan Penal Code) became the draconian piece of legislation it is today, whereby non-Muslims are very vulnerable to malicious false accusations that could lead to their execution.

The plan to use the Mujahideen to defeat the Soviet Union succeeded but with the unintended consequence of the Mujahideen later evolving into the Taliban and Al-Qaeda. Hillary Clinton admitted in 2017:

> The people we are fighting today we funded 20 (sic) years ago. We did it because we were locked in this struggle with the Soviet Union.

They invaded Afghanistan and we did not want to see them control Central Asia, and we went to work… [we said,] "Let's deal with the ISI and the Pakistani military, let's go recruit these Mujahideen … and let's get some to come from Saudi Arabia and other places, importing their Wahhabi brand of Islam, so that we can go beat the Soviet Union. And, guess what, they retreated, they lost billions of dollars and it led to the collapse of the Soviet Union. So there's a very strong argument: it wasn't a bad investment to end the Soviet Union. But let's be careful what we sow because we will harvest. [163]

Another unintended consequence of the US/UK actions was the near destruction of the Afghan Church. During the Soviet occupation, the Gospel could be preached and a number of Afghan Muslims converted to Christianity. After the Soviets retreated, Afghanistan was left to the Mujahideen, who were soon replaced by the Taliban, who did their best to kill all the converts. When informed, in a private conversation, of the near obliteration of the Afghan Christian community in the process of winning the Cold War, the CIA's chief historian put it this way: "It was a small price to pay."

Almost the same thing happened again about 20 years later when an evangelical Christian British general in Afghanistan authorised the creation and distribution of a fatwa, written by two Islamic judges, that called for the killing of all converts to Christianity. This was done to show the people of Afghanistan that President Karzai, supported by NATO, was at least as sharia-compliant as the Taliban and thus to win their hearts and minds.

In January 2019 an Israeli general admitted that Israel had been providing weapons to rebel groups in the Syrian civil war that began in 2012. These rebel groups included Islamists. Just as America in 1979 seemed indifferent to the ideology of those it planned to strengthen and use to fight its wars, so too Israel appeared not to have cared about the radical views of the groups it was arming.[164] Alex Fishman, chief military-security correspondent for *Yediot Achronot*, explained:

A not insignificant portion of the Syrian rebels in the Golan have adopted the extreme Salafist ideology of Jabhat al-Nusra, an offshoot of al-Qaeda…The Israeli view is that the religious extremist views of the Syrian rebels are less relevant [than their capacity to combat Israel's enemies – Iran and Hezbollah]. Israel believes that what interests them [the rebels] above all is survival; and that it's possible to buy their loyalty through material aid which helps guarantee their own security.

The [Wall Street] Journal article [in June 2017, reporting interviews with Syrian rebel fighters stating that Israel was providing them with weapons, ammunition and salaries] gives one the impression that Israel doesn't always examine closely the views of its allies as long as it gets from them a useful security exchange. According to Israel's perspective, the enemy of my enemy is my friend. And if Jabhat al-Nusra fights against IS in the southern Golan, and each of them in turn fights against Hezbollah and the Syrian army in the Deraa region – all the better."[165]

Islamist rebel groups, whether IS's competitors funded by Israel or IS itself, targeted Christians in Syria, kidnapping and killing them. In Iraq approximately 200,000 Christians and many Yazidis fled their homes when IS seized Mosul and the plains of Nineveh in 2014. Their churches were turned into prisons or IS weapons stores, or burnt and desecrated. IS fighters even cut out and ate the hearts[166] of some of their victims. It was IS who beheaded 20 Egyptian Christians and one Ghanaian Christian on a beach in Libya in February 2015 – migrant workers selected by IS for execution because they were not Muslims and refused to convert to Islam. Later in the same year IS repeated the process with a group of 34 Ethiopian Christians.

Examples from Africa

Though less well known in the West, many other Islamist organisations are notorious in their own parts of the world. Boko Haram arose in north-east Nigeria in 2002 and now causes terror in several countries of West Africa. It targets Christians, schools (except Islamic schools) and the security forces. Thousands have died, thousands have been kidnapped and tens of thousands have lost their homes and livelihoods because of Boko Haram.

On the other side of the continent, Al-Shabaab began in Somalia in 2006 but extends its violence into Kenya and elsewhere. Christians are a main target and many al-Shabaab attacks involve carefully separating those they have captured into Muslims (who are allowed to go) and Christians (who are killed). Elsewhere in Africa are smaller Islamist organisations such as Seleka (in the

Central African Republic) or the Allied Democratic Forces (in Uganda and the Democratic Republic of the Congo), both of which target Christians. Further north is the Islamist organisation called Al Qaeda in the Maghreb.

Some Islamists have succeeded in setting up states under strict sharia. Sudan has been ruled by sharia since 1983. Although the mainly Arab, mainly Muslim North accepted this decision, Southerners (mainly Africans, many of them Christians) fought long and hard to resist sharia being imposed on their part of the vast country. An estimated two million Southerners were killed and five million displaced before they gained independence in 2011. All this time, the Khartoum government severely persecuted the Christian minority in the North, especially those living in Darfur in the western part of Sudan. As in many parts of Africa (and also Myanmar), the persecution generally is a mixture of ethnic and religious, but many individual cases show a clear anti-Christian motive. So great was the killing of non-Arabs in Darfur by the pro-government Janjaweed militia that in 2004 US Secretary of State Colin Powell described the Darfur killings as genocide.

SECULAR HUMANISM[167]

The very twentieth-century ideology of secular humanism has roots going back more than 3,000 years. As long ago as 1500 BC an atheistic, materialistic belief system called Lokayata developed in India, which had many variants including a particularly popular one called Carvaka. Another Indian precursor of humanism was Theravada Buddhism, which rejects, or considers irrelevant, the concept of a creator God. Buddha is revered as a model of a fully enlightened human being. These and other Indian philosophies were incorporated into the modern humanist ideology in the 1960s and 1970s.

In China, a form of humanism began to emerge through the teaching of Confucius (551-469 BC). This was referenced in Europe during the fifteenth to eighteenth centuries by early promoters of humanistic ideas who sought to bring down the Church. Ideas and philosophies from ancient Greece and ancient Rome also had a significant impact on modern humanism; these teachings were preserved in medieval Islamic libraries and hence were accessible to European scholars who later began to explore humanist thinking.

The Renaissance emphasis on classical education, the Reformation emphasis on the individual and the Enlightenment emphasis on reason – all good things in themselves – combined to set the stage for a rejection of traditional Christian beliefs in the West and the growth of humanism. In 1860 the word "humanist" was used in print for the first time, and in the next four decades various secular and humanist societies were founded. But it was the mass killing by so-called Christian nations in two world wars and the gross inhumanity against Jews in the Holocaust which gave secular humanism the boost it needed to become a dominant force in the world. People began to question the validity of a religion whose followers could do such horrendous things.

Humanists define their ideology as follows

> Humanism is a democratic and ethical life stance, which affirms that human beings have the right and responsibility to give meaning and shape to their own lives. It stands for the building of a more humane society through an ethic based on human and other natural values in the spirit of reason and free inquiry through human capabilities. It is not theistic, and it does not accept supernatural views of reality.[168]

What perhaps strikes religious believers most about humanism is the fact that, with humankind set up in place of God, there are no absolute rights or wrongs. Each person can choose for themselves their own morality and how to live. When morality has become negotiable, truth itself is the next victim – a strange irony for an ideology which puts so much emphasis on science and rational thought. As Brenda Watson has pointed out, the very word "truth" now has negative overtones for some people, who link it with stubbornness, intolerance and violence. Other humanists look wistfully at the idea of "truth", which seems to them an unattainable dream.[169]

Not all humanists are opposed to religion. Some actively affirm the beneficial effects of Christian morals on society. But some humanists and other atheists consider that any formal religion is dangerous for society and they actively oppose religion, especially Christianity. Their efforts to spread humanism and atheism are deliberate and well planned. One of their established methods has four stages:

1. **Tolerance** – urge society to tolerate a humanist value or behaviour that is contrary to the society's cultural norms (and most likely contrary to Christianity).
2. **Equality** – pressure the authorities and society to put the humanist belief/behaviour on an equal level with the society's pre-existing belief/behaviour.
3. **Reversal of norms** – make the previous norms seem backward, silly or evil.
4. **Aggressive action** – make the previous norms (which may have been Christian values) illegal.

In the first three stages, Christianity may be weakened and damaged if Christians follow the rest of society in embracing the values of humanism and materialism – often without realising it – as humanists successfully promote their beliefs through education, media and popular culture. But this damage is self-inflicted. Wise, discerning, brave, well-taught Christians will not take on non-Christian beliefs and values, even if all around them do. It is only at the fourth stage that persecution of Christians begins.

In the fourth and final stage of establishing humanism in a society that previously had a Judeo-Christian culture, new laws are introduced to criminalise Christians who express or live out various aspects of their faith. These laws could also criminalise people who follow other religions, but at present the main target seems to be Christians.

One example is the development of "hate speech" laws. As regards Christian persecution, the key step in this progression is the point when the law changes from protecting people only from physical harm to protecting them also from mental or emotional distress. In England and Wales this happened in 1986 when the Public Order Act was passed. Section 5 of this Act made it an offence to say "threatening, abusive or insulting words" or display them within the hearing or sight of someone likely to be caused "distress" by them. If the law was only concerned with "threatening words" there would be no problem. It is the inclusion of the words "abusive", "insulting" and "distress" that makes the law a potential source of persecution of Christians. Indeed, pensioner Harry Smith was convicted in 2002 under the Public Order Act 1986 for carrying a placard around Bournemouth saying "stop immorality, stop homosexuality, stop lesbianism". There was nothing physically threatening in this, but some people may have felt insulted or distressed by Mr Smith expressing his personal beliefs.

Similar potential problems arise for Christians when laws against "incitement to violence" become laws against "incitement to hatred", especially if it is "incitement to religious hatred". In the UK, the House of Lords has worked hard to protect freedom of expression in a number of new laws from 2001 onwards, removing the most dangerous parts or adding clear guarantees of free speech. In 2013, Section 5 of the 1986 Public Order Act was amended by removing the words "or insulting" after a campaign by Christians and others.

But the genie is out of the bottle; the public mood has changed. Hurt feelings are now considered as important as hurt bodies, and, even if the law is not quite there yet, people – sometimes including the police – act as if it is. Many British Christians have been arrested for street preaching, or answering questions about what they believe on sexual ethics or other religions, or taking a stand in other ways for the traditional Biblical morality that was the norm in the UK until a couple of generations ago. Some of the cases come to court, and usually the Christians are eventually acquitted (unlike Harry Smith). But when the humanists finally establish the laws they want, Christians will be found guilty and punished.

Another kind of humanist persecution of Christians is beginning to occur at the level of nations. Countries with laws in line with traditional Christian beliefs and lifestyles are coming under international economic pressure, for example, cruise ships boycotting Caribbean islands.

All this comes on top of laws gradually enforcing humanist values and eroding the freedoms of Christians to live by Christian values. Forcing Christian medical staff to perform abortions and assisted suicides, banning Christian parents from fostering or adopting children, and suspending university students if they express Biblical views on sexual ethics or offer to pray for other students stressed by their workloads – these are all real and recent issues around the world, and there are many more.[170]

CONCLUSION

The twentieth century was a century of great persecution for Christians. As we have seen, much of this was due to political and ideological developments on the world stage. A recurring motif in this chapter has been the way in which the actions of Western politicians directly or indirectly, undermined the work of Western missionaries and led to distrust, harassment and persecution of the local believers. However, this persecution did not bring about the extinction of the Church as happened in certain times and places in the past. Rather, the twentieth-century Church seems to have grown best in some of the contexts of greatest pressure, such as China and Iran.

Christianity also spread wider than in any other century. By the end of the twentieth century there were indigenous Christian believers in every Muslim-majority nation, something that was unthinkable at the beginning of the century, or even half way through it. They may have been very few in number, as in Mauritania, Libya or the Maldives, but by the year 2000 they were there.

The first two decades of the twenty-first century have seen increased pressure on Christians. Some Middle Eastern countries with a continuous Christian presence for two millennia are now in danger of losing it, as desperate Christians leave their homelands to seek freedom, security and equality elsewhere. But the dwindling Christian communities remain — at least for now.

The early twenty-first century has also been marked by a belated recognition in the West that Christians in other parts of the world are suffering unjustly for their faith. The UK's Prince Charles has repeatedly drawn attention to the plight of Christians in the Middle East "who, with such inspiring faith and courage, are battling oppression and persecution".[171] It is to be hoped that this will soon be followed by a recognition of the pressures now facing Christians in many Western countries too, from the secular humanist agenda.

Some Western governments also have been active on behalf of Christians, for example, the German and Hungarian governments gave financial support to Christians in the Middle East. Both Cyprus and Hungary sought to offer safe refuge to Christian refugees from that region, though thwarted by European Union regulations.

In 2018 American Secretary of State, Mike Pompeo, announced his country's intention to promote religious liberty internationally and to find "concrete ways to push back against persecution and ensure greater respect for religious freedom for all". It is to be hoped that this policy will be pursued with great wisdom and caution, lest it backfires. Ironically, it is the very might of the US, the world's only superpower, which makes its efforts to promote religious liberty, at least for Christians, rather likely to do more harm than good. For it is often assumed that, to coin a phrase, "my enemy's friend is my enemy". Therefore, the overt support of America may simply create greater suspicion and hostility towards Christian minorities in countries that do not see eye to eye with the US. As we saw in chapter 5, when Roman Emperor Constantine decided to ask the Persian Emperor to look after the Christian minority in the Persian Empire in the fourth century, it brought down terrible persecution on the very Christians that Constantine was trying to assist.

Might it therefore be easier for second-ranking countries with less "clout" than America to be more effective in helping persecuted Christian minorities? On 30 January 2019 the UK government launched a review into the British response to the global persecution of Christians. Foreign Secretary Jeremy Hunt, who had ordered the review, acknowledged that in the past the UK had neglected the issue of persecuted Christians, recognising the complications of having been an evangelising and a colonising country at the same time:

> This is something I think in the past we have been a little bit shy to talk about for various reasons, but I suspect the main one is our colonial history and some of the association with (sic) some of the missionary activities with colonialism, rightly or wrongly.[172]

Philip Mountstephen, Bishop of Truro, who was appointed to head up the review, commented:

> I think there is a real sense that persecution of Christians has been a blind spot in government thinking and in Foreign and Commonwealth Office thinking. The figures suggest that 80% of religiously motivated discrimination and persecution worldwide is directed against Christians, and I think it is very simple to say they have not received 80% of the notice...[173]

Let the last word on the persecution of Christians in the "long twentieth century" be given to the Syriac Orthodox Patriarch of Antioch and All the East. Speaking of the savagery of Islamic State jihadists as they swept across Iraq in 2014-2015, barbarising Muslims and terrorising Christians, Mor Ignatius Aphrem II made the point that in the midst of the worst imaginable human behaviour there was also the best imaginable human behaviour, as individuals in appalling situations cared for each other at great cost and risk to themselves.[174]

Chapter 14

CHRISTIAN RESPONSES TO PERSECUTION

Christians can face pressure, discrimination, injustice or persecution in many types of context. This includes environments where non-Christian religions dominate and also environments where atheistic ideologies, such as Communism or secular humanism, hold sway.

IS RELIGIOUS LIBERTY A BIBLICAL CONCEPT?

Freedom of religion is set out as a universal standard in Article 18 of the 1948 United Nations' Universal Declaration of Human Rights (UDHR):

> Everyone has the right to freedom of thought, conscience and religion; this right includes freedom to change his religion or belief, and freedom, either alone or in community with others and in public or private, to manifest his religion or belief in teaching, practice, worship and observance.

This was followed in 1976 by the International Covenant on Civil and Political Rights (ICCPR), whose Article 18 reads:

> 1. Everyone shall have the right to freedom of thought, conscience and religion. This right shall include freedom to have or to adopt a religion or belief of his choice, and freedom, either individually or in

193

community with others, and in public or private, to manifest his religion or belief in worship, observance, practice and teaching.

2.   No one shall be subject to coercion which would impair his freedom to have or adopt a religion or belief of his choice.

3.   Freedom to manifest one's religion or beliefs may be subject only to such limitations as are prescribed by law and are necessary to protect public safety, order, health, or morals of the fundamental rights and freedoms of others.

4.   The States Parties to the present Covenant undertake to have respect for the liberty of parents and, when applicable, legal guardian to ensure the religious and moral education of their children in conformity with their own convictions.

But is the aspiration to religious freedom grounded in Scripture? How should Christians react to being persecuted, to their fellow-Christians being persecuted, or to living in a context of persecution? Is religious liberty central to Christian theology and faith, or is it a luxury, a gift, a privilege? Should Christians resort to human laws and declarations like the UDHR and ICCPR to ensure their religious freedom? Should such freedom cover everyone in society, or only Christians? Should all benefit from religious liberty, or just a few?

Freedom is rooted in God

The Bible shows us that freedom is rooted in God's nature and in His dealings with human beings. God made the universe, holds it together by His Word of power, and governs it through His law, in wisdom, truth and love. God made human beings in His divine image. He made us to glorify Him and enjoy Him forever (Westminster Shorter Catechism). He does not force His rule or love on us, but gives us a conscience and a desire for Him. In other words, He gives us the freedom to seek and find Him.

God's way of governance must be the model for human governance. Humans must deal with each other in wisdom, truth and love. Because each one of us is created in God's image and the Son of God came clothed in human flesh, we must treat each other with the dignity which this entails. Human dignity, based on the fact that we are created in God's image, is what gives us "human rights", including religious liberty. No one must be forced; no one must be hindered. Everyone must be free to worship as they choose. Each individual has the duty, and therefore the right, to seek the truth. With this right comes a responsibility – to treat others as equals, with dignity and justice.

Liberty of the spirit

Christian experience has shown that in times of intense persecution – torture, imprisonment or approaching martyrdom – God gives grace to His people. Many have testified to a bliss that transcends their physical environment.

Another gift from God is the spiritual freedom He gives to those who have put their faith in Christ: they are free from sin (Romans 6), from the law (Romans 7) and from death (Romans 8). "Christ has set us free" (Galatians 5:1).

Freedom and humanity

The Biblical understanding of freedom is based on the Biblical understanding of humankind as *imago Dei*, made in the image of our Creator God. This gives us not only the potential for inner freedom but also dignity as individuals free to make our own choices.

God gives us freedom to choose. Adam and Eve made a choice. So did Cain when he chose to kill his brother Abel out of jealousy and then asked a question: "Am I my brother's keeper?" Yes, he should have been his brother's keeper and taken responsibility for his brother's wellbeing, as we all should for each other.

God commands us to act with *tzedakah*. This beautiful Hebrew word means "righteousness". It is much broader than "charity" in the sense of "alms-giving". It is about right relationships with other people, as well as about our private morality. This is the "righteousness like a never-failing stream" that the LORD desires (Amos 5:24).

Closely linked to *tzedakah* is the Hebrew word *mishpat*, which in simple terms means "justice", a justice rooted in the nature of God. *Mishpat* means much more than punishing wrongdoing. *Mishpat* is about treating people the same, regardless of race, social status, sexual orientation or religion. God frequently commands us to do *mishpat* and the word occurs more than 200 times in the Old Testament. It means giving people their rights, what is due to them. So caring for the poor is not love, so much as it is justice. David Doty says, "The justice of God is sacrificial and active."[175] If everyone behaved with perfect *tzedakah* there would be no need for *mishpat*, because there would be no injustice or neglect to put right. *Mishpat* tops the list of things that are right and good in Isaiah 1:17 and Micah 6:8. *Mishpat* frequently describes helping widows, orphans, immigrants and the poor – "the quartet of the vulnerable"[176] – and we should note that there are no conditions laid down that these vulnerable people must worship Yahweh in order to be eligible for *mishpat*.

God also commands us to love, with *agape* love, the love of Christ. Love is the essential quality of the Christian, based on the sacrificial, self-giving love of Jesus. Love (for God and neighbour) is both the first and the second greatest commandment, Jesus said, thus redefining the boundaries of how we should deal with others (Matthew 22:34-40). We are not to treat others on the basis of skin colour, religious belief or sexual orientation, but on the basis of the fact that they are made in God's image. Jesus takes this teaching a stage further when He gives His disciples a new command: to love one another (John 13:34). When they have truly learned to love one another, in the way that Christ loved them, they will be able to love everyone else too.

The Gibeonites

The Gibeonites were a community from Canaan who "did work wilily" (Joshua 9:4 King James Version) and tricked the Israelites into swearing by the LORD to let them live, when all the other Canaanite peoples were to be eliminated (Joshua 9, especially v19). Therefore this community of non-Israelites, who apparently did not worship Yahweh, continued to live amongst the Israelites for generations.

The Canaanite religion was polytheistic, with idol worship and Baal worship at its heart. It was also militaristic and extremely violent. It emphasised sexuality, linking it to fertility, and it was occultic, involving child sacrifice.

How did the Israelites treat the Gibeonites? The Israelites allowed them to live, but enslaved the Gibeonites as woodcutters and water-carriers. They were "to provide for the needs of the altar of the LORD" at Israel's central sanctuary (Joshua 9:23-27).

How did God treat the Gibeonites? God protected them. It was on behalf of the Gibeonites that God sent giant hailstones and stopped the sun in the middle of the sky so that the Israelites could win a battle to defend the Gibeonites from their enemies (Joshua 10:5-14).

Centuries later, Saul violated the covenant with the Gibeonites. No doubt, his intention was to cleanse the land of their occultic religion, and thus he planned and began a genocide. But God, despite the evil practices of the Gibeonites, would not have them persecuted, killed or expelled. As punishment for ill-treating the Gibeonites, God sent a three-year famine on the Israelites. This was lifted only when the Gibeonites were given seven descendants of Saul to kill (2 Samuel 21:1-14). King David punished the descendants of Saul for unjustly attacking the Gibeonites.

Freedom for all?

God called Israel to be holy as a nation, separated from all the practices of the Canaanites. Yet they had to allow the unbelieving Gibeonites to live in their midst and not persecute them, even though the Gibeonites had used trickery to gain this status and Israel had failed to seek counsel from the LORD. For their part, the Gibeonites co-operated with Israel and agreed to obey her laws.

God created all human beings in His image, giving them dignity and choice. Dignity and the power to choose are linked. God intends that humans should act on their own judgment, enjoying and making use of a responsible freedom, not forced but motivated by their conscience.

God teaches us that His priorities of righteousness, justice and love override everything else. The Gibeonites were to live among the Israelites and freely follow their own polytheistic religion.

This is not just a principle from Old Testament times. Jesus tells us that our heavenly Father causes His sun to rise on the evil and the good, and sends rain on the righteous and the unrighteous. To be like Him, we must love our enemies (Matthew 5:44-45). We must be just to all who are created *imago Dei*, whether they are a fellow Christian, an agreeable neighbour, or an implacable foe.

Jim Campbell, senior counsel of the US-based Alliance Defending Freedom, explains that:

> Defending religious freedom is not, and must not become, a self-seeking quest to shield us [Christians] from inconvenience and trials as we practice our faith. Rather, it must be part of fulfilling the church's call to love our neighbors by righting fundamental assaults on our common humanity. [177]

So the Bible teaches that freedom of religion must be for all in society. We should not try to prevent followers of other religions from having places of worship, or access to their sacred books, for example.

But freedom of religion does not include freedom to be murderous or to incite others to violence. It does not override existing laws for the maintenance of a stable and peaceful society. It is not an excuse, either morally or in law, for any such destructive behaviour.

Furthermore, we have already pledged to ensure freedom of religion for all, or at least our governments did so on our behalf when they signed up to the UDHR and the ICCPR. We are duty bound, morally and legally, to put these commitments into practice. We have, quite literally, made a covenant (the International Covenant on Civil and Political Rights). We saw how seriously God expected the Israelites to take the covenant (Joshua 9:15 ESV) that Joshua made with the Gibeonites. We saw His severe displeasure when later generations, in their zeal for the LORD, broke it. Let us not make the same mistake.

WHAT DID THE CHURCH ACTUALLY DO?

It is remarkable how soon church leaders began to ask political leaders for freedom of religion. Justin Martyr, who was born in about the year 100, asked the Roman emperor for justice for Christians who were being persecuted.[178] Tertullian (150-230) wrote:

> ... it is a fundamental human right, a privilege of nature, that every man should worship according to his own convictions. [179]

During the fourth century, these hopes became reality under a series of Roman emperors. Galerius' Edict of Toleration (311) stopped the persecution of Christians, Constantine personally embraced Christianity (312), Constantine and Licinius' Edict of Milan (313) established freedom of religion, and Theodosius' Edict of Thessalonica (380) made Christianity the official religion of the empire. The state-approved church was now in a position to persecute others, and did so with gusto.[180]

The model of an established state church has continued from then until now. It has produced a shameful tally of cruel persecution, whether of other Christians or of non-Christians. In certain times and places it has been savagely anti-Semitic. Even when these shocking excesses are absent, there is a tendency for a state church to slip into nationalism. Surely it would have been better to establish a religion-state relationship rather than a church-state relationship, so that all religions were treated equally and none had pre-eminence.

The Reformers

The Protestant Reformers took a variety of attitudes to the church-state situation at their time, a situation in which the spiritual and secular powers were closely intertwined. Luther (1483-1546) held that the government should leave everyone to believe according to their individual conscience. On the other hand, Calvin (1509-1564) established a strict religious regime in Geneva and punished anyone who differed. The Anabaptists took the (then) radical line that the state should have nothing to do with church matters at all.

The Roman Catholics

The Second Vatican Council of the Roman Catholic Church issued a statement on religious freedom on 7 December 1965 entitled *Dignitatis Humanae* (On the Dignity of the Human Person). This affirmed that all humans have the right to religious freedom and must not be coerced into acting against their own beliefs. It states that this freedom applies to individuals and to groups, and lists five freedoms that religious communities should have, summed up by Jeff Mirus as follows:

- Religious communities may govern themselves, worship publicly, assist and instruct their members, and promote institutions for ordering their lives in accordance with religious principles.

- Religious communities are not to be hindered in selecting, training, appointing, transferring, or communicating with their ministers, or in acquiring funds, purchasing properties or erecting buildings for religious purposes.
- Religious communities "also have the right not to be hindered in their public teaching and witness to their faith", providing that they themselves refrain from acting in ways that are either coercive or dishonorably persuasive.
- Religious communities "should not be prohibited from freely undertaking to show the special value of their doctrine" to society as a whole, and so are free to hold meetings and establish charitable and social organizations "under the impulse of their own religious sense."
- The family in particular has the "right freely to live its own domestic religious life under the guidance of parents," who have the right to determine "the kind of religious education that their children are to receive." Government must guarantee and protect this freedom.

Since protection of rights is an essential duty of government, "government is to assume the safeguard of the religious freedom of all its citizens in an effective manner," and to "help create conditions favorable to the fostering of religious life." However, if special civil recognition is given to one religious community, the right of all citizens and religious communities to religious freedom must still be recognized and made effective. Government must never violate the freedom and equality of citizens before the law for religious reasons. Finally, it is "a violation of the will of God" when force is brought to bear in any way in order to destroy or repress religion.[181]

Dignitatis Humanae emphasised that all these rights must be limited by the rights of others, duties towards others, and the common welfare. It also stated that "society has the right to defend itself against possible abuses committed on the pretext of freedom of religion" and that governments should safeguard not only the rights of all, but also "genuine public peace" and public morality.

Today

"Freedom is never more than one generation away from extinction," US President Ronald Reagan famously said.

Every generation must fight for freedom, protect freedom and hand on freedom to the next generation. New laws, and new interpretations of old laws, are rapidly eroding freedom of religion, freedom of speech and other long-cherished freedoms in the West.

In some Western countries, such as the UK and Australia, there is no law specifically guaranteeing and protecting full religious freedom. Sir John Hayes, a British MP, has warned of the serious situation in the UK:

> This "golden era" of liberty may be ending and the United Kingdom risks regressing. Religious believers are, once again, facing increased pressure to restrict their faith to the "private sphere". We now see regular, and increasingly unapologetic, persecution of Christians who remain committed to Biblical teaching, refusing to bow to liberal, secular orthodoxies…
>
> So, although it is now Bible-believing Christians who face increasing discrimination today, radical secularists are every bit as determined to undermine the freedoms of observant Muslims and Orthodox Jews.[182]

Religious freedom is a right that is not conferred on humans by humans, and, therefore, cannot legitimately be denied to humans by humans. It comes from God.

HOW SHOULD INDIVIDUAL CHRISTIANS RESPOND TO BEING PERSECUTED?

The Bible and Christian experience show us a variety of ways that believers respond to persecution, and Church history is made glorious by the faithful men and women of God who served Him unswervingly and often paid the price in martyrdom.

State protection?

Ezra and Nehemiah faced similar problems from enemies hostile to the exiled Israelites returning to Jerusalem. But they reacted differently.

Ezra refrained from asking King Artaxerxes for a military escort as the large group of returnees began their journey from Babylon to Jerusalem. Instead, he relied on fasting and prayer for safety on the road (Ezra 8:21-23). By contrast, Nehemiah accepted the army officers and cavalry that the king sent with him for the journey (Nehemiah 2:9).

Like Ezra, Nehemiah organised the people to pray, but unlike Ezra, he also "posted a guard day and night" (Nehemiah 4:9). As threats increased and intelligence reports repeatedly warned of likely attacks, Nehemiah stepped up his military preparedness and had armed men standing ready to defend those who were re-building the wall of Jerusalem. Indeed, even the builders carried weapons (Nehemiah 4:11-23).

Centuries later, and in the context of a very different empire, the apostle Paul appealed to the state justice system for help against his religious enemies (Acts 25:7-12).

Escaping and avoiding?

Paul experienced repeated persecution,[183] but responded in a variety of ways. On one occasion he escaped and fled (Acts 9:23-25). Another time he used his status as a Roman citizen to avoid a flogging (Acts 22:24-30).

Accepting and enduring?

Before this there were many times when Paul faithfully endured terrible and violent persecution (2 Corinthians 11:23-24). Once when an earthquake broke his prison chains and opened the prison doors, Paul chose not to escape. By contrast, when Peter's chains miraculously fell off and the gates miraculously opened for him, he followed the angel out of prison and made his way to freedom (Acts 12:6-10).

Later, we see Paul setting off to Jerusalem, ready not only to be imprisoned but even to die there for Christ's sake (Acts 21:10-14).

Denying Christ?

Some converts from other religions choose to keep their Christian faith secret to avoid persecution. Some might even be killed if their families discovered their decision to follow Christ. It may mean they have to continue certain practices of their old religion, so as to avoid suspicion. This contrasts with converts who choose to proclaim their love for the Lord and take the risk of suffering for Christ.

Naaman, a Syrian army commander who had been miraculously healed of leprosy by following the instructions of the Israelite prophet Elisha, decided he would never again offer sacrifices to any god except Yahweh, who had healed him. But Naaman's job required him to accompany his master to a pagan temple and there bow down alongside his master to the god Rimmon. Naaman could not envisage doing anything else, despite his new faith in Yahweh. He asked for forgiveness in advance and Elisha assured him on this point (2 Kings 5:17-19).

Amidst all the possible responses to persecution, it might seem that the red line that can never be crossed is to reject Christ outright. Many Christians have been gloriously martyred for refusing to deny Him.

But what if the threatened suffering is going to fall on others, not on yourself? Around the turn of this present century, a group of Indonesian Christians, who had gone away together for a youth event, were confronted by armed Islamist militants. The militants said they would spare the young people if the leaders stepped forward. The pastor and elders made themselves known, no doubt expecting to be killed on the spot. But, having identified the spiritual leadership of the church, the militants then said those leaders must convert to Islam or the young people would be killed.

A similar dreadful dilemma has been forced on church leaders in other contexts, for example, Communist Czechoslovakia in the twentieth century, or Japan in the seventeenth century.[184] To deny Christ would save others from physical torture or death, but what of your eternal destiny? And what of *their* eternal destiny? What spiritual damage might it do to those others to see their leaders rejecting the faith? Would they understand your motive, or might they follow your example? Is it more loving to let them suffer in their bodies, sure that their souls are saved, or to save them from short-term physical suffering yet possibly imperil them in eternity? In these circumstances, if some commit apostasy with their lips but continue to love the Lord in their hearts, is that right or wrong? Only God knows.

The early Church suffered repeated bouts of persecution under various Roman emperors. Many Christians apostatised, especially in the 250s AD under the persecution of Emperors Decius and Valerian, but when the persecution eased off some wanted to resume their Christian faith. There was strong disagreement amongst those who had remained faithful about what should be done with these cases: should they be accepted back into the church or not?[185] No doubt some cited the example of the apostle Peter who denied Christ three times but repented and was reinstated by the Lord (John 18:15-27; 21:12-19). Others may have recalled strong warnings in Scripture, such as Hebrews 6:4-6, about those who fall away, or may have had practical concerns about whether these individuals would betray other church members if persecution re-started.

Each individual must choose

There is a wide variety of possible responses to persecution, and each person must make their own decision. The one response that seems to have no justification at all is to seize power and kill the persecutor.

The annals of church history have shown us that in the times of greatest peril, pain and persecution Christians, although they have not sought death, have often willingly embraced death. So great was the grace of God that they did not fear the fire, the lion or the sword. In the Egyptian church, martyrdom is seen as the greatest blessing that God can bestow upon His child and to be welcomed as such.

But for some others, to be a "living martyr", by continuing faithfully to confess Christ as Lord while living in an unbelieving world, can be a greater burden to bear than dying for Christ.

Chapter 15

CONCLUSION

Although it is impossible to predict what the future holds for the Church in the twenty-first century, it is clear that she will continue to suffer and to be persecuted simply because she bears the Name of Jesus Christ her Lord.

For over two thousand years, the Church has undergone persecution in various forms. At times it seemed as if her light had been extinguished, for the flame had grown so dim it was on the point of dying out. And yet the wind of the Spirit of God blew upon her and she caught alight again, perhaps not in the same location but somewhere else where she now burns bright. So her faithful witness continues. The Christian hope is that God will keep His Church and protect her, for Jesus said the gates of hell will not prevail against His Church.[186]

FOLLOWING IN HIS STEPS (1 PETER 2:21)

Christians have always found strength in times of persecution from the knowledge that Jesus understands what they are going through. He not only knows because He is omniscient, He also knows because He Himself suffered. He knows from His personal experience. The wonder and glory of God in Christ who suffers may leave us speechless – and often baffles followers of other religions – but it is one of the main sources of endurance and consolation for Christian believers. Although we can never know the spiritual suffering of bearing the sins of the whole world, our Lord's physical and psychological suffering reflect what His faithful followers have experienced from the first century until the twenty-first century, sometimes in surprising detail.

Many Christians know what it is to be rejected, despised, alone and falsely accused. Some have been betrayed by close colleagues in the ministry. A Romanian pastor discovered recently that for many years his assistant pastor had been methodically reporting on him to the secret police.

Falsely accused Christians are beaten and tortured while in custody, hounded energetically through the courts, or yielded up to angry mobs. In Pakistan, India and Egypt, where the law enforcement and judiciary are intimidated by frenzied crowds deliberately whipped up by religious leaders, it is rare for Christian victims to get justice; sometimes they are even arrested while their attackers go free. How often have civil and religious authorities combined to persecute Christians? In Malaysia today, Christians from a Muslim background know well the problem of their cases being passed to and fro between the secular courts, with greater powers, and the religious courts who are more strongly against them, just as Jesus experienced.

The sweeping charge of *majestas* on which Jesus was condemned is akin to the charges faced by many Christians today. In countries such as Sudan and Iran, Christians are charged with "crimes" like treason or espionage simply for believing in Christ, living as His disciples and sharing their faith. It also happens in places like North Korea and various Central Asian republics ruled by individuals who have developed a personality cult around themselves that is almost a religion, and who cannot tolerate anyone who worships Jesus. "Public order" is another pretext often used by governments to crush Christian witness.

Many of Christ's followers have been crucified, starting, tradition says, with the apostles Philip, Andrew, Peter and Bartholomew (who was crucified twice). In the Armenian, Syriac, Assyrian and Greek genocide a hundred years ago, crucifixion was one of the many barbaric methods which the Turks and Kurds used to kill the Christians of the Ottoman Empire. Even in our generation some Christians are crucified; reports in recent years have come from Iraq, Syria and Sudan, for example.

Today Christians walk the way of their Master Jesus – kangaroo courts and all. But those who endure physical, mental and emotional pain for His sake, whether or not it leads to martyrdom, can be sustained by the knowledge that their Lord and Saviour endured the same opposition from sinful men (Hebrews 12:3). As they bear ridicule and disgrace, they can remember that He scorned the shame of the cross (Hebrews 12:2). As their bodies are broken, maimed or burned, they can take comfort and hope in the fact that His wounded body is now glorified in heaven (Revelation 5:6) as He intercedes for His suffering people, perhaps showing His pierced hands and side as if to say, "Father, help them, protect them – this is the price I have paid for their salvation."

WHAT ELSE CAN WE LEARN?

This book is called *Hated Without a Reason*, reflecting the words of the Lord Jesus in John 15:25, quoting Psalms 35:19 and 69:4. His disciples must take care to be sure this can also be said of them. Christians should do nothing to deserve persecution. Over the centuries, many dreadful things have been done by those bearing the Name of Christ, things which have brought that Name into disrepute and brought down persecution on His people. Such things have been done because of ignorance or foolishness, or because of pride, arrogance, greed, callousness or a host of other tragically shocking motives. It is little wonder if Christians are then hated and persecuted, not just the Christian perpetrators of the unChristlike deeds but also others who are called by His Name.

Earlier pages of this book have described many occasions when Christians have been persecuted not for religious reasons as such, but for political reasons: the Church in Country A was targeted because of what the government in Country B was doing. Those persecuted Christians had been unable to convince their fellow citizens that they did not support the foreign government's actions. Those Christians were hated and persecuted without a reason that they had any control over.

So we Christians must take care that, if we are hated, it is only because we love the Lord. If we are hated, it must be without a reason except the reason that we are faithful to Him and to His Word.

We must be willing to embrace suffering – if it comes. This does not mean seeking it out, but simply accepting it from God if it is His will. We may not in this life understand His purpose but "we take it gladly, trusting though with trembling, out of so good and so beloved a hand," as Dietrich Bonhoeffer wrote from prison. When the Theban legion was decimated and then massacred under Emperor Maximian in the third century, people marvelled that the soldiers did not defend themselves, but laid down their weapons and offered their necks to the executioners. They had not looked for death, but they embraced it willingly rather than deny Christ or harm His people. They are a model of true martyrdom.

Those Egyptian Christians soldiers of the Theban Legion had put their loyalty to Christ first, then came their loyalty to their brothers and sisters in Christ and finally their loyalty to the Roman Emperor. This flags up the complicated issue of links between Church and state. Such links are dangerous for us as Christians. They create conflicts of loyalty. They draw us into compromising positions. They make us complicit with the acts of the state. They put both our wisdom and our courage to the test as we have to tiptoe around the many challenges created. The history of Christian persecution teaches us to be very cautious about links with the state.

It teaches us also that the best of intentions can inadvertently cause great harm. Emperor Constantine set out to help the Christian minority in Persia, but his wellmeant letter to the Persian Emperor, followed by his preparations for a military invasion of Persia, eventually led to the "Great Persecution" of Christians in Persia which lasted for 40 years. Similar disastrous misjudgments at international level are easy to envisage in today's world.

Another area requiring great caution in the age of the internet is publicity about Christian minorities. An article celebrating the work of the Holy Spirit in bringing many Muslims to Christ in a particular country, for example, may be seen by Islamists as humiliating and shaming for the cause of Islam. They may act to try to change the situation i.e. to reduce the number of converts by persecuting or killing them. Likewise, hopes and prayers expressed in phrases like "to win such-and-such a country for Christ" may alarm the country's government and cause it to take action against its Christian minority.

Looking at the history of Christian persecution we find many wonderful examples of faith, hope and love which we can strive, with God's help, to emulate. But, sadly, there are also examples of those who found the pressure too much, who fell away and denied Christ, either to save their earthly lives or for a lesser goal. The Christians in seventh-century Oman gave up their faith simply because they would otherwise have had to surrender half their possessions. If they had been willing to endure material deprivation for Christ's sake, perhaps the Church on the Arabian peninsula would not have been wiped out – only God knows. Let us learn from these sad examples and determine that we will never deny our beloved Lord, who died for us.

Countless other believers accepted the gift of martyrdom, often leaving their earthly bodies through a hideously agonising process. As we have seen, young and old were willing to endure unbelievable pain for the love of Jesus, the resurrection hope, and the heavenly joy that was set before them. One of those who remained faithful was Perpetua, a 22-year-old mother thrown to the beasts in a Roman arena to delight the crowds. Her last words ring down the centuries from 203 AD to us today. They sum up the message of this book. **"Stand fast in the faith and love one another."**

THE SILK LETTER

The "Silk Letter" was written by a Korean Christian called Hwang Sa-yeong (Alexander Sayông Hwang) to the Bishop of Beijing in 1801 on a piece of silk measuring 62cm x 38cm. It was written in Chinese, the language of educated Koreans at the time, and comprises 13,311 Chinese characters arranged in 122 columns. See chapter 11 (above) for more on why this letter was written and what happened to it.

Below is an abridged translation of the Silk Letter by Alexander Y. Hwang and Lydia T. Kim. The numbers in brackets indicate the columns. Paragraph breaks have been added by the translators for ease of reading in English. Korean names are presented with the Christian name followed by the first name and then the surname. (Note that there can be various spellings when transliterating Korean names into English e.g. Chou and Joo are two ways of spelling the same Korean name.)

(1-5) Sinner Thomas and others plead in tears to Bishop De Gouvea [Bishop of Beijing].

Through travelers from last spring, we had heard that you were enjoying good health, but time has passed since then, and as we approach the end of the year, we wonder how you are doing. When we ponder on our knees about how his holiness has been blessed by the grace of the Lord with health in body and spirit and how through the help of the Lord his virtues are increased, we are filled with great respect and love, and are overcome with abounding joy.

Because we are sinners filled with heavy sin and wickedness, spiritually, we have become the targets of the Lord's anger, and due to our lack of wisdom and understanding, we have lost the sympathy of other people. Due to these reasons, a persecution has risen, whose destruction has reached the priest [Chou]. Since we sinners have not been able to respond to our Lord's grace by sacrificing our lives how can we dare to plead to you in writing? However, when we ponder on our knees, even though there is the danger of the Church being turned upside down and people tormented with persecution, we are without leadership and have no place to plead, as we lost our loving priest and meek brothers, who have been scattered in four directions. Since your holiness, through grace, has become our parent and through loyalty upholds the heavy responsibility of pastoral leadership, we believe that you will pity us and save us. Who else are we to call upon in these times of great trouble?

Therefore, we dare to inform you of the details of the persecution. It is difficult to summarize, as it has been a complicated process that has been going on for sometime, but we inform you in the following details. We desire on our knees that you will pity us and consider our situation.

As the Church has crumbled down to nothing, only the sinners have escaped danger, and John [Ok-Chun Hee] has not been found either. Do you not agree that this indicates that the Lord's grace has not been completely cut off from our nation? Alas! Those who are dead have proven holiness through death, and those who are alive must hold onto the truth through death. However, we are lost as to what to do because we lack in knowledge and strength. We have secretly conferred with a few brothers about our recent events, and now we inform you of our situation in great detail. Please read and have pity and save us who have no one to rely on. We are like a group of sheep that has ran away — some have escaped into the mountains, and others are holding back tears in silent cries as they roam the streets, without a place to go. Our struggles have reached deep within us, and all that we hope for day and night is the grace of our Lord and the generous love of your holiness. We hope on our knees that you will pray for the help of the Lord and that you will generously extend human love by saving us from these troubles and allowing us to reside in peace.

Christianity has spread all over the world, and people of all nations are praising, and there is no one who is not drumming and dancing to the joy of the Lord's Church. Even when you consider our nation, who is not a child of God? However, due to distance and separation, we heard the Gospel late, and evil has led to unbearable difficulties and ten years of storm. However, we never dreamed of this year's cruel persecutions. It is truly pitiable. How can we face this situation? Because there has not been a special blessing bestowed upon this crisis, there is a danger of Jesus Christ's holy name being wiped away from this nation. Our hearts are torn to pieces as we consider the fact that our thoughts and words have reached this level. When our older brothers in China and Europe hear about our dangerous and troubled situation, how will they not feel the pain and have pity on us?

We dare to hope that our desperate efforts will be rewarded as your holiness follows the Lord's example of grace and the teachings of the Church, by informing the Pope and the nations about our situation and the ways to save us. As we quiet our hearts, shed tears, and implore you, we await good news with great anticipation. Please have mercy on us, as we are unable to tell you everything in writing.

(6-16) *The persecution of Christians of Choong-Chung Do by the king: Thomas Chai-Pil Gong, Martin Joon-Bae Lee, Chul-Shin Kwon, and Ahn-Jung Lee.*

(17) *Description of the rivalry of the familial factions and their support or opposition to Christianity.*

(19-21) *The immediate situation after the death of the king in 1795 and the persecution of Christianity by the queen regent.*

(22-23) *Arrests of Thomas Chai, Peter, Stephan, and John Chai-Hyun Chang.*

(24-25) *Decree of the queen regent against Christianity.*

(25-28) *Arrest of Augustine Jung.*

(29-30) *The arrest and imprisonment of Christians of Seoul to the federal court in the second month of 1801.*

(30-31) *Executions of Augustine Jung, John Chai-Hyun Chang, Thomas Chai, Francis Saberio Hong, Nak-Min Hong, Columba Kang, and Seung-Hoon Lee, and others.*

(32-69) *Biographies and martyrdoms of John Chang-Hyun Chai, Augustine Jung, Thomas Chai, Francis Hong, Nak-Min Hong, Peter Seung-Hoon Lee, Ga-Hwan Lee, Peter Pil-Jae Chai, Yosaphat Gun-Soon Kim, Baek-Soon Kim, Luke Hee-Young Lee, Philip Pil-Ju Hong, Colomba Kang.*

(69-70) *The execution of the king's brother for involvement with Christianity.*

(70-73) *Biography and martyrdom of Peter Cho.*

(73-74) *Details of Christians in Chun La Province.*

(75) Some say that since the beginning of our country, no civilians were killed as much as in this year, but we do not know if that is true or not. We do not know how many people died as martyrs among all those people. The people that the government really wants to kill are the learned scholars who have high positions. The government reasons that the people are not as guilty as these learned men, because they are ignorant. Many common people were saved from death because the government overlooked their offense. Because what occurred before February was witnessed by our own eyes, we know what happened. But the events after February are just hearsay.

The acts of martyrs (76) I have described were based on what people have said and on what I know. As for the rest of the acts, I dare not write them here. I am still worried that there might be reported facts that are untrue. They need further investigation.

(77) Since 1795, the priest had stayed in the house of Colomba. Once in a while, he went to other places, but only Colomba knew his whereabouts. When the persecution began, a male believer who wanted to protect the priest went down to a province, arranged a hiding place, and came back to Seoul to take the priest. But when he met with Colomba and told her about his plan, she told him that a safe place for him had already been found. The man pleaded to meet the priest several times, (78) but he returned without seeing the priest. After about a week, when that male believer sensed an imminent danger to himself, he took his family and fled.

When Augustine Chung was arrested and refused to reveal the identity of the priest, the magistrate arrested Colomba, with her son, and tortured them. When they did not give in, the magistrate took their servant and tortured the servant. The servant gave in to the torture, told them what she knew, and revealed the age and the facial features of the priest.

The magistrate demanded Colomba to tell them where the priest was hiding. She replied, "He was living at our house before, but he left a long time ago. I do not know (79) where he is now." The government had his face drawn and sent copies to all the provinces as a wanted man. In the middle of March, the priest turned himself in. He went directly into the government building and said to the surprised district soldiers: "I am a Catholic priest. I heard that the government is prohibiting Catholicism and is killing many innocent people. The fact that I am alive does not help these people. So I came to give my life." When they took the priest to the magistrate, he had him imprisoned. But he did not interrogate him nor torture the priest.

It is said that the priest wrote many letters while in prison, but I was not able to obtain any.

(80) A non-believer said that the one who turned himself in called himself a Chinese. After the priest was imprisoned, the people in Seoul said that a Chinese was advocating that Catholics are not traitors. They also said that the Chinese was not going to die before he had said all that he wanted to say. These rumors seem to be true.

In mid April, the government ordered one of the generals to execute the priest. But that general reported that he was sick and did not come out for four days. He was relieved of his duties, and a new one was appointed to carry out the execution. The priest was taken out of the prison, tortured — his knees were beaten thirty times — (81) and was made to pass through the crowd. He looked at the crowd and told them he wanted rice wine because he was thirsty. The federal soldiers gave him rice wine. After he finished his drink, he was taken to the river south of the city. An arrow was pierced through the ear of the priest, and he was made to read the charges against him. Quietly he read the charges and lowered his neck.

That was around three in the afternoon on April 19, which was the celebration day of the Trinity. When his head was cut off, suddenly great winds blew and dark clouds covered the whole sky. The great noise and the flashing lightning terrified everyone in Seoul. One believer (82) was three hundred miles away from Seoul and another believer was four hundred miles away from Seoul —

when they witnessed the extraordinary wind and thunder, they thought that something had happened. Later when they heard about the priest's death, they realized that it was that hour of that day.

The priest's head was raised on a stick for five days. It was guarded day and night so that people could not take it off. Later the general had it covered in a dirt mound, but it was still guarded. The believers planned to find his body and secretly transfer it for a proper burial. But an evil magistrate requested, "It is not right that his body be buried. Please order his body to be taken out and laid out in the open." The king's mother had granted the request. But the general (83) who had guarded the priest's head said, "The body has been already been buried. Do we really need to take it out again?" So his body was not taken out. His body was moved to somewhere. Believers searched all over but could not find where his body was buried.

When the priest was executed, the officer who pronounced his charges had said that the priest was from Jeju Do Island. The reason was that the government wanted to cover up the fact that they did not report it to the Chinese government and consult them on how to handle such a matter.

After the priest was martyred, the magnitude of the persecution decreased a little. But searches and arrests continued, and many people were still in prison. Someone had said that there were still nine more people who would be executed. But since it was hearsay, we do not know whether it was true or not.

(84) When the priest first came to our country, someone had already informed the king of his arrival. So, for seven years the priest had to be very careful about his movements and could not engage in public ministry. Therefore, not many people had received grace, and most converts were women. A number of people from the province and some merchants in Seoul were quite enthusiastic, but few people had received grace. They went through a lot of trouble, but they endured their hardships in expectation of something great. They could not even mention the word "priest" in their own house, let alone see his face.

(85) Now they finally got to see the priest, only after he was killed by the haters of the Holy Teachings. All their efforts for the past ten years came to nothing, and [now] they feel like their body and spirit are on the verge of perishing. The hearts of these people are broken. They have lost a sense of purpose. Not knowing whether they will live or die, they do not know what to do.

In consolation, we told them: "The priest came to our country to save many people. He could not see you nor show his love to you because there were too many obstacles. Now that he is martyred, the power of the Lord's protection over us will be greater than when the priest was here on earth. Our trust and hope will become greater than before, (86) so let us not be disappointed at all." But we knew that people were still oscillating between doubt and faith, grief and consolation. Such a scene was not seen in our past.

I know that in the West, the past persecutions were more severe than our own. But the lineage of the priests continued from generation to generation, and the Eucharist was continued. Therefore, Catholicism did not die out, and the souls of the living were saved. But in our country, the situation is so different that there is no hope for the future. Sheep may survive without the shepherd, a child may grow without a mother, but we have (87) no way of surviving.

We, the sinners, were born in the region of darkness, but fortunately by the grace of our Lord, we have become his people. We were so grateful for his special grace that we wanted to serve the Lord with all our hearts. But we had no idea that this would happen.

I have heard that the blood of the martyrs becomes the seeds of the Church. But unfortunately, our country is located next to Japan. Those islanders are cruel and have forsaken the relationship with the Lord on their own. Our government approves of it and plans to imitate what they have done. Is that not ridiculous?

Since our people are gentle and weak and the law is not strictly enforced, (88) the persecution should not be as atrocious as in Japan. But now, among the believers in this country, it is hard to find a person with a strong will and a discerning mind. Most believers are ignorant men, women, and children. They might number a couple of thousands. We have no leaders who can care for and oversee them. How can we last long in this situation? In this state, the Church will die out within ten years, even if there was no persecution from the government. Ah! It is a matter that draws nothing but lament and wailing. How can I witness the end of Christianity before I die!

We have escaped the wrath this year and are torn between gratitude and fear. We are thankful (89) because the Lord has protected us and saved our lives. We are fearful because we have not been chosen by the Lord, due to our sins.

We desire to do our best for the Lord with our remaining lives, but we lack wisdom and have reached the end of our strength. Do we have to swallow our anguish and die with *han*[16] in our hearts? In this dire situation, who will take pity on us and comfort us? I would like to throw myself before your majesty and plead in tears, but because mountains and waters make you inaccessible, it torments me all the more. What are we to do?

In addition to the pain of hearing the news of [the] priest's imprisonment and death, there was another matter that I greatly feared. (90) If the priest's incident was reported to the Chinese government, the blame might fall upon the Church there. Then there would be no hope of restoration of our Church. Day and night, I was more anxious about the events there than here. But fortunately, the foundation was not shaken, we are still living, and Yohan (Ok-Chun Hee) is safe. It must be that the Lord has committed the matters of our country to you. How can we not plead to you in all earnestness and look for your favor? We reveal everything to you. Please take us into your consideration.

Among all nations, our country (91) is the poorest, and among our people, the believers are even poorer. We can count with our hands the number of believers who are fortunate enough to avoid starvation and [exposure to] winter. Ever since the arrival of the priest in 1794, we have not been able to work well with the priest, and many things have not been accomplished. Some think that is because we lack experience, but in reality it is because we are powerless and poor. This year, the number of people who entered the Church has increased [a] little, and our financial condition has improved slightly. But we have not been able to do the basic things (92) because we lacked financial power. Even the cause of our present dilemma can be traced back to our financial difficulties.

In this year's persecution, those who were afflicted have lost their whole estate, and those who survived have escaped with nothing but their own bodies. The poverty among believers is worse than in 1794, and even if we had a plan to relieve the situation, we do not have the power to carry it out. Already many works have been destroyed, but if we had some material wealth, there are still things that could be done.

Among the believers who were not found out, there are a few who are still capable. If all of us unite our strength, we can still start a new work. In regard to the political situation, it has gotten worse and worse since 1795. (93) But after this year, I hope the persecution will dwindle, because all those who have been held under suspicion have died or gone away.

This is how Catholicism has survived until today. (94) In Kyung gy, Choong chung, and Chunla provinces, there were many believers. In Kyung Sang and Kang Won provinces, there were a number of believers who had fled from persecution. An investigating official is traveling around in these five provinces. In Hwang Hae and Pyung An provinces, there were no Christians, and no Christians immigrated into them. There is nothing going on in those two provinces. People say that there still is surveillance, but if things are quiet for a year or two, the watch will relax. Then we will be able to do something.

(95) Before, Catholics were not afraid to reveal their religion, but now we cannot afford to. In the future, we have to plan everything in detail and protect ourselves to preserve the faith. If we bring the old believers to maturity and teach the new believers as we pray for the Lord's help, then an opportunity will come and we will be able to preserve the Church.

The believers' mistake in 1794 has come to this. Since the first attempt was unsuccessful, if we are very careful, persecution will not rise again. Of course, we should not (96) just sit around and wait to die in this situation. But everything else can be discussed after we have had financial stability. We had no idea that the survival of the Church in a nation depended upon that despicable mammon. If the Church were to die out just because of a lack in material wealth, how horrible would that be?

That is why I dare to kneel before you in humble request. Please make a plea for us to other Western nations. If enough funding is provided to maintain the Church and save souls, I will ask your permission after every preparation has been made to manage it uprightly. Please have mercy (97) on us and help us.

I know that such a request is burdensome, but if we do not make a request and remain silent, it will mean eternal death. I speak these words before you because it is better, even if we get nothing, to die having made a request than to die with a regret of not having made a request.

We want to reveal to you that our bodies and our hearts are empty. I hope that your majesty will resemble the merciful Lord above and consider the poor fate of our people down below. If you comfort us and fulfill our wish, it will be a great benefit to the cause of the Church and our people. If you do not abandon us in your grace and open up a way of life (98) for us, we will do our best to follow in that path. But it cannot be done in a few months. It will take at least three years.

There are two things that make it difficult to cross the border. One is hair, and the other is language. Hair can easily grow back, but language is not an easy matter.[17] If one were fluent, it would not be dangerous. We thought that one of our men could go to the Cathedral in Beijing and teach our language to young people so that their language skills can be used in the future. But we want to know what you think.

If you allow it, we can (99) set a secret sign or sound, and the two can meet at the Eastern gate. If the Eastern gate is not good, then the two can proceed over to the Choon-gate [Check Gate]. The most convenient way would be to have a prudent Chinese believer reside within the Check Gate and open up a store to serve people that are passing by. Then it would be easy to exchange letters through him.

We have come to a point where the road divides between death and life, but executing the above plan would not be too hard. If people had a merciful heart (100) toward our country, like you do, our proposal would be accepted with gladness. I bow before you and make this plea: would you take charge and see that it gets accomplished?

Our country is in a perilous state, and whatever the Chinese emperor orders, no one will dare oppose. If your majesty were to send a word to the Chinese emperor and say, "I want to spread the Catholic faith to Chosun [Korea], but I hear that Chosun belongs to China and that it does not communicate directly with other nations. So I write to you. Would you order a special decree to Chosun, and let her receive Western missionaries to teach loyalty (101) and reverence so that she can be faithful to you," then the emperor would not deny your request since he knows that the Western missionaries are hardworking and faithful. This would be possible, but in view of the current situation in China, I do not know if it would be a good time or not.

The grace of our Lord in this country is special. From the beginning, Christian teaching came to us without an evangelist. (102) We cannot count all the special blessings we have received. The punishment this year was to root out our sinful shortcomings. But the Lord, in his grace, has not abandoned us and [has] left us a way out in the midst of atrocious destruction. That is a sign that the Lord will protect and save this country. Since the Lord is helping us, if China and Western nations also unite in helping our country, then how can catastrophe not be turned into a blessing and this tiny land the size of one's palm be unsaved? We comfort ourselves and others with such thoughts and maintain ourselves against death. I implore your majesty and the Pope to carry out the Lord's will (103) and save this country.

Bowing down, I continue. I hear that there is continuous rising of thieves in western China, against whom the Chinese army has been defeated several times, but that China keeps losing land. The Chinese emperor is clearly anxious about it. If there is someone whom the emperor trusts, someone who is good with words and is familiar with the matters of the state, he can say to the Emperor: "Being urgent in complacency and sensing danger in security is an eternal truth. Your dynasty has risen from the East two hundred years ago and has possessed the whole world. But dynasties rise and fall. If something unfortunate happens in later generations, they would have to go back to Yong Go Top.[18] But Yong Go Top is not a good place. (104) Chosun is right across the river. You can see their houses and you can hear the shouts across the river. The land on the other side is about three thousand li's in length and width. In the southeast, the land is fertile, in the northwest, the soldiers and horses are powerful, and mountains stretch down to a thousand lengths, providing endless timber. Since the sea on three sides surrounds the land, there's always plenty of fish and salt. In Kyung Sang province, ginseng abounds. In Tamlado (Jeju Island), there are good horses. It is a country with many natural resources, and the Yi Dynasty is very weak, like a string that is about to break. The king's mother is acting as regent, and powerful nobles are wielding arbitrary control. In this chaos, the people are grumbling and sighing. At this time, (105) make Chosun a vassal country. Make the king wear the same robe and free the traffic on the border. Then you can make Chosun part of Yong Go Top and enlarge the royal dynasty's lands. Between Pyungyang and Anju, establish a diplomatic center and let the king manage the country. If you show kindness to the people, they will be loyal to you. If a base is established on the east side of Yoyang and Shimyang, the great distance and roughness of the area in between will give protection even when the whole world rebels. Soldiers can be trained and employed when the opportunity comes. That will establish a foundation for a dynasty for 10,000 years. Moreover, I hear that the king of Chosun is still young and does not have a wife yet. If one of the royal princesses becomes his wife, the king will be a blood relation, (106) and his son will be considered a grandson of the emperor. He will be very loyal to your dynasty. Also Chosun can be a power to check Mongolia. If you miss this opportunity, another might take the place. And if that country settles down and becomes strong, it will not be good for us. This is the time. If you do not decide and act now, you will regret it later."

If the Chinese emperor allows it and believers help, the Church will expand greatly. (107) In China, there already are many believers and there would be ways to speak to the emperor. I hear that Hak-Sa Young, who came a few years ago as an imperial messenger, is a relative of the emperor's wife. I also hear that he is close to your majesty. One of the servants in his house is a believer. Maybe the plan can be carefully executed through a person like Hak-Sa Young. If a person like him insists on such a view, the emperor might accept it.

Even if the emperor accepts such a request, it would be hard to make Chosun a vassal without a reason. It can be done after one or two punishable offenses have been made known. In our country, (108) there is no justice and people do not follow the law. I cannot tell you all of them one by one. This plan would be beneficial to the household of the emperor and would not be harmful to this country. Currently, the condition of our country is perilous and will not last long. If Chosun becomes a vassal of China, the evil-minded officials' power will dwindle and the Yi Dynasty's power and fame will double. How is this pursuing only the security of the Church? It will be a blessing to the nation. (109) Please do not think that the plan is unrealistic or that I am blind to circumstances.

In your instructive letter of last year, we read that a large ship would be sent a few years later, but things have changed much now, and it would be hard to hope for success without a scheme. There is such a plan that will make people of Chosun to obey without any resistance. But it would be very difficult to execute. However, I want to inform you about it.

The military strength of this country is very weak, the weakest among all nations. We have had peace and tranquility for two hundred years, and people do not know what an army is. There is no competent king and there are no virtuous officials. So, if one unfortunate (110) event occurs, the whole nation will crumble like dirt and scatter. If a few hundred armored ships and fifty or sixty thousand troops came to our shore with a few Chinese scholars who were accomplished writers and were to send a letter to our king stating: "We are evangelists from the West. We have not come here for wealth but to save lives according to the order of the Pope. If your country agrees to accept just one missionary, we will go back without firing one single shot and without any demands. (111) We will just sign an agreement of friendship and go back rejoicing. But if you do not accept the messenger of the Lord, we will not go back even after you have died as a result of the Lord's punishment. Is the king willing to save the whole nation by accepting one missionary, or is the king not going to accept one person and lose the whole nation? Make your choice. The teachings of the Lord emphasize love, loyalty to the king and honoring of one's parents. The Lord's teachings will be a great benefit to this kingdom. We do not gain any profit by spreading this teaching. Our intentions are sincere. Please do not doubt us."

If they keep telling the king that the Western nations have had peace and comfort for a long time because they have honored the Lord and that accepting a (112) Western missionary is not harmful but beneficial, the whole nation will be awed and comply. It would be great to have all those ships and troops, but if that is too hard, several tens of ships with five or six thousand troops might be enough for the task. Several years ago, a Western ship came drifting on our shore and one of our believers went aboard. He said that that one ship would be able to fight against a hundred of our ships.

The reason why the people of our nation interfere cruelly with the progress of Catholicism is not that their characters are cruel and evil. (113) There are two reasons: the fight between political factions is intense. They are using Christianity to slander and exclude each other from power. The other is that what they have seen and learned do not go beyond Song Hak [Chinese philosophy], and anything that differs from themselves, they think of it as the greatest mutation ever seen in the whole world.

People of Chosun can be compared to a child in a remote countryside who has never gone outside the house. When he sees a stranger, he will be shocked and cry very loudly. That is what is happening these days. In reality, the people of Chosun are afraid, suspicious, and ignorant. Their characters are very gentle and weak. They delayed the execution of the priest after his self-surrender because they were afraid of a riot by the believers. (114) After they had made sure that the believers would not do anything, they grew bolder and carried out the execution. But even then their suspicion and fear did not subside. That is why this is an opportune time to carry out such a plan, because they are afraid. Even if they do not want to accept the missionary, they will not refuse, because they fear great power and seek peace. This plan is difficult to carry out, but if it is executed, it will succeed.

(115) A few say that it is too difficult to accomplish and that it does not befit the reputation of the Church. But some of us sinners do not think so. In this country, there have been many martyrs in the past ten years. Even the priest and high officials of the government were executed. The haters of Christianity slandered them as traitors, but they were not able to offer a single piece of evidence. People already know that the martyrs were gentle and good-natured people, and they are sympathetic to the believers. If the believers in this country rise up in rebellion, that act would destroy the good reputation of the Church.

The West (116) is where the Church originated. In two thousand years, the faith has spread to all nations in the West, and all have turned toward the Lord. But only this small sized country is disobeying the command of the Lord, cruelly killing the believers and even executing the priest. Would it not be right to raise up an army to inquire after their offense? Even if our country is destroyed, the reputation of the Church will not be harmed. This plan is only (117) to raise the magnitude of the threat so that they would accept the Church. It will not harm the common people. It will not extort any wealth. It is modeled after mercy and righteousness. It reflects the most excellent image of the Church. We do not have to worry about her reputation. I am only worried that we do not have enough strength for this plan.

Another one says that if this plan is reported to China, it will harm the Church there. But I think this can easily be solved. In the letter it can be said: "Years ago, the Pope had ordered so and so priest to evangelize Chosun, but Chosun has not only refused to accept the faith but even killed the priest. If they do not accept the faith, we will send a message (118) and inform China about the sins of Chosun and we will punish the offenders to comfort the people." Then the sin of killing the Chinese scholar will be exposed. Because they are afraid of China's punishment, they would not dare report it.

Opening up a store inside the Check Gate would be the most urgent matter. The subsequent plans would have to be executed within three to four years. If this time passes, we will have the opportunity again. For us, (119) one day seems like a year, and we have no power. We can only wish in our hearts with fervency. Have mercy on us and come to the rescue soon.

In this year's persecution, most of those who were known to be Christians did not escape wrath. Those who escaped have become traveling merchants or have moved to other places. Many believers are wandering on the road. Believers do not practice the faith out in the open, but on the day of ancestral worship, their identity as believers is easily discovered, so if there are any Chosun believers on the road, (120) please let them be hidden from the sight of the people to save their lives.

One person vowed to offer worship to the Lord twice a week from last Lent to next Lent. But during the persecution, he fled into the mountains and was not able to have worship. He vowed, but did not keep it. Please forgive him. Are unfulfilled vows of the past (121) also a sin?

(122) On the 1801st year after the birth of the Lord, and one day after the day of Simon Thaddaeus, Thomas sinner and others bow twice before you.[19]

NOTES

16 *Han* is the feeling of anguish and frustration

17 Chinese shaved the front of their heads, while Koreans did not.

18 The birthplace of the Chung Dynasty. It is today's Yung An Hyun in Manchuria.

19 St Simon's feast day is April 26, thus the letter was completed April 27, 1801.

Source: Alexander Y. Hwang and Lydia T. Kim, "The Silk Letter of Alexander Sayông Hwang: Introduction and Abridged Translation", *Missiology: An International Review*, Vol. XXXVII, No. 2, April 2009, pp.168-177. Reproduced by kind permission of the editors of *Missiology*. (Some of the translators' notes have been omitted.)

NOTES

1 Acts 5:41.
2 For examples, see pages 28, 44-45, and 184.
3 The Coptic Orthodox Church Centre UK, Coptic Orthodox Diocese of London, "The Coptic Orthodox Church", http://www.copticcentre.com/the-coptic-orthodox-church/ (viewed 31 January 2019).
4 See p.147.
5 See pp.162-163.
6 At the Lutheran World Federation's eleventh assembly, held in Stuttgart, Germany.
7 John 15:18-25.
8 See chapter 4.
9 See p.131.
10 *The Times*, 8 October 1857, p.5, column 4, cited in Brian Stanley, "Christian Responses to the Indian Mutiny of 1857", in W.J. Sheils (ed.), *The Church and War: Papers Read at the Twenty-First Summer Meeting and Twenty-Second Winter Meeting of the Ecclesiastical History Society*, Studies in Church History, Vol 20, Oxford, Basil Blackwell, 1983, p.280.
11 From a Latin poem by Arnulf of Leuven (died 1250). This English translation is by James W. Alexander in 1830.
12 Isaiah 53.
13 Herbert B. Workman, *Persecution in the Early Church: a chapter in the history of renunciation*, 1906, London, Charles H. Kelly, p.10.
14 See p.15.

[15] Judea and Samaria had been ruled by another son of Herod the Great until 6 AD when, unable to bear King Archelaus' cruelty any more, the people asked the Romans to remove him and rule them directly through procurators sent from Rome.

[16] Septimus Buss, *Roman Law and History in the New Testament*, 1901, London, Rivingtons, p.224.

[17] Johann Heermann, translated by Robert S. Bridges.

[18] See chapter 4.

[19] *Foxe's Christian Martyrs of the World: From the Celebrated Work by John Foxe and Other Eminent Authorities: Newly Revised and Illustrated*, Chicago, Moody Press, no date, p.30.

[20] More details of his story are on pp.119-121.

[21] Eusebius, Bishop of Caesarea in Palestine, lived from c. 260 to c. 339 and wrote his famous ten-volume *Ecclesiastical History (History of the Church)* over many years, probably completing it in 323 or 324.

[22] Alexander Walker (trans.) "Apocrypha of the New Testament", in Alexander Roberts & James Donaldson (eds.), *Ante-Nicene Fathers: The Writings of the Fathers Down to A.D. 325: Volume 8: The Twelve Patriarchs, Excerpts and Epistles, The Clementina, Apocrypha, Decretals, Memoir of Edessa and Syriac Documents, Remains of the First Ages*, Peabody, Massachusetts, Hendrickson Publishers, 2004, p.556.

[23] Tertullian, *The Prescription Against Heretics*, trans. Peter Holmes, in Alexander Roberts & James Donaldson (eds.), *Ante-Nicene Fathers: The Writings of the Fathers Down to A.D. 325: Volume 3: Latin Christianity: Its Founder, Tertullian, I. Apologetic; II. Anti-Marcion; III. Ethical*, Peabody, Massachusetts, Hendrickson Publishers, 2004, p.260.

[24] Eusebius, *History of the Martyrs in Palestine*, edited and translated by William Cureton, London and Edinburgh, Williams and Norgate, 1861, p.2.

[25] *Crimen laesae majestatis* (usually called *majestas*) was the crime for which Jesus was executed. See p.12.

[26] The prolific Christian writer Tertullian, one of the "early church fathers", was born in Carthage (in modern-day Tunisia) around 150 AD.

[27] Augustine (354-430) was Bishop of Hippo (in modern-day Algeria). This quotation comes from his book *The City of God*, ii.3.

[28] *Dialogue with Trypho*, Number 110.

[29] See p.78.

[30] He was first Caesar and then Augustus of the western Roman Empire from 284 to 305, while Diocletian was Augustus of the eastern Roman Empire (see below). Not to be confused with Maximin, another persecuting emperor, who ruled the eastern half of the Empire from 311 to 313.

[31] It was not the only Theban legion in the Roman army.

[32] *Coptic Church Review*, Vol. 25, No. 2, Summer 2004.

[33] Roger Bussey, "The Theban Legion Massacre AD 286", Weapons and Warfare: History and Hardware of Warfare, https://weaponsandwarfare.com/2018/03/21/the-theban-legion-massacre-ad-286/21 March 2018 (accessed 13 January 2019).

[34] Eusebius, *History of the Martyrs in Palestine*, edited and translated by William Cureton, London and Edinburgh, Williams and Norgate, 1861, pp.26-28.

[35] H. Broadbent, *The Pilgrim Church*, 1931 (2014 edition), USA, Resurrected Books, pp.62-63.

[36] See p.46.

[37] Eusebius, *The History of the Church*, Book 9, chapter 8, translated by G. A. Williamson, 1965, revised and edited by Andrew Louth, London, Penguin Books, 1989, p.289.

[38] This is a different Caesarea from the one where Gregory's contemporary, the historian Eusebius, was bishop. Eusebius' bishopric was the Caesarea on the coast of modern Israel.

[39] Eusebius, *Life of Constantine*, Book 4, chapter 13.

[40] See p.46.

[41] Although Constantine's Christianity was probably not a genuine personal faith, his powerful mother Helena does appear to have been a committed Christian.

[42] Tertullian wrote: "*Plures efficimur, quoties metimur a vobis; semen est sanguis christianorum.*" A plain translation of his Latin is: "We multiply whenever we are mown down by you; the blood of Christians is seed." It comes from the final chapter (chapter 50) of his most famous book, *Apologeticus pro Christianis* [*Apology on behalf of Christians*], which was a defence of Christians against the defamation and persecution they were suffering at the hands of the Roman authorities.

[43] Tertullian, *Apology*, chapter 37.

[44] Eusebius, *Life of Constantine*, Book 4, chapter 54.

[45] Robert Markus, "From Rome to the Barbarian Kingdoms (330-700)" in John McManners, *The Oxford Illustrated History of Christianity*, New York, Oxford University Press, 1990, pp.62-63.

[46] Markus, "From Rome to the Barbarian Kingdoms (330-700)", p.66-67.

[47] ὁμοούσιος (*homoousios*) in Greek.

[48] The Nicene Creed, produced at the Council of Nicea and used in many churches today, emphasises this in the passage: "We believe in one Lord, Jesus Christ, the only Son of God, eternally begotten of the Father, God from God, Light from Light, true God from true God, begotten, not made, of one Being with the Father."

[49] The Council of Constantinople made some amendments to the Nicene Creed, creating the version used today.

[50] Other Germanic tribes such as the Franks and Anglo-Saxons (who migrated to what are modern France and England respectively) were never Arians, but converted from paganism straight to a Trinitarian form of Christianity. See p.80.

[51] Syriac Orthodox Archdiocese for the Eastern United States, "Syriac Orthodox Church of Antioch – General History" http://syrianorthodoxchurch.org/general-history/ (viewed 3 February 2019).

[52] Philippa Adrych and Dominic Dalglish, "Religions in the Roman World" in Ja Elsner and Stefanie Lenk, *Imagining Divine: Art and the Rise of World Religions*, Oxford: Ashmolean Museum, University of Oxford, 2017, p.41.

[53] See p.80.

[54] John Foster, *Church History 2: Setback and Recovery AD 500-1500*, London, SPCK, 1974, p.11.

[55] The Byzantine Empire (324-1453) was the eastern part of the Roman Empire, which lasted nearly a thousand years after the western Roman Empire had come to an end. Its capital was Constantinople (previously called Byzantium, now called Istanbul), its language was Greek and its religion was Christianity.

[56] Before the advent of Islam, the Christians of Najran had suffered severe persecution by Jews. See p.55.

[57] This flight or migration to Medina took place in the year 622 AD, which was later chosen as the start of the Islamic calendar.

[58] See chapter 8.

[59] Letter to Shimʿun, Metropolitan of Riwardashir, approximately 650 AD. Letter 14:2,7. English translation by William G. Young in *Handbook of Source-Materials for Students of Church History*, Madras, Senate of Serampore College, 1969, pp.317-318.

[60] Letter to the people of Qatar, approximately 651 or 652 AD. Letter 18:3. English translation by William G. Young, pp.318-319.

[61] *The Chronicle of Ibn al-Athir for the Crusading Period from Al-Kamil Fiʾl-Taʾrikh* Part 1, translated by D.S. Richards, Farnham, Ashgate Publishing, 2010, p.104.

[62] Stated by the French geographer Conrad Malte-Brun in his posthumous work *Précis de la Géographie Universelle*, Vol. 10, Book 171, 4th edition, Paris, Le Normant, 1837, pp.638-639.

[63] J.R. Wellsted, "Memoir on the Island of Socotra", *Journal of the Royal Geographical Society*, Vol. 5, 1835, p.218.

[64] Britannia was smaller than today's Britain, and Germania was larger than today's Germany.

[65] His book *An Ecclesiastical History of the English People* was finished in 731, when Bede was about 59. Bede spent most of his life in Jarrow, Northumbria (north-east England).

[66] John Foster, *Church History 2: Setback and Recovery AD500-1500*, London, SPCK, 1974, p.2.

[67] See p.61.

[68] Earle E. Cairns, *Christianity Through the Centuries*, 3rd edition, Grand Rapids, Michigan, Zondervan, 1996, p.171.

[69] Paulinus taught Roman Christianity, Aidan taught Celtic Christianity.

[70] To tie up some loose ends: in the eleventh century the Gospel reached Finland, and in the twelfth century Christianity at last became fully established in Sweden.

[71] There is anecdotal evidence that the Gospel may have reached China in the first century AD but 635 is generally accepted as the earliest date for which there is firm evidence.

[72] The name for Syriac Christianity at this time in China was *Jingjiao*, a word with many nuances. It is sometimes translated as "Luminous Religion" indicating the sense of shining with light, or as "Illustrious Religion" indicating the sense of great and glorious.

[73] Today's Triad gangs can be seen as a legacy of the White Lotus Society.

[74] See p.157.

[75] For more details, see pp.156-161.

[76] The five-family group (*gonin gumi*) was a system of local neighbourhood associations comprising units of five households. The families in a group were obliged to denounce any Kirishitan family among them; the remaining four families would then be exempt from punishment. However, the five families were all held responsible and executed if one was accused of being Kirishitan by someone from outside the group.

[77] Those who came out of hiding were referred to as "resurrected Kirishitans". Some however chose to continue with the distorted form of faith they had practised in their underground days; they were called "hidden Kirishitans".

[78] Richard Fox Young, "Early Responses to Christianity in Japan and Korea (1549-1854/1876)" in Mark R. Mullins and Richard Fox Young (eds), *Perspectives on Christianity in Korea and Japan*, 1995, New York, The Edwin Mellen Press, p.6.

[79] This document had been signed by Emperor Meiji on 30 October 1890. It set out the government's policy on education, with a focus on Confucian principles and loyalty to the emperor. It was read aloud at important school events and pupils had to memorise the text. It was considered the basis of public morality and to have its own spiritual power.

[80] Jesus was accused of the same two crimes. See chapter 2.

81 John Breen, "Shinto and Christianity" in Mullins, *Handbook of Christianity in Japan*, 2003, Boston, Brill, p.266.

82 Likewise in North Korea today, whole families are punished for the "offence" of one Christian.

83 Persecution had greatly impoverished the Church, as its wealthy members had had their property confiscated.

84 Korea had a China-centred worldview and was very respectful and subservient towards its powerful neighbour to the west, paying tribute to China every year. Koreans felt it natural that they, as a small country, should depend on and serve the larger country.

85 Meaning without a foreign evangelist.

86 Hwang is referring to the famous words of Tertullian, who died in the early third century. See p.58.

87 Koreans did not look on Japan as a country that it was proper or necessary for them to submit to. Korea's relationship with Japan was therefore not as peaceful as its relationship with China.

88 For details of what the Japanese government had been doing to Christians in Japan, see chapter 10.

89 The number of Christians increased from 6,000 to 9,000 in the three years 1836-1838.

90 Translated by Sebastian C.H. Kim and Kirsteen Kim, *A History of Korean Christianity*, New York, Cambridge University Press, 2015, p.42.

91 Newly planted churches should become self-propagating, self-supporting and self-governing as soon as possible.

92 See p.95.

93 The chains of the *General Sherman* still hung on Pyongyang's main gate.

94 See p.97.

95 For further information on the early Church in South Asia, see Patrick Sookhdeo, *A People Betrayed: the impact of Islamization on the Christian Community in Pakistan*, Christian Focus Publications and Isaac Publishing, 2002.

96 See pp.28-29.

97 Recorded in *The Anglo-Saxon Chronicle* (edited and translated by B. Thorpe, 1861, Vol. 2, p.66), cited in John Rooney, "Exploring St. Thomas", *Al-Mushir*, Vol. 25, Nos 1&2, 1983, p.83.

98 We have already seen in chapter 7 that the Christians of the island of Socotra, near Yemen, believed that they too were descended from converts made by Thomas.

99 John Rooney, *Shadows in the Dark*, Rawalpindi, Christian Study Centre, 1984, p.45.

[100] The details of the martyrdom are different from those of the oral traditions in South India.

[101] In ancient times the word "India" could be used for a broad range of geographical locations including the whole of the sub-continent, parts of the Arabian peninsula and even the Horn of Africa.

[102] The Mughal emperors were descendants of Timur.

[103] Most of them were Bunts, descendants of Saraswath Brahmin converts, who had very fair skins and blue – or more often green – eyes. Nowadays many Bollywood film stars and Miss Indias are Bunts.

[104] It is said that Wellington learned from Tipu Sultan's example the military tactics that he used later to defeat Napoleon. Ironically, it is also said that Tipu Sultan himself learned these tactics from his French allies.

[105] R.G. Burton, *Wellington's Campaigns in India*, Indian Army Intelligence Branch, 1908.

[106] Indian soldiers recruited to fight for the East India Company.

[107] "Indian mutiny was 'war of religion'", interview with William Dalrymple, BBC News website's Soutik Biswas, last updated 6 September 2006.

[108] William Owen, *Memorials of Christian Martyrs and other Sufferers for the Truth in the Indian Rebellion*, London, Simpkin, Marshall and Co., November 1858. Examples of Indian Christians suffering for Christ and being martyred are throughout the book (see pp.46-59, 120 for some mentions of Delhi). For other issues see pp.27-30 (apostasy); pp.30-32 (Indian Christians' loyalty to British); pp.32,138 (Hindus protecting Indian Christians); pp.153-159 (example of a British Christian refusing to convert to Islam, in a situation where persecuted Indian Christians and British Christians suffered together and encouraged each other).

[109] Owen, pp.28-29.

[110] Brian Stanley, "Christian Responses to the Indian Mutiny of 1857", in W.J. Sheils (ed.), *The Church and War: Papers Read at the Twenty-First Summer Meeting and Twenty-Second Winter Meeting of the Ecclesiastical History Society*, Studies in Church History 20, Oxford, Basil Blackwell, 1983, pp.279-281.

[111] Patrick Sookhdeo, *A People Betrayed: the impact of Islamization on the Christian Community in Pakistan*, Christian Focus Publications and Isaac Publishing, 2002, pp.55-57.

[112] For further information on the situation of Christians in modern Pakistan, see Patrick Sookhdeo, *A People Betrayed: the impact of Islamization on the Christian Community in Pakistan*, Christian Focus Publications and Isaac Publishing, 2002.

[113] Speech as president of the Constituent Assembly, 11 August 1947, i.e. three days before independence.

[114] For more details, see pp.170-173.

[115] See pp.109-110.

[116] The attacks were recognised as genocide by the Parliamentary Assembly of the Council of Europe (January 2016), the European Parliament (February 2016), the US State Department (March 2016) and the UK House of Commons (April 2016).

[117] Syriac Orthodox Church of Antioch, Archdiocese for the Eastern United States, "General History – The Syriac Orthodox Church of Antioch – A Brief Overview" http://syrianorthodoxchurch.org/general-history/ (viewed 3 February 2019).

[118] See Yusuf Malek, *The British Betrayal of the Assyrians*, Warren Point, New Jersey, The Kimball Press, 1935.

[119] Giles Milton, *Paradise Lost: Smyrna 1922 The Destruction of Islam's City of Tolerance*, London, Hodder & Stoughton Ltd, 2008, p.227.

[120] Giles Milton, pp.230, 268-269.

[121] Giles Milton, pp.235-237.

[122] Giles Milton, p.372.

[123] David B Barrett (ed.) *World Christian Encyclopedia: A Comparative Study of Churches and Religions in the Modern World, AD 1900-2000*, Oxford, Oxford University Press, 1982, pp.1,6.

[124] Patrick Johnstone and Jason Mandryk, *Operation Word: 21st Century Edition*, 6th ed., Carlisle, Paternoster, 2001, p.2.

[125] Brian J Grim, Todd M Johnson, Vegard Skirbekk, Gina A Zurlo (eds.), *Yearbook of International Religious Demography 2017*, Leiden, Brill, 2017, pp.246-247.

[126] Barrett, 1982, pp.686-687.

[127] Bengt Sundkler and Christopher Steed, *A History of the Church in Africa*, Cambridge, Cambridge University Press, 2000, p.860.

[128] 88.7% in 2001 according to David B Barrett, George T Kurian & Todd M Johnson, *World Christian Encyclopedia: A Comparative Survey of Churches and Religions in the Modern World: Volume 1*, 2nd ed., Oxford, Oxford University Press, 2011. p.762. The Christian percentage is now declining as Islam advances.

[129] David Reynolds, *The Long Shadow: The Great War and the Twentieth Century*, London, Simon & Schuster Ltd, 2013.

[130] See pp.95-96.

[131] Kathleen Carter, "Sixty Years On: Reflection on the Practical Relations Between Christianity and Marxism-Leninism in the Soviet Union" in Alan Scarfe & Patrick Sookhdeo (eds.), *Christianity and Marxism*, Exeter, The Paternoster Press, 1982, p.48.

[132] The Cheka was the usual term used for the All-Russian Extraordinary Commission, a Bolshevik secret police organisation, created by Lenin in 1917.

[133] This quotation taken from an adapted version published as an article in *National Review*, 22 July 1983, republished in *National Review* 11 December 2018 https://www.nationalreview.com/2018/12/aleksandr-solzhenitsyn-men-have-forgotten-god-speech/ (viewed 2 January 2019).

[134] From an address by 540 Lithuanian Catholics to the Lithuanian Supreme Soviet, published in *The Chronicle of the Lithuanian Catholic Church*, No. 7, August 1973.

[135] Quoted in George Paterson, "The Spiritual Marxism of Mao Tse-Tung" in Alan Scarfe & Patrick Sookhdeo (eds.), *Christianity and Marxism*, Exeter, The Paternoster Press, 1982, p.82.

[136] Paterson, pp.85-86.

[137] Quoted in Paterson, p.90.

[138] Paterson, p.95.

[139] Chris Buckley, "Xi Jinping Thought Explained: A New Ideology for a New Era" in *New York Times*, 26 February 2018, https://www.nytimes.com/2018/02/26/world/asia/xi-jinping-thought-explained-a-new-ideology-for-a-new-era.html (viewed 5 February 2019).

[140] Carmine Napolitano, "The development of Pentecostalism in Italy" in William Kay and Anne Dyer (eds.), *European Pentecostalism*, Leiden, Brill, 2011, pp.192-193.

[141] https://www.assembleedidio.org/ (viewed 5 February 2019).

[142] "Pope apologizes for Fascist era persecution", *The Local*, 29 July 2014, https://www.thelocal.it/20140729/pope-asks-forgiveness-for-fascist-era-persecution (viewed 5 February 2019).

[143] https://en.wikipedia.org/wiki/Clerical_fascism (viewed 3 February 2019).

[144] The first two empires were the medieval Holy Roman Empire of the German Nation and the German Empire of 1871-1918.

[145] 22 August 1939, Obersalzberg, in a speech to his generals before the German invasion of Poland. He ordered them to kill every Polish man, woman and child, the same aim as he had for the Jews.

[146] *Mit brennender Sorge, Encyclical of Pope Pius XI, on the Church and the German Reich*, 14 March 1937, official English translation by the Vatican, from paragraphs 3 and 4, http://w2.vatican.va/content/pius-xi/en/encyclicals/documents/hf_p-xi_enc_14031937_mit-brennender-sorge.html (viewed 29 January 2019).

[147] Quoted in Andrew Chandler (ed.), *Brethren in Adversity: Bishop George Bell, the Church of England and the Crisis of German Protestantism, 1933-1939*, Church of England Record Society No. 4, Woodbridge UK, The Boydell Press, 1997, p.140.

[148] M. S. Golwalkar, *We or Our Nationhood Defined*, Nagpur, Bharat Publications, 1939, p.35.

[149] Julius J. Lipner, *Anandamath or The Sacred Brotherhood: A Translation of Bankimcandra Chatterji's Anandamath, with Introduction and Critical Apparatus*, Oxford, Oxford University Press, 2005.

[150] Chhattisgarh, Gujarat, Himachal Pradesh, Jharkhand, Madhya Pradesh, Odisha and Uttarakhand. Arunachal Pradesh and Rajasthan have produced similar laws but they are not fully enacted.

[151] Dharmapala is using the word "Aryan" in its proper sense, to describe people who speak a certain group of Indo-European languages. He is not using it in the Nazi sense.

[152] Dharmapala, *History of an Ancient Civilization: Ceylon under British Rule*, Los Angeles, 1902, in Ananda Guruge (ed.) *Return to Righteousness: A Collection of Speeches, Essays and Letters of Anagarika Dharmapala*, Colombo, The Government Press, 1965, p.482.

[153] Donald E. Smith, *Religion and Politics in Burma*, New Jersey, Princeton University Press, 1965, p.83.

[154] Theodore Lim and Dengthuama, "An Overview of Christian Missions in Myanmar" in *Global Missiology*, Vol. 3, No. 13, April 2016, http://ojs.globalmissiology.org/index.php/english/article/view/1884 (viewed 2 February 2019).

[155] Khup Za Go, "A Brief History of Christianity in Burma (Myanmar)", 1993, https://sialki.wordpress.com/the-stories-of-zomi/a-brief-history-of-christianity-in-burma/ (viewed 20 February 2019).

[156] Carine Jaquet, *The Kachin Conflict: Testing the Limits of the Political Transition in Myanmar* [online]. Bangkok: Institut de recherche sur l'Asie du Sud-Est contemporaine, 2015, chapter 1, "Kachin history, perceptions, and beliefs: contextual elements", pp.17-32, paragraphs 5 to 8, http://books.openedition.org/irasec/273 (viewed 10 February 2019).

[157] For more details, see Patrick Sookhdeo, *Faith, Power and Territory: A Handbook of British Islam*, McLean, Virginia, Isaac Publishing, 2008, pp.35-57.

[158] Sunni Muslims are followers of the main branch of Islam, comprising at least 80% of all Muslims worldwide.

[159] There is debate about whether "Wahhabism" and "Salafism" are two very similar but different ideologies, or whether they are two names for the same thing. Other terms in use are "neo-Wahhabism" and "neo-Salafism" but there is no clarity about how these are defined.

[160] For more information on *dawa*, see Patrick Sookhdeo, *Dawa: The Islamic Strategy for Reshaping the Modern World*, McLean, Virginia, Isaac Publishing, 2014.

161 Shias are the second largest branch of Islam, comprising at least 10% of all Muslims. The split from Sunni Islam took place when there was a leadership dispute in 657 AD, after which the two branches developed a somewhat different theology from each other. Shias are often persecuted by Sunnis.

162 Jackie Thornhill, "How the United States Created Al-Qaeda", 23 January 2017, https://medium.com/@jackiethornhill/how-the-united-states-created-al-qaeda-2bbe129faf57 (viewed 2 February 2019).

163 "Hillary Clinton: We created al-Qaeda/ISIS" https://www.dailymotion.com/video/x5vf3i4 (viewed 3 February 2019).

164 Elizabeth Tsurkov, "Inside Israel's Secret Program to Back Syrian Rebels", *Foreign Policy Magazine*, 6 September 2018, https://foreignpolicy.com/2018/09/06/in-secret-program-israel-armed-and-funded-rebel-groups-in-southern-syria/ (viewed 2 February 2019); Rafiq A. Tschannen, "Israeli military finally admits supplying arms to Syria militants" in *The Muslim Times*, 15 January 2019, https://themuslimtimes.info/2019/01/16/israeli-military-finally-admits-supplying-arms-to-syria-militants/ (viewed 2 February 2019).

165 Richard Silverstein, "The Syrian war's worst kept secret that could become Israel's nightmare", *Middle East Eye*, 28 June 2017, https://www.middleeasteye.net/opinion/syrian-wars-worst-kept-secret-could-become-israels-nightmare (viewed 3 February 2019); https://www.yediot.co.il/articles/0,7340,L-4979649,00.html.

166 Mor Ignatius Aphrem II, Syriac Orthodox Patriarch of Antioch and all the East, speaking at the inauguration of a new Archdiocesan Residence in Erbil, Iraqi Kurdistan, 26 January 2019.

167 For more details, see Patrick Sookhdeo, *The New Civic Religion: Humanism and the Future of Christianity*, 2nd edition, McLean, Virginia, Isaac Publishing, September 2016.

168 Bylaw 5.1 of the International Humanist and Ethical Union, an umbrella organisation for the global humanist movement with 116 member organisations from over 50 countries.

169 Brenda Watson, "The Need for Responsible Religious Education in the Light of the 'Value Free' Society" in Marius Felderhof and Penny Thompson (eds.), *Teaching Virtue: The Contribution of Religious Education*, London, Bloomsbury, 2014, p.77.

170 For some specific examples, see Patrick Sookhdeo, *The Death of Western Christianity: Drinking from the Poisoned Wells of the Cultural Revolution*, McLean, Virginia, Isaac Publishing, 2017, pp.112-129.

171 Prince Charles was speaking at a special Advent service for persecuted Christians at Westminster Abbey on 4 December 2018. https://globalchristiannews.org/

article/prince-charles-praises-extraordinary-grace-and-capacity-for-forgiveness-of-persecuted-middle-eastern-christians/ (viewed 2 February 2019).

[172] Interviewed on 30 January 2019 at the Foreign and Commonwealth Office, "Sunday" programme, BBC Radio 4, 3 February 2019, https://www.bbc.co.uk/sounds/play/m00029fg

[173] Interviewed on 30 January 2019 at the Foreign and Commonwealth Office, "Sunday" programme, BBC Radio 4, 3 February 2019, https://www.bbc.co.uk/sounds/play/m00029fg

[174] Mor Ignatius Aphrem II, Syriac Orthodox Patriarch of Antioch and all the East, speaking at the inauguration of a new Archdiocesan Residence in Erbil, Iraqi Kurdistan, 26 January 2019.

[175] David B. Doty, "On Justice and Righteousness (mishpat & tsadaq)- Strong's 4941 & 6663", https://edensbridge.org/2012/01/11/on-justice-and-righteousness-mishpat-tsadaq-strongs-4941-6663/ (accessed 2 March 2018).

[176] This phrase was coined by Nicholas Wolterstorff.

[177] Jim Campbell, "Why Christians Should Support Religious Freedom for Everyone", 22 April 2017, https://www.thegospelcoalition.org/article/why-christians-should-support-religious-freedom-for-everyone/ (accessed 2 March 2018).

[178] In his *First Apology*, chapters 2, 68.

[179] *Ad Scapulam*, chapter 2, translated by Sydney Thelwall. This was an open letter from Tertullian, who lived in Carthage (in modern Tunisia), to Scapula, the Roman Proconsul of Africa, who began persecuting Christians, some time after 14 August 212. The letter urged Scapula to stop his persecution, not because the Christians were unwilling to die for their faith, but so that he might avoid the disasters which seemed to befall other persecutors of Christians. https://en.wikisource.org/wiki/Ante-Nicene_Fathers/Volume_III/Apologetic/To_Scapula/Chapter_II (accessed 2 March 2018).

[180] See chapter 6.

[181] Jeff Mirus, "Vatican II on Religious Freedom", 13 September 2010, https://www.catholicculture.org/commentary/otc.cfm?id=700 (accessed 2 March 2018).

[182] Rt Hon Sir John Hayes, Foreword to Barnabas Fund's *How Britain led the world in developing freedom of religion*, McLean, Virginia, Isaac Publishing, January 2019, p.1.

[183] See pp.26-27.

[184] The Japanese situation is powerfully portrayed in Martin Scorsese's 2016 feature film *The Silence*, based on a 1966 book of the same name by Shūsaku Endō.

[185] See chapters 4 and 6.

[186] Matthew 16:18.

INDEX